483

Hewens

£8

D1066174

*The Alliterative Tradition
in the Fourteenth Century*

The
Alliterative Tradition
in the
Fourteenth Century

Edited by
BERNARD S. LEVY *and* PAUL E. SZARMACH

✠

The Kent State University Press

Library of Congress Cataloging in Publication Data

Main entry under title:

The Alliterative tradition in the fourteenth century.

Includes bibliographical references and index.
1. English poetry—Middle English, 1100–1500—
History and criticism—Addresses, essays, lectures.
2. Alliteration—Addresses, essays, lectures.
I. Levy, Bernard S., 1927–   II. Szarmach,
Paul E.
PR317.A55A45 1981   821'.1'09   80–28821
ISBN 0–87338–255–2

Manufactured in the United States of America

Contents

Contents

Introduction

IN the fall of 1973 Rossell Hope Robbins organized a symposium on "Chaucer, Ricardan Poet," the papers of which have appeared in the volume *Chaucer at Albany*. The success of this symposium, and particularly the interest in fourteenth-century poetry it generated, made a second conference, on the non-Chaucerian tradition, desirable and appropriate, if not necessary. Consequently, another Chancellor's Conversation in the Disciplines was held at Binghamton from October 31 to November 2, 1975, on "The Alliterative Tradition in the Fourteenth Century."

The program was partly organized along certain traditional lines, viz., a concern for the origins of the Alliterative School and the necessary consideration of the generally acknowledged masterpieces *Sir Gawain and the Green Knight* and the monumental *Piers Plowman*. The process of invitation and negotiation, however, uncovered a significant inclination on the part of the scholars concerned to extend the discussion beyond *Gawain* and *Piers*. Thus this volume has a special focus on other works in the tradition. This interest in a number of different works has its counterpart in the interest in different methodologies represented in these essays, such as the historical, formalist, patristic, and iconographic.

In the first essay Derek Pearsall proposes a new context for the origins of the Alliterative Revival. The standard explanation

tends to suggest an evolution of alliterative verse rather than a
continuum of alliterative writing of wide currency and varied
function. However, it seems likely that a tradition of unrhymed
alliterative verse, in written copies, has been lost and that these
written copies were made, preserved, and made available to later
generations of writers in the monasteries of the Southwest Midlands. This Southwest Midlands context, Pearsall argues, provides the Alliterative Revival with its roots, the continuity for its
provenance, and a strong direction for its development.

In "The Characterization of Women in the Alliterative Tradition," Maureen Fries considers several works in the light of a
humane feminism. She describes three modes of characterization
and applies these categories to the *Morte Arthure, The Awntyrs
off Arthure, Sir Gawain and the Green Knight*, and generally but
briefly to other works. These three modes, developed from the
work of Sr. Ritamary Bradley, are archetype, stereotype, and the
depiction of reality. The Arthurian poems of the Alliterative Tradition offer varieties of female characterization, ranging from the
limited but realistic representation of Gaynour in the *Morte Arthure*, through the striking presentation of Gaynour as an archetype of combined courtly and spiritual significance in *The
Awntyrs off Arthure*, to the fascinating mixture of archetype,
stereotype, and realistic behavior which contributes to the excellence of *Sir Gawain and the Green Knight*. In *Sir Gawain*
Guinevere is not an important character; rather another courtly
lady, Bertilak's wife, functions as both a courtly and a spiritual
archetype of evil. Thus, despite the so-called masculine meter
and matter that others have found, the alliterative poets actually
included all of humanity as their subject.

Ruth M. Ames and David Lampe discuss the tradition of
Piers Plowman. Ruth Ames points out that critics are still puzzled
over the way the pardon given to Piers was impugned by the
priest. She believes that Langland goes out of his way to suggest
that the views of both are true. The dispute between Piers and the
priest thus propounds a riddle: What is understood by some as
justice and by others as mercy? What is read by one as letter and
another as spirit? The answer, which is only explained gradually

over the course of the poem, is to be found in the law of God, and the argument is over its interpretation. Langland's vision of the law embraces the Old and New Laws both as historical periods and timeless morality. He sees the realization of justice and mercy as accomplished by Christ, but also as a perennial riddle, the answer to which must be sought by every man. The conflict between Piers and the priest represents the prophetic and the priestly ways of interpreting the law of God in every age. Basic to Langland's handling of the theme is his belief that the essential law had not changed, but in practice Christians slipped into their own legalism. As he tells the story of mankind Langland constantly affirms the prophetic emphasis. Ames concludes that the quarrel between the priest and Piers dramatizes the conflict between those interpreters of the law who deny and those who desire God's pardon for mankind.

David Lampe offers a fresh look at the Lollard *Peres the Ploughmans Crede*. He finds that "a careful consideration of the different language patterns, especially the contrasting usages of praise and blame and ethical appeal [reveals] the various layers of irony which allow for the poem's sharp satire." In the first half of the poem the representatives of the four orders engage in bitter attacks against each other while in the second Peres inveighs against mendicants and possessioners. The difference in the attacks of the respective parts is that Peres, unlike the disputatious friars, is closer to the ideas and spirit of the founders of the respective orders. Peres uses the Beatitudes as a point of departure for his criticism; indeed Peres exemplifies the Beatitudes. His is the new voice of a simple Christian whose real words and action transcend feigned belief. Because Peres has no self-interest in the reform, his moral perspective ironically contrasts with the friars who use similar argumentative techniques without an appropriate moral starting point.

John Fleming, John Friedman, and Earl Schreiber offer new approaches to the study of the "homiletic poems" of the *Gawain*-poet. Fleming focuses on the centuple structure of *Pearl*. He studies its "one-hundred-and-oneness"—the fact that the poem has exactly one hundred and one stanzas. The scriptural source for the hundred and ones which show up in the structural schemes of medieval books can be found in Matthew 19:29: "And every one that hath forsaken houses, or brethren, or sisters, or father, or mother, or wife, or children, or lands, for my name's sake, shall receive an hundredfold, and shall have everlasting life." An exegetical approach to the hundredfold, the spiritual centuplum of religious consolation, involves an increase by one hundred. The number for religious consolation thus becomes one hundred and one, and would have felicitous overtones for *Pearl*. That such a possibility was at work in *Pearl*, Fleming argues, can be demonstrated by an architectural history of the number 101. *Pearl* is thus a poem for which no juster shape could be imagined than that of centuple consolation.

John Friedman argues that although Biblical exegesis traditionally interprets Jonah as a type of Christ, the *Patience*-poet presents Jonah as notably un-Christlike. The poet thus stresses the ways in which Jonah fails to live up to the ideals represented by Christ. The poet's audience would be familiar through their parish worship with homiletic and liturgical materials that stress the perfective aspects of Christ, namely the way in which Jesus fulfills and goes beyond what Jonah does unwillingly and imperfectly. Early in the poem Jonah's rejection of his mission and the cross indicates the poet's determination to present Jonah from such a perspective. An examination of the poem reveals a wealth of material that gives form to or elaborates the perfective view. Such a view accounts for the prophet's unappealing personality in the poem and would provide the medieval audience with a constant homiletic contrast between the English prophet and the "True Jonah."

Earl Schreiber seeks to demonstrate that *Clannesse* is a more fully unified and coherent poem than most readers realize. He sees the poem as following a simple homiletic structure; that is, the prologue gives a moral principle and the rest of the poem amplifies it. The poem rises above a mere schematic unity because it has interlocking metaphors and structures that tie the major parts together. The prologue is a narration of the parable of the Wedding Feast. Through this narration the poet introduces the major themes of the poem: "priests, feasts, clothing, marriage, vessels, spatial descents, deformity and perversion in contrast to beauty and cleanness; and estrangement, destruction and sorrow in contrast to union, eternal life and joy." In his discussion of the amplification, Schreiber suggests, among other things, an aesthetic justification for the story of Belshazzar's Feast, which Dorothy Everett saw as a blemish: Belshazzar's Feast is an apocalyptic warning to those who would reject the perfect example of *clannesse*, who is Christ. The story is part of the overall moral vision of a poet whose skill in poetic structure has created a well-wrought vessel.

Finally, Russell Peck and A. C. Spearing consider important aspects of two quite different alliterative poems. Russell Peck studies the *Alliterative Morte Arthure* as a Boethian tragedy. Peck contends that the *Morte Arthure*, like much of the literature of the late fourteenth century, is concerned about the nature of virtuous behavior. Its author espouses the idea that the chaos man sees about him is caused by man himself. The poet, furthermore, singles out the will as the faculty that most determines an individual's life. The poem, a masterful study of willfulness and the wonders it can conjure, falls into two major parts. In the first half Arthur is mostly concerned with defending his lands, title, and people from a usurper. After his victory, his motive becomes revenge, which is not a lawful reason for war. From a Boethian point of view, revenge stems from a willful misunderstanding of what rightfully is one's own. Consequently, the actions in the first half tend to reflect deluded judgments and to parody the more rationally ordered events of the first half. In the second half of the poem, Arthur fails to accomplish his will because, instead of fighting with the strength of God, he tries to win battles on his own. Peck contends that Arthur becomes a tyrant and disposseses himself. Willfulness not only makes him victim of fortune but also removes him from the security of his rightful place. It is clear that Arthur shaped his own fate. The wonder is the bleak scene of his death.

In the concluding essay, Spearing argues for greater aesthetic appreciation of *The Awntyrs off Arthure*. Like Schreiber on *Clan-*

nesse, Spearing explains a hitherto unnoticed structural principle
that invests the poem with coherence and meaning. *The Awntyrs
off Arthure* is analogous to a diptych in medieval painting or to a
montage in contemporary film. The poet has juxtaposed two parts
in order to evoke a theme. This structural pattern occurs generally
in medieval English literature, but "structural parallel with variation" is far more common in alliterative poetry. In *The Awntyrs
off Arthure* this juxtaposition celebrates a noble way of life that
when challenged, displays its limitations. The apparition of
Guinevere's mother, for example, highlights Guinevere's shallowness in a number of ways. Galeron of Galway's unsuccessful
challenge to the Arthurian court nevertheless merits him a generous admission to the Round Table, but Spearing finds the ending
of the poem as enigmatic as that of *Sir Gawain and the Green
Knight*. Is there psychological and spiritual fulfillment? Life goes
on in the Arthurian court.

We must thank several people who made the Conference and
this volume possible. Our first thanks go to the Chancellor of the
State University of New York, Ernest L. Boyer, for supporting
the Conversations in the Disciplines program, and to Everard
Pinneo, assistant to the Vice-Chancellor for Academic Programs,
who made administration of the grant less burdensome than it
might have been. The Conversation received additional support
from SUNY-Binghamton, viz., the Provost for Graduate Studies
and Research, first Norman F. Cantor and then John LaTourette,
and the Chairman of the English Department Zack Bowen.
Dorothy Huber, the secretary of the Center for Medieval and
Early Renaissance Studies, organized many of the details of the
Conference, as she has so patiently and efficiently done for the
Center for so long. Several graduate and undergraduate students
worked for us with cheerfulness and enthusiasm. We owe special
thanks to Virginia Darrow Oggins for her careful preparation of the
index. Rossell Hope Robbins and his wife Helen Ann gave encour-
agement. The editors and their contributors had hoped to see this
volume published in 1978 or at the latest 1979. Unfortunately the

publisher with whom we had first contracted experienced technical delays and then financial difficulties. We therefore owe special thanks to The Kent State University Press and its Editorial Board for accepting the special problems associated with a volume that was in final page proofs elsewhere for quite some time. Of course, without cooperative and patient contributors there would have been no volume.

BERNARD S. LEVY
PAUL E. SZARMACH

1

The Origins of the
Alliterative Revival

DEREK PEARSALL

THE title of this paper is not a new one. Literary scholars have addressed themselves on a number of occasions to the question of what happened in the early and middle years of the fourteenth century to produce the remarkable efflorescence of alliterative poetry in the latter half of the century.[1] They have returned with a variety of answers, some of them mutually contradictory, but the energy of their interest in, and engagement with, the question is enough to suggest that something did happen that needs explaining. Perhaps the nature of the phenomenon and the questions it provokes can best be suggested by a simple statistic, namely, that from the seventy-five years between the second recension of Layamon's *Brut* in the Otho manuscript and the writing of the earliest poems of the revival, that is, roughly 1275–1350, there are extant 28 lines of unrhymed alliterative verse, while from the seventy-five years that follow, roughly 1350–1425, there are over 40,000. Something clearly did happen. Whether it should be called a "revival" is more doubtful. To "revive" a tradition would normally imply that the tradition was dead; it would also imply a degree of conscious intention on the part of those responsible for resuscitation. Neither implication can be fully substantiated. Arguments for the continuity of the alliterative tradition have often taken an unfortunate turn, especially insofar as they have concerned themselves with the "heroic spirit" or "English-

ness'' of alliterative verse,[2] but there can be no doubt that the
survival of the basic verse form, and of a vocabulary and formulaic phraseology associated with it, constitutes a form of continuity. The argument for conscious intention needs more delicate
handling, since we are clearly dealing with sophisticated poets
who were perfectly capable of making artistic decisions as to
choice of verse form. All one can say at the moment is that the
intentions behind the choices have not in the past been satisfactorily displayed. On the whole, it would seem that some word such
as ''renewal'' or ''reflourishing'' would be more appropriate than
''revival,'' but I shall nevertheless go on using ''revival.''

There is of course an explanation of the origins of the Alliterative Revival which appears in most standard accounts of the
phenomenon. It goes something like this. In early Middle English
alliterative verse, such as *The Proverbs of Alfred* and the *Bestiary*, the addition of rhyme at half-line and end-line, which had
always threatened the internal rhythmical structure of the alliterative long line, eventually broke the line into a couplet, of waver-
ing rhythm and two or three stresses, which eventually fell in
with the four-stress couplet derived from French octosyllabic.
Meanwhile, in another and more legitimate line of descent, the
alliterative long line, having ''shaken off'' (like the sturdy native
animal it was) the tendency to rhyme, established itself with re-
newed strength as an integral unit, end-stopped, with the first
half-line rhythmically and rhetorically dominant over the second.
Something mysterious happened to this line: it seems to have
gone underground with the poetic *maquis* of the western marches,
to have been kept alive through oral transmission, to reappear
triumphant when the Anglo-Norman poetic usurpation was over-
thrown.

What is wrong with this explanation is its dynamic, evolutionary, and essential xenophobic character, the way it conceives of
the development of poetic form as a battle between native and
alien elements. It may be that we should abandon evolutionary
language and think instead of a ''continuum'' of alliterative writing of wide currency and varied function, a set of flexible and
unformulated procedures within which writers could work accord-

ing to their knowledge and inclinations. This is certainly the case in the late Old English period, where we have a wide spectrum of alliterative writing, including the "classical" type of alliterative verse, various modifications of the classical type such as *Maldon*, a number of looser popular forms evidenced in the poems inserted in the *Anglo-Saxon Chronicle*, and the whole range of rhythmical alliterative writing in Aelfric and Wulfstan for which "prose" is such an inadequate term.[3] All these forms survive into the early Middle English period, some of them enriched and strengthened, as in the rhythmical alliterative writings of the Katherine-group.[4] Sometimes we find a poet using more than one kind of alliterative verse within a single poem, as happens in the *Bestiary* and, more significantly, in Layamon. It is difficult to believe that a battle between native and alien verse forms is going on in the verse form of the *Brut*: we should at least expect, in such a long poem, signs that the battle was being won or lost. But Layamon's choices between different forms of rhymed and unrhymed alliterative verse remain much the same at the end as at the beginning of the poem. It is important to stress this activity of choice in such a poet, and to set it against the usual "dynamic" theory which has Layamon floundering along for 16,000 long lines amidst the wreckage of the alliterative line without discovering any systematic principle of versification.

The currency of a wide variety of alliterative writing, a "continuum," needs to be recognized too in the period with which we are more particularly concerned, the late thirteenth and the early fourteenth centuries. In its most basic form this may be no more than a penchant for two-stress alliterative phrases deriving from the most fundamental rhythmic characteristics of the language itself. Such we find in much of the prose of the period, and we see it in traditionally heightened and elaborated form in the prose of Rolle. On a more formal level, alliterative verse with rhyme is used on occasions in the friars' miscellanies of the late thirteenth century, in the early fourteenth-century manuscript Harley 2253, and in the poems of Minot and of Rolle.[5] The influence of the alliterative tradition or "continuum" is strong also in metrical rhymed verse, by which I mean that kind of verse derived from foreign models with more or less regular alternation of stressed and unstressed syllables as opposed to the rhythmic type-patterning of alliterative verse. One form of this influence is the use of alliteration, irregular but often heavy, as an additional ornament within nonnative but firmly established couplet and stanzaic forms. There are poems of this kind in Rolle and Minot, while the examples in Harley 2253 provide a full ancestry for *Pearl*.[6] Characteristic of this form is the variation in the traditional patterns of alliteration that it induces: rhyme is now the significant determinant of structure, and alliteration, no longer structurally necessary, may lapse, or be confined to half-lines, or be extended to all four staves of the long line to compensate for loss of function. This last variation, which is virtually unknown in Old English alliterative verse, is encouraged by the tendency of rhyme to draw the weight of the line toward the last, rhyme-bearing stress, which can less easily in such a situation be a nonalliterating stress. Another form of the influence of the alliterative tradition in metrical rhymed verse is the marked tendency of the loose septenary/alexandrine long line, of mixed Anglo-Norman and Latin descent, to fall into the cadences of the native four-stress line, with or without alliteration. We see this in the poems of Jesus College, Oxford, MS 29 and Harley MS 2253,[7] in the *South English Legendary*, in the *Tale of Gamelyn*, and in a poem from the Auchinleck manuscript, *The Simonie*, which has been specifically associated with *Piers Plowman*.[8]

Further examples could be given of the strength of diverse alliterative traditions in poetry of the period 1275–1350, but perhaps the point is clear enough. The traditions, it will be seen, are not confined to the West, though their strength is greatest there. The only casualty in this process of adaptation and development is apparently the unrhymed alliterative line itself. From the period in question, only a few debased and dubious remnants survive. *Thomas of Erceldoune's Prophecy*, in Harley 2253, qualifies more because it lacks rhyme—and indeed any other mark of poetic identity—than because it is recognizably alliterative, though its descendants, the political *Prophecies* of the fourteenth, fifteenth, and sixteenth centuries, are important evidence of the preservation of a loose, popular, and probably partly oral alliterative tradition.[9] A fragment of unrhymed alliterative verse quoted in Rolle's *Ego Dormio* has a more authentic ring:

> Alle perisches and passes þat we with eghe see;
> It wanes into wrechednes, þe welth of þis worlde.
> Robes and ritches rotes in dike,
> Prowde payntyng slakes into sorow.[10]

This is evidently verse, different in vocabulary, cadence, and above all in poetic self-consciousness from even the most elaborate of Rolle's alliterative prose. Even so, all the lines except one conform to the alliterative patterns of rhymed rather than unrhymed alliterative verse, namely *aa/aa, aa/bb, aa/xx.* If we had no evidence from after 1350, we should find it easy to understand how the old alliterative verse had been superseded, except in a few forms barely on the fringe of literate verse making, and how its rhythmical and formal characteristics had been either rejected or totally absorbed into rhymed verse.

All this makes the sudden flowering or "revival" of unrhymed alliterative verse in the second half of the century not a bit easier to explain. I am not here referring to an explanation of the reasons for the resurgence of alliterative poetry, but to an explanation of the processes by which it took place. The former has been provided by Elizabeth Salter in her two essays on "The Alliterative Revival."[11] Here, after first dismantling Hulbert's hypothesis that the poetry of the revival was the propaganda of baronial discontent,[12] she gives a persuasive account of the provenance of alliterative poetry among the noble households and gentry of the West. If we ask what might have prompted those nobles and gentlemen to extend their patronage to alliterative verse, the answer may be simply that Anglo-Norman verse, which hitherto absorbed nearly all courtly and aristocratic patronage, was now, about 1350, in a state of rapid decline. Alliterative verse would have offered itself as a ready substitute, suitable, like the alexandrine in *laisses,* for long and ambitious poems, and untainted by the hack professionalism of current forms of rhymed verse. It probably had an archaic flavor, just as Layamon's *Brut* did even in its own day,[13] but this may not have been altogether, if at all, a disqualification.

Such an explanation makes it even more difficult to believe that the processes of transmission for this high-caste poetry were oral. There was probably an orally transmitted alliterative verse, but its products, when written down, would have the debauched character of the *Prophecies* I have already mentioned. All the evidence we have suggests that oral transmission makes wretched what it touches, and that the longer the process the more debased the product. The range of evidence, from the Lincoln's Inn romance-manuscript[14] to the Percy Folio, is complete, and confirms what we might, in common sense, expect. There is no mystery about oral transmission, and I should make it clear that I am not invoking the higher mysteries of oral formulaic composition, which are even more irrelevant to Middle English than to Old English alliterative verse.

Yet continuity of a kind there must have been, and it is not entirely explicable in terms of the extant written documents. For all that has been said above about the strength and variety of alliterative tradition in the late thirteenth and early fourteenth centuries, it can provide precedent only for some of the secondary poetic activity of the revival, such as *Pearl,* and perhaps a partial precedent for *Piers Plowman.* Two things about the classical poetic corpus of the revival (in which I include the *Alexander* poems, *The Destruction of Troy, The Siege of Jerusalem, Morte Arthure, Gawain, Cleanness, Patience, St. Erkenwald, Winner and Waster,* and *The Parlement of the Thre Ages)* remain difficult to explain, and they may be related. One is the unanimous adoption of the traditionally authentic alliterative pattern based on *aa/ax,* where all the tendencies of alliterative verse with rhyme and of metrical rhymed verse with alliteration were to the breakdown of such patterns. The other is the rejection of rhyme itself, and for this, which I take to be a significant act of choice, the scraps of rhymeless verse we have noticed provide only a pathetic precedent. Alliterative prose can be cited as a model, but it is as difficult to believe that the alliterative poets disentangled a regular, systematic, and traditionally authentic versification from the looser rhythms of prose as to believe that they achieved the same object by stringing together accidentally regular alliterative lines from the detritus of the septenary/alexandrine tradition. In addition to these metrical features, there are, in the "classical" poems, a traditional diction and formulaic phraseology which are often archaic and often exclusive to alliterative poetry, and which constitute further proof of the continuity of a stricter alliterative poetic.

At this point, it is probably necessary to invoke the fragmentary state of our knowledge of much Middle English poetry. Most of the alliterative poems of the revival exist in unique copies, some of them survivals of the most fortuitous kind. Only *Piers Plowman* and *The Siege of Jerusalem* exist in more than two, and these have the sanction of a popular religious subject matter. Take away a handful of manuscripts, and there would be no alliterative revival to be explained. If we transfer this situation to the late thirteenth and early fourteenth centuries, the period for which records fail us, and reckon with the added uncertainties of an earlier date, the disadvantaged status of English and, by presumption, a predominantly secular subject matter, it will not seem impossible that a tradition of unrhymed alliterative verse, in written copies, has been lost. The tradition would have to be located in the West Midlands, the base, though not the exclusive home, of the revival.

I should like now to propose the principal argument of this essay, which is that these written copies were made, preserved, and made available to later generations of writers in the monasteries of the Southwest Midlands.[15] The positive evidence for this hypothesis is well known, though it does not seem to me that its significance has been fully displayed. It is that in the second recension of the English verse *Chronicle* attributed to Robert of Gloucester, there is extensive borrowing from a written text of Layamon's *Brut*.[16] The *Chronicle* exists in two versions, an earlier and a later. The two versions have a common text up to line 9137, the end of Henry I's reign, but thereafter diverge. The earlier version continues with a detailed account, in a further

3,000 lines, of events up to 1270; the later version presents a different and drastically abbreviated continuation, of only 600 lines, taking the story up to just after the accession of Edward I in 1272. At the same time, the later version interpolates extensively in the first part of the poem, and it is among these interpolations that the borrowings from Layamon occur. The *Chronicle* as a whole is in a Southwest or Southwest Midland dialect and shows detailed knowledge of and interest in events around Gloucester, particularly in the thirteenth century. The Gloucester affiliation is less strongly marked in the later version, because of the reduced scale of treatment of more recent events. The author of the longer continuation, and probably therefore of the whole of the earlier version,[17] names himself in line 11,748, "roberd/ þat verst þis boc made," as one who saw and was affrighted by the darkness that covered the land for thirty miles around while the battle of Evesham was being fought in 1265. It has been presumed that Robert was a monk of Gloucester or some nearby monastic house.[18] He shows a keen interest in monastic affairs, and his work is of a kind that seems appropriate, indeed possible, only within the monastic tradition of chronicle writing and historical compilation. It is obviously intended, being in English, for a wider audience than the cloister,[19] though there can be no suggestion that it is designed for popular consumption. Its very length, as compared, for instance, with the genuinely popular *Anonymous Short English Metrical Chronicle,*[20] as well as its serious and detailed treatment of history, would argue against such an assumption. It is important, in any case, to distinguish between provenance and destination in discussion of literary works,[21] and the argument I am putting forward here has primarily to do with provenance. It is not that the *Chronicle* was intended exclusively for monks, only that the writing of it necessitated a monastery's resources. All that I have said about the monastic affiliations of the author of the earlier version of the *Chronicle* would apply to the later abbreviator and interpolator. If the earlier writer was at work sometime between 1297, a date confirmed by internal evidence,[22] and about 1330, the date of the earliest manuscript, the later writer must be placed within the same period, since the earliest manuscript of the later version, though itself about 1400, must go back to an original of about 1330.[23]

The borrowings from Layamon are confined to three of the forty-seven interpolations in the later version,[24] though these three interpolations contain nearly three-quarters of the total number of interpolated lines (562 out of 873). The first is short and gives further detail on King Bladud's attempt to fly. The other two are long, one dealing with a sequence of events including the feuds of Ferrex and Porrex and of Belinus and Brennus, the other with a sequence of minor kings between Gorgont and Lud. Comparison shows conclusively that the interpolator had before him a written text of Layamon, though he often treats it freely. Here are some specimen lines from the second interpolation:

Robert:

þo gan here wexe werre
    & echman slou oþer
& robbede & reuede
    þei he were his broþer
Her was hunger & hete
    wo was þe vnstronge
Her was muche manqualm
    wrake was in londe
Fewe lefde alyue. . . .

Layamon:

Elc mon ræuede oþer
    ðeah hit weren his broðer
Wrake wes on londe
    wa wes þone vnstronge
Her wes hunger & hete
    her was alre hærmene
    mest
Her wes muchel
    mon-qualm
þat lut her quike
    bi-lefden. . . .[25]

The text used by the interpolator is one very close to the Caligula manuscript,[26] though it seems to have been through an intermediary with more strongly marked western characteristics.[27] It is particularly interesting that the interpolator should have been using the older text of Layamon, apparently understanding fully its archaic diction.[28] His reason for using Layamon was presumably that Layamon, in these passages, gives a more expansive and lively account of incidents recorded fairly briefly in Geoffrey of

Monmouth's *Historia,* which is the source of the original chronicle in these passages. This interest in the pre-Arthurian kings and the descent of the British would argue for a continuation of Layamon's own concerns and provide a link with the alliterative poets, who return significantly on a number of occasions to the theme of Brutus and the legendary history of Britain.[29] It may be worth recalling that the great western family of the Mortimers had a particular interest in Arthur because of their claims to Arthurian descent.[30] These are larger issues, however, and should not distract attention from the main one here. Although no argument can be made that the interpolator was interested in alliterative verse as such—in fact, most of his close borrowings are of couplet material more readily assimilated into his own septenary/alexandrine couplet—it is nevertheless clear that a text of an important alliterative poem was available to and understood and being used by an English poet in the Southwest Midlands, almost certainly in a monastery, in the 1320s.

Another important literary affiliation for Robert's *Chronicle* is in its use of the *South English Legendary.* The common text of the first part includes extensive borrowing from the lives of Kenelm, Edward the Martyr, and Alphege, while the longer continuation uses the life of Becket.[31] All these are English saints, of course, and it is obvious why the author of a chronicle of English history should go to a legendary to supplement his historical sources when the saints concerned are important historical figures. The borrowing is again based on a written text, though the originals are very freely treated, and material that is not of obviously historical interest is omitted. The borrowing is demonstrably from the *Legendary* into the *Chronicle,*[32] and not vice versa, which confirms the usually accepted date, about 1275,[33] for the earliest version of the *Legendary,* and agrees with its presumed origins, from dialectal evidence, in the Southwest Midland area. It casts some doubt, however, on the mendicant provenance usually assumed for the *Legendary.*[34] The friars have been held responsible for much English poetry in the late thirteenth and early fourteenth centuries, but it is clear that their interests in vernacular poetry, whether expressed through religious lyrics or verse-sermons, are dominated by professional and homiletic concerns. They are the professional preachers and penitencers of the age, and it is difficult to understand their particular interest in the long, circumstantial, and quasi-historical lives of figures such as these English saints. History, on the other hand, was the traditional and dominant preoccupation of monastic writers, and the deduction of a monastic provenance for the *Legendary* would seem to be a natural one, confirmed by its use here as a source text within a monastic environment. The relevance of these arguments here is to confirm the existence of extensive vernacular poetic activity in the monasteries of the Southwest Midlands. None of this activity, admittedly, is in alliterative verse, but there is one small shred of evidence that may have significance in relation to my central argument.

The *Life of St. Kenelm* in the *South English Legendary* is long and circumstantial. It tells how the infant King Kenelm of Mercia was murdered (A.D. 819) by his sister and buried in an obscure cow-pasture in the Clent hills in Worcestershire.[35] A dove was the only witness and carried a small writ to the Pope at Rome with an inscription in English which no one could read at first. It contains two lines of good alliterative verse without rhyme:

> In Clent Coubach Kenelm Kinges bern
> Liþ vnder [haȝ] þorn heued bireued.[36]

The boy's body was disinterred and carried with great ceremony to the abbey, founded by his father Kenulf, at Winchcombe, which was later a center for the cult of the boy saint. Two lines are not much to go on, and it is certainly true that these two lines have a wide currency in Latin chronicles of the twelfth and thirteenth centuries as a kind of "commemorative snatch"[37] rather than as the accidental debris of a lost alliterative poem, and also appear separately, copied on the flyleaf of Pembroke College, Cambridge, MS 82 (before 1207).[38] But it is interesting that the *Legendary*, in introducing the quotation of the two lines, offers a specific comment on the absence of rhyme:

þe writ was iwrite pur Engliss . as me radde it þere
And to telle it wiþoute rime . þis wordes riȝt it were.

(265–66)

This suggests, at least, some awareness of a different verse form, important in contrast to the silence on such matters usually observed by early Middle English poets.

Robert's *Chronicle* makes no use of the couplet: in fact, its main borrowing from the *Life of St. Kenelm* is from its initial account of the early shrines and dioceses of England, which is lifted out of context and placed at the beginning of the *Chronicle*. Only a few lines are spent, at the appropriate point, on Kenelm himself. The later interpolator, however, expands on this brief account with a slightly different version of the legend, according to which Kenelm's corpse spoke after forty years and gave away its whereabouts. The corpse speaks in two perfect lines of alliterative verse, rhymed this time:

& seide her liþ Kenelm . of his heuede bireued
þat þoru his soster & þe stiward . so was igreued.[39]

One can be skeptical about the importance of such scraps, but scraps are all we are likely to get at this stage. Several such alliterative couplets and odd lines are gathered together by Wilson in his *Lost Literature of Medieval England*,[40] mostly from monastic chronicles in Latin, some of them actually quoted in English, others more or less plausibly recoverable from Latin paraphrase. Some of them may be the product of genuine oral transmission, like the line quoted by Giraldus Cambrensis (1194) as an example of the popularity of alliteration among the English—"God is to gedere gamen and wisdom"[41]—which sounds like a proverbial saying,[42] but it is hard to resist Wilson's deduction that there is a lost corpus of historical alliterative poems. The texts of these poems, preserved in monastic houses, along with Layamon, would provide the evidence of continuity for which we seek, and some precedent for the historical interests of many of the poems of the revival.

Beyond this, the argument has to fall back on more general considerations. The dozen poems that I have referred to as constituting the classical core of the revival are all poems of learned provenance, especially those based on Latin sources. They presuppose poets moving among books in a fairly knowledgeable way, with a freedom that one would associate primarily with monastic writers. The poet of *Alexander A*, for instance, interpolates material from Orosius into his paraphrase of the *Historia de Preliis*[43] in exactly the way that is habitual with the scrupulous and bookish monastic compiler. He also interpolates a long catalogue-description of Olympias,[44] for which the most obvious source is the description of Helen in Guido della Colonne's *Historia Destructionis Troiae*.[45] This work is the source of *The Destruction of Troy*, of course, and it has been argued elsewhere that it is a work of special importance to the poets of the alliterative revival in the development of a particular *topos*, that of the alliterative storm.[46] The poet of *Alexander A*, speaking of the ancestry of Nectanabus, refers to his practice in the gathering of source materials in a way that may be thought to be characteristic of the monastic historian:

> Of what kinne hee comme . can I nought fynde
> In no buke þat i bed . when I beganne here
> þe Latine to þis language . lelliche turne.[47]

The poet of the *Siege of Jerusalem*, likewise, weaves together materials from the *Polychronicon*, the *Vindicta Salvatoris*, the *Legenda Aurea*, and the *Bible en francois* of Roger d'Argenteuil,[48] very much in the manner of Robert of Gloucester. It is probably true to say that monastic libraries were the only libraries where such a range of historical source materials could be found, and the catalogues and records of the monastic houses in the Southwest Midlands, where they survive, provide ample evidence that these and related materials were indeed available. Writers like Orosius, Josephus, Guido della Colonne, Geoffrey of Monmouth, and Higden appear regularly in the extant catalogues and among the surviving manuscripts of known provenance, as do works on Alexander, not always clearly identified, and rather less commonly, the writings of the twelfth-century historians such as William of Malmesbury, Henry of Huntingdon, and Florence of Worcester.[49] One would be very interested, of course, in evidence of other kinds of library resource relevant to the poetry of the revival, but works in English do not appear in monastic records as a matter of standard practice until the fifteenth century.[50] An exception may be made for Old English manuscripts, those of Worcester in particular, but it seems to me that the importance of these has been exaggerated. Certainly, Old English prose manuscripts were being copied and annotated in the Worcester library as late as the early thirteenth century by the scribe of the tremulous hand,[51] and there are scattered evidences of interest in Old English, here and elsewhere, until well into the fifteenth century.[52] This kind of antiquarianism, however, does not seem to hold much promise for a vigorous reawakening of alliterative poetry.[53] One would be more intrigued by the existence of a copy of the *Ancrene Wisse* in Wigmore priory in the thirteenth century[54] as evidence of vernacular interests (especially since Wigmore was under the patronage of the Mortimers), or by the evidence that a chaplain attached to Lanthony priory in the thirteenth century, who was also a schoolmaster at the local grammar school, was a collector of English religious lyrics.[55] Recent work on the relationship between the alliterative poem of *William of Palerne* and its patron, Humphrey de Bohun, has raised the possibility that the author of the poem was a canon of Lanthony, which was in the patronage of the Bohuns.[56]

One could go on from this to argue that the serious historical and didactic concern of nearly all the alliterative poetry of the revival[57] is itself a product of monastic culture, but it may be thought that I am contradicting my earlier argument about the importance of aristocratic patronage. To make it clear that there is no essential contradiction it is necessary to recur to a consideration of the nature of these monastic houses, primarily Benedictine and Augustinian, in the later Middle Ages. Though they doubtless provided opportunities for many devout and holy lives, the main spiritual impetus of the age was exerted elsewhere, and these houses, great and small, were very much part of the social, economic, and cultural life of the age. Their records are preoccupied, like the records of the great magnates, with "the acquisition and disposal of property and privilege,"[58] and the abbots and priors of the great houses kept court in a manner little different from secular lords. This was especially true in Worcester, where the bishop was also *ex officio* head of the cathedral priory; he had a household like that of a great baron, with many esquires and members of the gentry attendant upon him, and went on his many travels with a hundred horse.[59] The records of episcopal visitation,[60] to take another approach, cannot be taken entirely at face value, since the language of rebuke is often excessively colorful, and there were many old scores to settle, but they point to a rich variety of secular practice in monasteries. This does not apply only to notoriously disorderly houses, like Abergavenny, where the monks "were in the habit of entertaining their guests with nocturnal travesties of the Crucifixion,"[61] nor to occasionally unruly ones like Leominster, Wigmore, and Great Malvern, but also to the great black abbeys. The metropolitan visitation of the diocese of Worcester by Archbishop Winchelsea in 1301 is free from all suspicion of local prejudice or favor, and here we find Winchelsea confirming that the abbot of Gloucester may keep six esquires in his household, as well as a chief huntsman and assistant to look after his hunting dogs and harriers.[62]

More important than all this, however, is the function of the large monastic houses as the four-star hotels of the age, the staging posts for royal and aristocratic as well as episcopal progresses. The old traditions of hospitality counted for something here, though the need to cultivate powerful patrons counted for more. Worcester and Gloucester, placed on the only two bridges over the lower Severn and vital therefore for access to the southern Marches and South Wales, were in particularly heavy demand.[63] Edward I, for instance, was a frequent visitor at Worcester, and he held parliament there in 1282, on his way to quell a disturbance among the Welsh.[64] Edward II was sumptuously entertained at the abbey of Gloucester, and a few years earlier, in 1306, the abbey had put on a splendid banquet for the king's jus-

tices, who were sitting in Gloucester on an inquisition of trailbas-
ton. There were seventy guests, including knights of the realm as
well as local priors. In 1378 parliament was held at Gloucester,
royalty being accommodated at the abbey, while the great hall of
the abbey served as the parliamentary chamber.[65]

Without pressing speculation too far, one might say that these
are very natural occasions for the presentation of sophisticated but
uplifting entertainments, with perhaps a historical and moral bias
and a local flavor (one aspect of which would be presentation in
English rather than French). Another circumstance concurs: true
courtly poetry deals almost exclusively with love, in some form
or other, as we see in Machaut or Chaucer, and this has to do
with its mixed audience, in which women were prominent. Alliterative verse of the revival, for all its courtly and sophisticated
nature in poems like *Gawain*, never deals with love in this same
way. Love may be a snare, as in *Gawain*, a biological imperative, as in *Clannesse*, but it is never the main business of life,
and it might be suggested that the kind of monastic context I
have sketched in, from which women of course were rigorously
excluded, was peculiarly appropriate for such perversity. Hard
evidence of these entertainments is, as always, lacking, unless we
can allude to the entertainment at St. Swithun's, Winchester, for
the visit of Adam of Orleton, the bishop of Winchester, in 1338,
when a minstrel named Herebert sang of Colbrond and of the
deeds of queen Emma,[66] but I would not wish to suggest that the
alliterative revival, which is monolithic neither in origins nor nature, was stimulated solely by the needs of these monastic entertainments. All the argument needs at this point is evidence of
close contact between the world of aristocratic sophistication and
the world of monastic learning. It would be natural to suppose
that clerks educated in monastic schools often moved out into the
secular world as clerks or chaplains to noble households and there
exercised their skills in alliterative verse on appropriate occasions. There is also movement in the other direction, in the kind
of books that often found their way into monastic libraries. The
books bequeathed by Guy of Warwick to the Cistercian abbey of
Bordesley in Worcestershire in 1305[67] are rich in the French and

Anglo-Norman romance which would have provided an aristocratic leavening for the sterner reading matter that filled most monastic libraries. Somewhat later than our period, but perhaps not entirely irrelevant, there is a bequest by Prior Nicholas Hereford to his abbey of Evesham in 1392, the catalogue of which reads like the library of an alliterative poet, with three copies of a *Bellum Troianum* and a *Vita Alexandri*, as well as a *Mort de Arthur cum Sankreal*, presumably in French.[68]

There are many ways, in fact, in which the kind of context I have tried to suggest could have stimulated the writing of the alliterative poetry of the revival, and I would not wish to eliminate the possibility that the revival was in the last analysis the responsibility of one man, who saw the potential of the unrhymed alliterative line and put it to new uses. Who this man might have been I do not know. It can hardly have been the author of *William of Palerne*, whose verse, though early enough, is not representative of the revival, and not really very good. It might have been the poet of *Winner and Waster*, if that poem is securely dated 1352–53. It may have been Langland, who after all was probably educated at a Southwest Midland monastery.[69] It was in any case, I suggest, in a Southwest Midland monastic context that the alliterative revival had its roots and it is this context that provides continuity for its provenance and a strong directive for its development. As Professor Hilton points out, the diocese of Worcester, in which nearly all the monastic activity I have talked about took place, was "an ancient nucleus . . . which persisted as a unit of economic, social, and cultural life throughout the Middle Ages," and within this diocese, as he says, "no center is more likely to have stimulated the West Midland school of poets than Worcester itself."[70] If we had the documentary evidence that we lack, one might guess that it would point to Worcester.

NOTES

1. Most recently, Charles Moorman, "The Origins of the Alliterative Revival," *Southern Quarterly,* 7 (1969), 345–71.

2. E.g., J. P. Oakden, *Alliterative Poetry in Middle English* (Manchester, 1930–35), II, 85–87; Moorman, loc. cit.

3. For important recent discussion, see *Homilies of Aelfric: A Supplementary Collection*, ed. John C. Pope, EETS 259, 260 (1967–68), Introduction, pp. 105 ff; Sherman M. Kuhn, "Was Aelfric a Poet?" *Philological Quarterly*, 52 (1973), 643–62.

4. See Dorothy Bethurum, "The Connection of the Katherine Group with Old English Prose," *Journal of English and Germanic Philology*, 34 (1935), 553–64; N. F. Blake, "Rhythmical Alliteration," *Modern Philology*, 67 (1969), 118–24.

5. See Oakden, *Alliterative Poetry,* I, 103–9.

6. See Oakden, *Alliterative Poetry,* I, 119–30.

7. E.g., *Hwon holy chireche is under uote, Death,* and *A Lutel soth sermun* in Jesus 29 in *An Old English Miscellany*, ed. Richard Morris, EETS 49 (1872); *The Flemish Insurrection* and *The Execution of Sir Simon Fraser* in Harley 2253 in *Historical Poems of the XIVth and XVth Centuries*, ed. Rossell Hope Robbins (New York, 1959), nos. 3, 4.

8. See Elizabeth Salter, "Piers Plowman and *The Simonie,*" *Archiv*, 203 (1967), 241–54. Auchinleck text in *Political Songs*, ed. Thomas Wright (Camden Society, 1839), pp. 323–45. Comparative edition from 3 MSS by Thomas W. Ross, *A Satire of Edward II's England,* Colorado College Studies no. 8 (Colorado Springs, 1966).

9. *Thomas of Erceldoune's Prophecy* is no. 8 in Robbins, *Historical Poems*; see also nos. 43–47 and *The Romance and Prophecies of Thomas of Erceldoune*, ed. J. A. H. Murray, EETS 61 (1875), Introduction.

10. *English Writings of Richard Rolle*, ed. Hope Emily Allen (Oxford, 1931), p. 64. Rossell Hope Robbins and John L. Cutler, *Supplement to the Index of Middle English Verse* (Lexington, Ky., 1965), no. 197.8.

11. Elizabeth Salter, "The Alliterative Revival I," *Modern Philology*, 64 (1966–67), 146–50, and "The Alliterative Revival II," *Modern Philology*, 64 (1966–67), 233–37.

12. James R. Hulbert, "A Hypothesis concerning the Alliterative Revival," *Modern Philology*, 28 (1931), 405–22. Hulbert's view still appears to be accepted by Moorman, in the article cited above (note 1), p. 351.

13. See E. G. Stanley, "Layamon's Antiquarian Sentiments," *Medium Ævum,* 38 (1969), 23–37.

14. See *Kyng Alisaunder*, ed. G. V. Smithers, EETS 227, 237 (1952–57), Introduction, p. 12.

15. Principally, that is, the Benedictine houses at Worcester, Gloucester,

Evesham, Tewkesbury, Winchcomb, and Leominster; the houses of Austin canons at Cirencester, Lanthony, Bristol, and Wigmore; and the Cistercian house at Bordesley. Most of these are within the diocese of Worcester.

16. W. Aldis Wright draws attention to this borrowing in his edition of the *Chronicle*, Rolls Series 86, 2 vols. (1887), Introduction, pp. xxxiii–xxxvii.

17. Wright (Introduction, p. xxxix) considers that at least two writers, and perhaps a team, were involved, though there has been a tendency to reintegrate authors since his day. For further comment on matters of authorship and provenance, see J. A. W. Bennett and G. V. Smithers, eds., *Early Middle English Verse and Prose* (Oxford, 1966), pp. 158–59; Anne Hudson, "Tradition and Innovation in Some Middle English Manuscripts," *Review of English Studies*, NS 17 (1966), 359–72. In the latter there is an up-to-date list of MSS of the *Chronicle*, as there is again in the same author's "Robert of Gloucester and the Antiquaries, 1550–1800," *Notes and Queries*, NS 16 (1969), 322–33.

18. The evidence is by no means overwhelming, since the name appears only in two MSS, both of the earlier recension, of course. It could be the name of a scribe, though this would be unusual in the body of a text. The name, in any case, is all we have. One possible identification might be Robert of Aldsworth, a monk of Gloucester (ca. 1275), whose name appears on the cover of a Bible he had made for himself, together with a list of his books. The Bible is now Corpus Christi College, Cambridge, MS 485: see Montague Rhodes James, *A Descriptive Catalogue of the Manuscripts in the Library of Corpus Christi College Cambridge*, 2 vols. (Cambridge, 1912), II, 438. Among the books listed is a "Summa Gaufridi," perhaps a digest of Geoffrey of Monmouth's *Historia*, which is a major source for the *Chronicle*. Another possibility, if we can assume that Robert was a child in 1265, is the Robert of Gloucester, canon of Lanthony, who was unsuccessfully presented as prior in 1324 and subsequently, in 1326, permitted to enter the abbey of St. Thomas in Dublin, and (an unusual provision) to take his books with him (*VCH, Gloucester*, II, 89); see also J. N. Langston, "Priors of Lanthony by Gloucester," *Transactions of the Bristol and Gloucestershire Archaeological Society*, 63 (1942), 1–144, esp. 77–80. This is presumably the R. de Gloucester, canon of Lanthony, who owned the copy of Aristotle's *Metaphysica* which is now Lambeth MS 55: see Montague Rhodes James and Claude Jenkins, *A Descriptive Catalogue of the Manuscripts in the Library of Lambeth Palace* (Cambridge, 1930).

19. The explanation offered for the omission of the more recondite prophecies of Merlin suggests a nonclerical audience: "Of þe prophecye of merlin . we ne mowe telle namore/ Vor it is so derc to simplemen . bote me were þe bet in lore" (2819–20). The assumption of monastic provenance for a work such as this in English argues that English had a higher status in western monasteries than one might expect. The argument is borne out by M.

Dominica Legge's comment that the western houses are but thinly represented as centers of Anglo-Norman (*Anglo-Norman in the Cloisters* [Edinburgh, 1950], p. 125), and by the famous lines in the *Chronicle* itself on the status of the English language (7542–47).

20. EETS 196 (1935), ed. Ewald Zettl. *The Chronicle of Robert Mannyng,* translated (1338) from the Anglo-Norman of Peter of Langtoft, and designed "not for þe lerid bot for þe lewed" (Frederick J. Furnivall, ed., Rolls series 87, 1887, line 6), is somewhat closer to this popular audience than Robert of Gloucester's *Chronicle*.

21. Especially since one MS of Robert's *Chronicle* (B.L. MS Addit. 19677) also contains the *Short English Metrical Chronicle*.

22. See Wright, Introduction, p. xi.

23. See Wright, Introduction, p. xliii.

24. In Wright's edition, Appendix E, of 12 lines, corresponding to Layamon's *Brut*, ed. G. L. Brook, Vol. I, EETS 250 (1963), lines 1437–47; Appendix G of 268 lines, corresponding to *Brut*, 1950–3036; and Appendix H, of 282 lines, corresponding to *Brut*, 3132–3525. The suggestion that the *Chronicle* borrows elsewhere from Layamon is briefly dismissed by R. H. Fletcher, *The Arthurian Material in the Chronicles*, Harvard Studies and Notes in Philology and Literature, 10 (1906); rpt. with additions by Roger Sherman Loomis (New York, 1966), p. 195.

25. *Chronicle*, Appendix G, 47–51; *Brut* (Caligula MS), 2015–18. Further examples of detailed borrowing include (*Chronicle* references first): in Appendix E, 3–5, 1438–41; 7–8, 1446; 12, 1447; in Appendix G, 8–9, 1956–57; 62–64, 2032–34; in Appendix H, 13–16, 3155–60; 21, 3168; 31–33, 3179–81; 65–69, 3224–28; 73–78, 3236–40; 119, 3308; 216, 3455; 233, 3479.

26. As is suggested by the copying of the significant Caligula error, *wif* for *wit* (3179), in Appendix H, 32 (see also Wright, Introduction, p. xxxvii).

27. As is suggested by the error *duc* (Appendix H, 54) for Caligula *deor* (3209), presumably through an intermediary *dur*.

28. E.g., *feþerhome* (Appendix E, 2: *Brut* 1438), recorded in *MED*, after Layamon, only here and in two poems of the Alliterative Revival, *The Wars of Alexander* and *The Siege of Jerusalem* (presumably by direct descent), before its appearance in late fifteenth-century Scots; *weþelede* (Appendix E, 5: *Brut* 1441), for which *OED* records only the Layamon reference; *cousti* (Appendix G, 63: *Brut* 2033), a favorite word in Layamon, for which *MED* (s.v. *kisti*) adds an interesting reference in the Worcester glosses to Aelfric, though neither *OED* nor *MED* record any use of the word after Layamon; *chiuese* (Appendix H, 21 [see Wright's errata, p. 1017]: *Brut* 3168), which *MED* (s.v. *chevese*) records in the Worcester glosses and the Katherine-group *St. Margaret* but after that, apart from Layamon, only in the life of St. Theophilus in the *Northern Homily Cycle*. The *Chronicle* writer also of course modernizes Layamon a great deal, and in the process

often hits upon the same reading as the similarly modernized Otho text (e.g., Appendix H, 119: *Brut* 3308).

29. E.g., *Winner and Waster*, 1–4; *Sir Gawain and the Green Knight*, 1–36, 2522–28; *St. Erkenwald*, 207; *Morte Arthure*, 1694–99, 4342–46.

30. See Mary E. Giffin, "Cadwalader, Arthur and Brutus in the Wigmore Manuscript," *Speculum*, 16 (1941), 109–10. But note the criticism of this essay in R. S. Loomis, "Edward I, Arthurian Enthusiast," *Speculum*, 28 (1953), 114–27, particularly of the early date (1279) proposed by Giffin for a political interest on the part of the Mortimers in the Arthurian legend. Loomis gives a good account of the general interest in Arthur in the late thirteenth and early fourteenth centuries. See also the comment by Archbishop Peckham (1284) on the popularity of tales of the Trojan descent of Britain, noted in R. M. Wilson, *The Lost Literature of Medieval England* (London, 1952; 2d ed., 1970), p. 111.

31. The *South English Legendary* is edited from two MSS by Charlotte d'Evelyn and Anna J. Mill, EETS 235, 236 (1956); the earlier edition, from Laud MS 108, by C. Horstmann, EETS 87 (1887), is not relevant here. The closest parallels (*Chronicle* references first) are as follows: 91–110, *Kenelm* 21–39; 115–34, *Kenelm* 47–70; 5812–27, *Edward* 14–32; 5840–77, *Edward* 41–92; 5896–5907, *Edward* 97–108 (Wright, Introduction, p. xx, associates these lines with the life of St. Dunstan, but in the edition used here they are part of the continuation of the life of St. Edward); 6051ff., *Alphege* 89ff. (the borrowing here is less close); 9603–11, *Becket* 206–14; 9618–21, *Becket* 285–88; 9626–29, *Becket* 319–23; 9655–9725, *Becket* 544–614; 9768–81, *Becket* 2130–44; 9782–91, *Becket* 2153–62; 9792–97, *Becket* 2171–76. For the fullest recent discussion of the borrowings, see M. Görlach, *The Textual Tradition of the South English Legendary* (Leeds Texts and Monographs, NS 6, 1974), pp. 40–45.

32. The direction of the borrowings, in the case of the life of St. Kenelm, is shown by Beatrice Daw Brown, "Robert of Gloucester's *Chronicle* and the *Life of St. Kenelm*," *Modern Language Notes*, 41 (1926), 13–23. See further Görlach, p. 40.

33. Görlach, pp. 37–38.

34. See the Introduction by Beatrice Daw Brown to her edition of the *Southern Passion*, EETS 169 (1927), chap. V. For full discussion of the question of provenance, see Görlach, pp. 45–50, where it is suggested that the *Legendary* was of Benedictine authorship, possibly for a community of nuns or for parish use, and probably from the Worcester area (pp. 32–37).

35. For some account of the origins and development of the legend, see E. S. Hartland, "The Legend of St. Kenelm," *Transactions of the Bristol and Gloucestershire Archaeological Society*, 39 (1916), 13–65.

36. *Kenelm* 267–68, with emendation of *a* to *haȝ* (cf. line 187, and line 282 in MS Harley 2277), as suggested by Bennett and Smithers (*Early Middle English Verse and Prose*) in their editions of the Laud 108 text of the *Life* (p.

104), on the basis of other extant versions of the couplet (see below).

37. The descriptive phrase quoted in the text is from Bennett and Smithers, p. 96. For quotation of the lines in Latin chronicles, see the *Chronica Maiora* of Matthew Paris, ed. Henry Richards Luard, Rolls Series 57, 7 vols. (1872–84), I, 373; the continuation of the St. Alban's *Chronicle* known as *Flores Historiarum*, ed. Henry Richards Luard, Rolls Series 95, 3 vols. (1890), I, 412; Higden's *Polychronicon*, ed. Joseph Lawson Lumby, Rolls Series 41, 9 vols. (1869–86), VI, 306. See Wilson, *Lost Literature*, p. 99.

38. This manuscript, a twelfth-century copy of Bede, comes from Tynemouth priory, a Northumberland cell of St. Alban's, whence, presumably, the historiographical connection. See *Medieval Libraries of Great Britain: A List of Surviving Books*, ed. N. R. Ker, 2d ed. (London, 1964), p. 191.

39. Wright, Appendix X, 5–6.

40. Wilson, pp. 28–30, 38, 96, 114, 125.

41. The line can be found in *Descriptio Kambriae*, I. xii: ed. James F. Dimock, *Opera* (Rolls Series 21, 1861–77), VI, 188. Giraldus gives two further examples of alliteration in English, but they are not lines of alliterative verse.

42. Bartlett Jere Whiting considers the line proverbial; see his *Proverbs, Sentences, and Proverbial Phrases from English Writings mainly before 1500* (Cambridge, Mass., 1968), p. 222 (no. G17).

43. *The Gests of King Alexander of Macedon*, ed. Francis Peabody Magoun (Cambridge, Mass., 1929), pp. 18–22.

44. *Alexander, fragment A*, ed. Walter W. Skeat, EETS ES 1 (1867), lines 178–99.

45. Guido de Columnis, *Historia Destructionis Troiae*, ed. Nathaniel Edward Griffin (Cambridge, Mass., 1936), pp. 71–73.

46. Nicolas Jacobs, "Alliterative Storms: a Topos in Middle English," *Speculum*, 47 (1972), 695–719.

47. *Alexander A*, lines 456–58.

48. *Siege of Jerusalem*, ed. E. Kölbing and Mabel Day, EETS 188 (1932), Introduction, p. xix; Phyllis Moe, "The French source of the alliterative *Siege of Jerusalem*," *Medium Ævum*, 39 (1970), 147–54.

49. See James Westfall Thompson, *The Medieval Library* (Chicago, 1939), pp. 267–310, 373–413; R. M. Wilson, "The Contents of the Medieval Library," in *The English Library before 1700*, ed. Francis Wormald and C. E. Wright (London, 1958), pp. 85–111, esp. 99–100; Ker, *Medieval Libraries of Great Britain*, passim; K. Humphreys, "The Distribution of Books in the English West Midlands in the Later Middle Ages," *Libri*, 17 (1967), 1–12.

50. See Wilson, *Lost Literature*, pp. 151–53.

51. See *Homilies of Aelfric*, ed. Pope, Introduction, pp. 185–88; *Homilies of Wulfstan*, ed. Dorothy Bethurum (Oxford, 1957), pp. 104–6; N. R. Ker, *Catalogue of Manuscripts Containing Anglo-Saxon* (Oxford, 1957), p. xlix.

52. See Angus F. Cameron, "Middle English in Old English Manuscripts," *Chaucer and Middle English Studies in Honour of Rossell Hope Robbins*, ed. Beryl Rowland (London, 1974), pp. 218–29.

53. See S. J. Crawford, "The Worcester Marks and Glosses," *Anglia*, 52 (1928), 1–25.

54. Ker, *Medieval Libraries of Great Britain*, p. 198.

55. Carleton Brown, "A Thirteenth-Century Manuscript from Lanthony Priory," *Speculum,* 3 (1928), 587–95. The manuscript, Corpus Christi College, Oxford, MS 59, appears to be a personal miscellany and workbook; its contents are mostly Latin, and include verses in praise of Humphrey de Bohun (d. 1275).

56. Thorlac Turville-Petre, "Humphrey de Bohun and *William of Palerne,*" *Neuphilologische Mitteilungen,* 75 (1974), 250–52. Lanthony had an exceptionally large library for such a small house, as appears from the early fourteenth-century catalogue (T. W. Williams, "Gloucestershire Medieval Libraries," *Transactions of the Bristol and Gloucestershire Archaeological Society*, 31 [1908], 78–195, esp. 139–78), and acquired a further fifty-seven volumes from the bequest of John Leche, a king's clerk and great pluralist, in 1361: see A. B. Emden, *A Biographical Register of the University of Oxford to 1500*, 3 vols. (Oxford, 1957–59), II, 1119. Many of these books are now in Lambeth Palace Library (see the catalogue of M. R. James, passim).

57. For the serious concerns of this poetry, see G. T. Shepherd, "The Nature of Alliterative Poetry in Late Medieval England," *Proceedings of the British Academy*, 56 (1970), 57–76.

58. R. H. Hilton, *A Medieval Society: The West Midlands at the End of the Thirteenth Century* (London, 1966), p. 34.

59. *VCH, Worcester*, II, 101.

60. See David Knowles, *The Religious Orders in England 1216–1340* (Cambridge, 1948), pp. 78–112.

61. Knowles, p. 101.

62. Rose Graham, "The Metropolitan Visitation of the Diocese of Worcester by Archbishop Winchelsey in 1301," in *English Ecclesiastical Studies* (London, 1929), pp. 330–59 (see p. 345).

63. A plea from the prior and convent of Worcester: "The claims on their hospitality increase by reason of the number of people who come to Worcester both for law-suits and to cross the river by the bridge, which is the only one for 48 leagues" (*The Register of Walter Reynolds, Bishop of Worcester 1308–13*, ed. R. A. Wilson, Dugdale Society Publications 9 [1928], p. 75). Complaints about the burden of hospitality were, admittedly, standard procedure in making requests for the appropriation of benefices.

64. *VCH, Worcester*, II, 101.

65. *Historia et Cartularium Monasterii Sancti Petri Gloucestriae*, ed. W. H. Hart, Rolls Series 33, 3 vols. (1863–67), I, 38, 44, 52.

66. Thomas Warton, *History of English Poetry,* ed. W. C. Hazlitt (London, 1871), II, 97; P. Christophersen, *The Ballad of Sir Aldingar* (Oxford, 1952), pp. 33–36. Emma, widow of Cnut, was a great benefactress of St. Swithun's, and her anniversary was regularly kept there: *Computus Rolls of the Obedientiaries of St. Swithin's Priory, Winchester,* ed. G. W. Kitchin, Hampshire Record Society (London and Winchester, 1892), esp. p. 232.
67. Madeleine Blaess, "L'abbaye de Bordesley et les livres de Guy de Beauchamp," *Romania,* 78 (1957), 511–18.
68. *Documents relating to the Priory of Penwortham,* ed. W. A. Hulton, Chetham Society 30 (Manchester, 1853), pp. 94–97.
69. *The Vision of William concerning Piers the Plowman,* ed. Walter W. Skeat, 2 vols. (Oxford, 1886), II, xxxii–xxxiii.
70. Hilton, *Medieval Society,* pp. 25–26.

2

The Characterization of Women in the Alliterative Tradition

MAUREEN FRIES

When I began investigating the subject of this paper, I was suspicious of the blanket statements everywhere encountered on the supposed "masculinity" of both content and tone in the fourteenth-century Alliterative Tradition. Considering the alliterative poets as a whole, Dorothy Everett held that their avoidance of "love-romances" and preference for "historical, or pseudo-historical, subjects" was an instinct the rightness of which was proven by the "essential unsuitability" of their medium for sentimental passages detailing male-female love relationships, "made ludicrous by the heavy insistence of the alliterative lines."[1] More recently, Charles Moorman has asserted that these poets "re-established much of the stern, ringing masculinity" of the heroic age of English poetry.[2] Such statements could be multiplied, but through them all run two implicit and unproved assumptions, one related to literary theme, the other to the alliterative meter itself. The first implies that the only characterization of a woman possible in fourteenth-century poetry is as the heroine of romance operating in a chivalric milieu; the second, that there is something innately unsuitable for characterizing females in the alliterative line itself. However, such assumptions fail to account for the striking feminine portraits in fourteenth-century alliterative poetry, particularly the balanced pairs of opposites: Gaynour and her mother's ghost in *The Awntyrs off Arthure at the Terne*

25

Wathelyn, Bertilak's Lady and Morgan le Fay in *Sir Gawain and the Green Knight*, Lady Holy Church and Lady Mede in *Piers Plowman*. Nor do such assumptions provide for the rich allusiveness of the Pearl in the poem which bears her name, nor for the sprightly maneuvers of Bertilak's wife in her dalliance with Gawain. Above all they exclude the varied tapestry of social life among women of all classes that weaves its way through the pages of *Piers Plowman*.[3]

My present subject embraces primarily some of the Arthurian romances: to discover how far the concerns common to the alliterative poets, such as an interest in contemporary manners and mores, and a ubiquitous moral seriousness, extend to the characterization of women in the Alliterative Tradition and in what fashion such concerns may have emerged.

Analysis of the characterization of women in medieval literature has generally suffered from a misleading oversimplification. A recent critic of *Piers Plowman* calls Lady Mede "second only to Criseide as the most fascinating female in medieval English literature"—not only overlooking the Wife of Bath (a slight I am sure she would greatly have resented) but speaking of Mede as if she were a personality created for her own sake, as in the modern psychological novel.[4] Yet, as Erich Auerbach has shown, medieval characterization moved from representing "the remote legendary hero" or "abstract or anecdotal . . . ethical type" only gradually to the depiction of "man as we know him in his living historical reality."[5] Derek Brewer has suggested that such characterization exists on a line stretching from the pole of "character as role" on the one hand to "character as personality" on the other (a pole he feels medieval authors rarely and only partially reached).[6] Sister Ritamary Bradley has refined these concepts further in a recent unpublished paper suggesting the modes of archetype, stereotype, and reality, as methods of approaching the characterization of women in medieval literature.[7]

Archetype, in the sense it had in the Middle Ages (which preferred the title *speculum*) means the reflection of Divine Consciousness in language.[8] Directly, the Image of God in human consciousness illuminates by Divine Wisdom and should lead to the grasping and love of the Good; indirectly, its darkening by human folly and/or satanic guile produces evil, which we should shun. Language is a desirable medium because of the pervasive doctrine of the Incarnation of the Word as Flesh, so conceived and used by the theologians and even secular poets. Archetypes in medieval literature may include men, women, things, and events, but Sister Bradley's statement that female archetypes "are used generally without discrimination" needs qualification. The primary source for archetypes, biblical exegesis, was notoriously unsympathetic to women and produced more negative or neutered than positive female archetypes. In medieval illustrations of the Fall, the serpent was consistently depicted with the face of a beautiful woman, because of Eve's supposedly greater blame for Original Sin and in spite of the Old Testament's assignment of blame on Adam equally with Eve (Genesis 3:16–24). Like her successors, Delilah, Bathsheba, and Potiphar's Wife, Eve became known as the source and symbol of lust and the dangers of the Flesh; it was she who led Adam astray (I Timothy 2:14). Opposed to Eve and her tribe was the influential but unique archetype of the Virgin Mary, who had achieved the highly desirable condition of motherhood of Christ without the questionable act of sexual intercourse; she was the second Eve, the perpetual virgin, the Divine Mother.[9] In the writings of Justin Martyr, Irenaeus, and Tertullian, just as Christ is juxtaposed with Adam, so is Mary juxtaposed with Eve; but there are few positive archetypal analogues for Mary in the Old Testament to balance the Christological precursors—Isaac, Samson, David, and others.[10] Strong Old Testament women were often neutered into abstractions, Judith the Church, for instance, and Sarah the Old Testament itself.[11] Although Christ had displayed everywhere in the New Testament his love and respect for women, not only his Mother but Mary and Martha, Mary Magdalene, and his other female disciples, and although women had remained loyal to Christ when men had wavered, such females were rarely accorded a positive significance.[12] Mary Magdalene is the only exception of importance, constituting as she does a sort of transition from the bad woman (the tradition of Eve) to the good (although never equal to the Virgin).[13]

A second and more positive influence upon female archetypes was personification allegory, where, from classical precedent, Christian writers portrayed the virtues as well as the vices as feminine.[14] In the decisive work in this tradition, the *Psychomachia* of Prudentius, female archetypes appear as suggesting the relative strengths and weaknesses of the vices and virtues they represent. Superbia is as valiant a warrior as any man, while Ira perishes by her own hand because Patientia is reluctant to engage her in combat.[15] But while the archetypes are all female, most of the exempla cited are male, with the interesting exceptions of Judith and the Virgin Mary as victors over lust.[16] This tendency continues in Boethius' *Consolatio*, with the balanced figures of Lady Philosophy and Dame Fortune, and in the allegories of Martianus Capella and Alanus de Insulis. In all these works, as in the bulk of exegetical writings, women appear as forces for good as well as forces for evil. Allegory was thus potentially fair to both sexes, although it could become antifeminist in a woman-hating environment.

A third source for female archetypes arose from the very nature of the romance itself.[17] With the rise of the European vernaculars and what used to be called "courtly love,"[18] the lady of romance, that tantalizing and unattainable figure, becomes the ambivalent mirror in which the knight pictures his own potential for moral achievement or moral failure in terms of the male warrior ethos such literature was designed to glorify. As Frederick Goldin shows, while many courtly poets never question "the moral indispensibility of this figure they praise . . . , the most interesting consider everything that a mirror is, recognizing, along with its . . . passivity, its mendacity, its dangerous innocence, its soullessness."[19] How little such romances are really about women appears from the ease with which Arthur's knights, in the French *Prose Vulgate*, turn their attention from their ladies to the pursuit of the Holy Grail, a mirror of the ideal rather than a mirror mixed with matter such as the courtly lady. Recognition

of the lady's role as an instrument for the perfection of a male
warrior class may force, as Sister Bradley has noted, "a revision
of opinion about the apparent shift from idealization to misogyny
in attitudes toward the female" in the Middle Ages: we should
recognize that antifeminism is always a danger whenever "a
female figure"—whether she be the Virgin Mary or the courtly
lady—"is idealized as a cult object."[20]

Closely related to archetype is the second category for studying
female characterization, stereotype, or the assumption that behavior is sex-linked. Although the Argument About Women, as
Francis L. Utley called it, originated in classical times, it prolif-
erated in the medieval period and provided a separate class of
medieval satire.[21] To all women were ascribed the sins of Eve:
women as a class represented, as she did, the Flesh or Lower Reason, while men, like Adam, stood for Higher Reason. Because
Adam had failed to guide his wife properly, and because all
women shared in Eve's sin, women should be silent and submissive to their husbands. So runs the argument from the random
(and sometimes contradictory) remarks of Paul, whose expectation of an imminent *parousia* colored his view of women and
marriage, through St. Augustine down to St. Bonaventura.[22] St.
Thomas attempted to reconcile science and reason with the teachings of the Church and recognized the differences in human per-
sonalities in body as well as in soul. He nevertheless concluded
that differences between male and female are substantial: that
woman is inferior to man, since man represents perfection while
woman comes into being *per accidens* as *mas occasionatus* ("the
male gone awry"); that woman depends on man in the act of
procreation (of which man is the only active and form-giving
principle) and for guidance, whereas man needs woman only for
begetting his children; and that even the rights to marital intercourse are not equal, since man is the master and woman by nature his servant.[23] Such teachings penetrated into every sphere of
life.

Aquinas' prejudices derived in large part from the teachings
of Aristotle; and, as Vern L. Bullough has recently noted, "the
clerics themselves were reflecting not only their own prejudices

but also those of ancient and medieval science,'' which considered women inferior anatomically and physiologically.[24] Besides the lust associated with Eve, women were accused of vanity, pride, and insubordination, and treatises on them suggested that the only hope for their salvation was to train them to be pure, humble, and submissive. Paradoxically, the weak Eve was somehow stronger than Adam, and so all men were warned to avoid the snares of woman's beautiful body, which was in reality, as St. Odo declared (and Bromyard after him), a sack of dung.[25] Such themes may be found in sermon collections, marriage manuals, penitentials, instructions for wives and children, and (whether we take it satirically or not) even in the third book of Andreas Capellanus' *De arte honeste amandi*.[26]

Often contradistinct from stereotype is the third category of female characterization, the depiction of reality, which I propose to study both in its Auerbachian sense of *figura* and in its reflection of everyday fourteenth-century life.[27] *Figura* is the linking of events or persons neither temporally nor causally but vertically to Divine Providence. In figural reality, the Incarnation represents the center of history, and all else radiates out from that center: ''an occurrence on earth signifies not only itself but at the same time another, which it predicts or confirms, without prejudice to the power of its concrete reality here and now.''[28] As such, figural reality is intimately linked with archetype as we have already defined it; but from the time of Dante's *Commedia,* figural reality has been undermined by a concern with the human for its own sake: in Auerbach's terms, the image of man has eclipsed the image of God.[29] Thus woman's behavior is often presented in fourteenth-century literature not only in figural terms but also in terms of historical reality. Fourteenth-century women in real life often varied considerably from their stereotypes.[30] While canon law and civil law (especially its English version) implied a subjection for women which must have been applauded by their theological critics, in practice woman's position depended more upon her social rank than upon her sex.[31] A number of women did very occasionally exercise (because of royal birth or marriage) extraordinary power, but Eleanor of Aquitaine's bare-breasted crusading and royal politicking are offset by dismal decades of imprisonment by her royal husband.[32] In spite of women's supposed limitations, middle-class as well as noble women acted as agents but had little freedom in the choice of a marriage partner, as the Paston Letters demonstrate.[33] Eileen Power has asserted that women of the upper ranks, where feudal ties determined such human relationships as marriage as well as much else, were actually *less* free than poorer women, who seem to have enjoyed in practice equality with men.[34] Vanity in dress in women was frequently decried from the pulpit, but the male courtiers of Richard II were apparently equally vain.[35] Lust is harder to document, but historical records indicate not only that men were as lustful as (if not more so than) women, but far more likely to get away with it.[36] Reality, then, transcended stereotype and frequently gave it the lie.

From this extended but necessary introduction, I now turn to the alliterative poems themselves and to the characterization of women in that tradition. In the Arthurian poems of the Alliterative Tradition there is a refreshing range of female characterization, from the limited but realistic representation of the *Morte Arthure* through the striking archetypes of *The Awntyrs off Arthure* to the fascinating mixture of archetype, stereotype, and realistic behavior that contributes so much to the excellence of *Sir Gawain and the Green Knight*.[37] William Matthews has correctly noted that "even those few traces" of "women and love" which appear in "the chronicle sources are minimized" in the *Alliterative Morte*.[38] Yet Gaynor, the only female character in the poem (if we exclude the undeveloped archetype of the Duchess of Metz, and Lady Fortune of the Dream), is treated not only with respect but even with almost unprecedented sympathy. Arthur carefully instructs Mordred, here his unwilling regent, that she must be held in worship, and that—while only she may hunt his game—she must take this solace only at fixed times (652–53, 657–59). To his sources the poet has added the realistic and moving leave taking between king and queen (695–716). The initial impression is thus of a dignified, loving, and believable relationship. When Sir Craddock, who brings the news of Mordred's having wed Gaynor and gotten her with child, tells his tidings to Arthur, neither man blames Gaynor (3550–52, 3575–76). Even Mordred is solicitous of Gaynor, writing her to flee with her (presumably their) children (3904–10). That Gaynor thinks herself guilty appears from her taking the veil, because of her falsehood and fear of her lord (3918). Yet, though ordering the slaying of Mordred's children, Arthur refuses to pass judgment upon her: " 'Yife Waynor hafe wele wroghte, wele hir betydde!' " (4325). In spite of a purposeful choice of a male warrior ethos, then, the poet of the *Morte* displays neither stereotyped antifeminism nor concomitant biased attitudes toward women. That he maintains this stance anent a woman already widely reviled in the French romances he obviously knew is even more remarkable.

This dignified treatment of Gaynour (as her name becomes) continues in *The Awntyrs off Arthure*, where she is transformed into an archetype of combined courtly and spiritual significance. The poet, greatly rationalizing his plot from its apparent source(s), indicated androgynous instincts in his portrayal of Gawayn and Gaynour in similar archetypal terms.[39] Each represents a special form of *superbia* as the root of all sins: Gawayn primarily *avaritia* and Gaynour *luxuria*. As the poem opens, their status as courtly archetypes is emphasized in the description of Gaynour's costume (14–26), Gawayn's gaiety (12, 68), and the badinage of courtly flirtation in which they indulge (92–99). This sophisticated veneer contrasts grotesquely with the appearance of Gaynour's mother's ghost as she rises from the "loghe . . . In the lyknes of Lucyfere, layetheste [in helle]" (83–84), with her reminder of her kinship to Gaynour couched in a curse, " 'I bane þe body me bare' " (89). The ghost's present state is a gruesome reminder of the end to which Arthurian courtly pride must come, and a striking juxtaposition of the spiritual reality of eternity and the artificial banality of courtly pretensions. In the dialogue which follows, the ghost tells Gaynour that the "baleful bestes" (211) which now circle and sting her head are the courtly hazards of "luf paramour, listes and delites" (213) in which she had herself indulged, and which she warns her daughter to avoid. Incidentally, this ghost, who stresses the dangers of lust in conversation with her daughter, places charity before chastity among the virtues (252). That she explicitly represents a *speculum* for her daughter emerges from the bob-and-wheel in which she calls herself Gaynour's "mirrour" (166–69). While she is Gaynour's exemplum, France (recently conquered by the Arthurians) is Gawayn's—and by extension Arthur's.

Gaynour exercises charity in the latter part of the poem, not only in the " 'thritty trentales' " (218) of masses requested by her mother, but in action as well: at the request of Sir Galerone's lady she intervenes to halt his battle with Gawayn over lands wrongfully given to Gawayn by Arthur (636–37). This charitable impulse spreads to both Arthur and Gawayn, but it stemmed from Gaynour's example. Seen as theme expressed through the strikingly rich juxtaposition and amalgamation of courtly and spiritual archetype, and subsequent *exempla* in all three Arthurians' actions, the *Awntyrs* does not exhibit the assumed cleavage between two supposed "halves" of which it has been accused, but emerges as a unified entity.

Like the *Awntyrs, Sir Gawain and the Green Knight* rejects the stereotyped *descriptio pulchritudinis feminae* of Guinivere which had become a romance commonplace, and chooses the same detail to indicate awareness of its triteness: the *Awntyrs*-poet cites her "grey eyen" (598), the *Gawain*-poet her "yʒen gray" (82). Guenore (the name-variant here) is not an important character in *Gawain*, although supposedly Morgan le Fay has set in motion the action of the poem to frighten her to death (2459–61). But another courtly lady, Sir Bertilak's Wife, functions both as a courtly and a spiritual archetype for Gawain. As she displays to him in words and action her assessment of his reputation, Gawain realizes what he might (and almost does) become: an unchaste lover of women, debasing both earthly and heavenly *cortayse* to which he is dedicated by betraying chastity and "trawþe."

In perhaps the most interesting variation on the female *descriptio* in medieval romance, the poet first presents the lady in an elaborate double *effictio* juxtaposed to the other female archetype of the poem, Morgan, already the most famous mirror of moral evil in Arthurian romance, even though she could also be a

beneficient fay.[40] In this double portrait (943–69), in which the
lady appears to Gawain "wener þen Wenore" (945), for every
feature which now enhances the younger woman's beauty, the
poet gives us not only its opposite in the older one, but suggests
what the lady herself is bound to become in moral as well as in
physical terms. Her "riche red . . . chekez" will turn "rugh"
and "ronkled" like those of Morgan; her "kerchofes . . . with
mony cler perleȝ" which now display "hir brest and hir byrȝt
þrote bare" will needs be covered by "a gorger . . . ouer hir
blake chyn" and a high gown "treleted with tryflez" to disguise
her body's decay. The lady whom Gawain now finds "lykkerwys
on to lyk" will become as "soure" and "sellyly blered" as her
companion (952–69 *passim*). This change is not only inevitable in
the course of nature, but unavoidable in moral terms, if we remember the French anecdote that Morgan lost her looks precisely
when "elle fu aspiree et de luxure et de dyable."[41] The lady's
pronounced tendencies in the poem toward *luxure,* and her motivation at the command of her husband, who has been identified
by several critics with the devil (and whose intentions toward
Gawain are, to say the least, diabolic), suggest a similar fate.
Here stereotype is transcended by archetype as the *Gawain*-poet
uses *effictio* to suggest *notatio* in a manner worthy of Chaucer's
in the *General Prologue.*

But the lady's function as an archetype of evil emerges not
only from this paratactic comparison with static Morgan, but also
in her actions toward the hero. The lady of romance is a "good"
archetype only when she prods the knight out of the indolence
which is one side of *luxure* and into that life of chivalric activity
through which he must constantly prove his own worth, as romances had illustrated from the time of Chrétien de Troyes. As
has often been noted, Bertilak, the lady's husband, is leading just
such an active life during the three days Gawain spends in
luxurious indolence—an indolence which seems extreme even in
terms of his long and hazardous journey to Bertilak's castle, and
the ordeal he must presently face. Not only does the poet frame
Gawain's indolence within these scenes of Bertilak's activity, but
he also constantly contrasts the lives led by the two men:

þe lede with þe ladyez layked alle day,
Bot þe lorde ouer þe londez launced ful ofte.

(1560–61)

Metaphors of capture emphasize the lady's role in Gawain's inactivity. On her first day's visit to his bedroom, she says:

"Now are ȝe tan as-tyt! Bot true vus may schape,
I schal bynde yow in your bedde, þat be ȝe trayst."

(1210–11)

Gawain takes up this metaphor, attempting to rise, and asking the lady to release her prisoner; but she replies with her mock courtesy that he may not rise, because she has "kaȝt" him (1223–25). On the following two days of her assault, Gawain also remains a slugabed; his only actions are the negative ones of avoiding her advances, reluctantly rendering the requested kisses, and sharing daily masses, meals, and games with the two ladies (1309–13, 1558–60, 1885–92). Besides reminding him of the side of his reputation he thus discloses, his ability to bring "blysse into boure" (1519), the lady also tells Gawain how "trwe knyȝtes" usually behave (1514–18), reminding him of the more necessary side he is now neglecting.[42] Yet all of her actions are designed to deprive Gawain of any chance of behaving in the properly chivalrous fashion. Even her giving him the green girdle he reluctantly accepts suggests that he will be passive in his coming and dreaded encounter.

The *Gawain*-poet's obviously wide reading in romance may imply that he purposely gives us in Bertilak's lady the opposite of our usual expectations of the lady's courtly function. Rather than acting as a means for the man she claims to love to achieve self-realization, she successfully *prevents* him from doing so. Moreover, as a putatively adulterous woman caught between husband and would-be lover, she further epitomizes the destructive side of womanly love familiar, from the stories of Isode and Guinivere as well as from numerous exegetical interpretations, to the poet, his audience, and us. Her behavior is similar to the stereotyped archetypal enchantresses of romance, like Morgan, with whom, however, I do not think she should be identified: she is, as the Green Knight explicitly informs Gawain, his and Morgan's instrument rather than the Fay's other self.[43] The reversal of the lady's expected archetypal role is given further point by the poet's amusing reversal of male and female sex roles between Gawain and the lady. However we interpret the lady's first day's offer of her "cors" to Gawain, she obviously takes the initiative on all three days, even while attempting to make Gawain into the bold lover she imagines (or pretends to imagine) him to be.[44] As J. F. Kiteley notes, she "speaks in the person of the woman when it furthers her purpose" (e.g., 1297–1301); but finding Gawain unresponsive, "she uses the terms of the courtly lover" as recommended by Andreas Capellanus.[45]

This double reversal of ladylike behavior in archetypal function and stereotyped sex role helps lend the poem its air of comedy of manners. But we must ultimately read it as a serious work, and of course the lady is an evil archetype in spiritual as well as in merely courtly terms. I believe this deeper meaning of her role emerges in Gawain's much commented-upon "antifeminist" speech to her husband near the end of the poem.[46] Here he has discovered that her motivation has not been the mere courtly dalliance which might be forgiven in a bored and provincial lady but an attempt upon his *cortayse* in its eternal as well as earthly sense. Earlier, the *poet* had hinted at Gawain's moral peril, and suggested that the lady was a spiritual as well as a courtly archetype by invoking an antitype, the Virgin (1768–69). But at that point, when Gawain's courtesy and loyalty (to say nothing of his chastity) had been tempted by the lady's advances, *he* did not project his anger upon her, but turned it inward, blaming himself (1657–62). Now, discovering that she has acted not upon her own initiative but as an instrument of evil, he compulsively compares her to that standard list of stereotyped archetypes developed by the Fathers, including Eve, Delilah, and Bathsheba (2414–78). Of course this passage may well represent Gawain's traditional role in the *blasme des femmes* tradition.[47] I think, however, that it also suggests the poet's vision of the lady as a religious as well as courtly archetype. Good-humored as it seems, the passage may even be a parody of the stereotyped pronouncements upon women familiar to the poet and his audience. In a more serious vein, it is necessary for Gawain's self-realization that he should understand the lady's moral as well as her courtly significance.

Because of her grouping with this exemplary company of female deceivers, we might have expected the lady's actions within the poem to be as stereotyped as medieval conceptions of them. How delightful, then, to find in her interplay with Gawain the result of a keen and steady observation of the actualities of fourteenth-century courtly life. The lady may be Morgan's or her husband's instrument, the role that the Fathers envisioned for all women. However, rather than behaving like a puppet, presumably remotely controlled with some sort of medieval radar by Morgan or Bertilak, the lady invariably and acutely assesses her own situation and changes tactics. She does so, for instance, when she considers Gawain's response to her initial flirtation: " 'þaȝ I were burde bryȝtest,' þe burde in mynde hade, / 'þe lasse luf in his lode' " (1283–84). She then switches from her initial ploy—suggesting that she would prefer his lordship above all others—to her first attack on his courtesy (1291–1301). In their second interview, she adopts the pose of student of "trewelof craftes" while still managing to suggest her availability: " 'Dos, techeȝ me of your wytte, / Whil my lorde is fro hame' " (1533–34). Realizing finally that the combined attack upon his chastity and good breeding is not going to work, again she changes tactics in the middle of a conversation and appeals to his love for his life with the offer of the girdle (1787–1867), which he reluctantly accepts.

Not the least of the delicious humor of these scenes arises from the reader's awareness of the double reputation of Gawain in the Middle Ages. His celibacy in this poem as compared with the promiscuity of his conduct elsewhere is not a "major gaffe," as one critic has called it, but one of the deliberate ambivalences in which this puckish poet delighted.[48] Since so many romances of the period concerned themselves with the plight of a chaste

heroine in constant peril from the lustful intentions of an evil villain (Chaucer's *Man of Law's* and *Physician's Tales* are only two
examples), what could be more amusing to a sophisticated poet
and his sophisticated audience than a reversal of that situation,
especially as it involved a man who, in the French *Prose Vulgate*
with which they may have been familiar, jumped into bed with
almost every available nubile lady he encountered?[49]

Looking back upon the poem from its ending, we see that this
"realism" of the lady is largely verbal; yet, as we read the
scenes between her and Gawain, they somehow work, making the
lady a complex combination of realistic, reversed-courtly and
spiritual archetypal, and stereotypical (in her function as the
femme fatale) behavior. The same cannot be said of the much-
debated presence of Morgan in the poem, but her passivity contrasts nicely with the lady's frantic activity.[50] Morgan is a convenient archetype of (Arthurian and moral) evil, now perhaps too
old and ugly to do her own dirty work. Moreover, the complex
contrast in appearance and function between Morgan and the
lady, as in that between Gaynor and her mother's ghost in the
Awntyrs, allows an interplay of courtly and spiritual archetype,
and rejection of stereotype, rarely equaled in medieval literature.
This theme is counterpointed in one poem by the realism of
Gaynor's charity, and in the other by the lady's seductive sallies.

Much of the richness of *Pearl* is due to a similar combination
of archetype, transmuted stereotype, and reality.[51] *Pearl* thus displays the same concern with woman as archetype, stereotype, and
reality as do the Arthurian poems of its own tradition. This presentation I have discussed elsewhere.[52]

How does this characterization of women in the Arthurian
poems of the Alliterative Tradition compare with that to be found
in the other poems of their day, those of Chaucer? We notice
a distinct difference in the courtly ambiance of *The Knight's Tale*
and *Troilus and Criseyde* and that of the alliterative Arthurian
poems. In the latter, the castles and the life within them seem
more solid and real, and hunts more functional (even when they
are analogues to courtly action as in *Gawain*). In the veri-
similitude of architecture and furnishings, the references to mass-

es and the feasting which seem so integral to the action, we sense much more than in Chaucer's courtly works the "felt life" of the century.[53] With the exception of the endings of the *Canterbury Tales* or of *Troilus*, there is in Chaucer little of the sustained tone of moral seriousness that we find in the Arthurian poems and *Pearl*. One has only to compare *The Book of the Duchess* with *Pearl* to see the difference in the elegiac tone: as Moorman has pointed out, the *Duchess*, "brilliant as it is as a literary exercise . . . expresses no moral nor does it even convey a sense of the seriousness of its ostensible subject, the death of a beloved wife."[54] It seems significant that there are no fabliaux in the Alliterative Tradition, and that only one of Utley's long catalogue of antifeminist satires is in the alliterative meter.

More to my purpose, the stereotype of the *descriptio pulchritudinis feminae* which Chaucer stylizes almost into emblem in his portrait of Emily, and then mercilessly satirizes in the following picture of Alison, is dismissed by the poets of the *Awntyrs* and *Gawain* with the reference to the grey eyes alone. That says it all for them: it is as if the requisite *effictio* might waste time more profitably spent upon more serious concerns. Chaucer's courtly women, Emily, Dorigen, even the incomparable Criseyde through most of the *Troilus*, are moved around as pawns in a chess game played by men. Women in the alliterative Arthurian poems and *Pearl* act upon and even change the men with whom they are connected: it is Gaynour's charity which begets Gawayn's and Arthur's, Bertilak's lady's temptations which almost cause the downfall of Gawain's earthly and heavenly *cortayse*, the Pearl's patient explanation of her existence in the afterlife which reconciles her father/lover to a Boethian acceptance of his loss. Archetypal women operate as forces for good (the Pearl) and for evil (Bertilak's lady), as do all human beings, and they are even matched with similarly endowed males (Gaynour and Gawayn).

We find similar tendencies in *Piers Plowman*, though with a difference of courtly ambiance: a courtly-spiritual archetype in Lady Mede, for instance, and a picture of daily life among all classes of fourteenth-century women that is unequaled in any poem of its age. Why the treatment of women in the Alliterative Tradition should be so unusual, not only from that of Chaucer but also from that of other romances of the period, remains (as Elizabeth Salter has said of this poetry as a whole) "something of a mystery." The serious treatment of women in Anglo-Saxon poetry, comparatively untouched by the French tradition, may have survived along with the meter; the isolation of the castles and/or monasteries in or for which these poems were written, or the influence of Richard Rolle and his school with its unique spirituality, may have been factors. Additionally, the favorite reading of Langland, the *Gawain*-poet, and other of these authors was the Bible. Perhaps they took seriously those few passages in which St. Paul talks of the equality of man and woman in Christ (Galatians 3:28; I Corinthians 10:11). In any case, the Alliterative Tradition was "masculine" neither in meter nor in matter; we have waited too long to recognize that its subject was all humanity.

NOTES

Research and writing of this paper were completed under a National Endowment for the Humanities Fellowship in Residence, at the University of Chicago, 1975–76. I would like to thank members of the NEH Residential Seminar, and especially its supervisor, Professor Stuart Tave, and Sr. Marie Brinkman, for helpful suggestions.

1. Dorothy Everett, "The Alliterative Revival," *Essays on Middle English Literature*, ed. Patricia Kean (Oxford, 1955), pp. 53–54.

2. Charles Moorman, *The Pearl-Poet* (New York, 1968), p. 22.

3. *Piers Plowman*, excluded here because of exigencies of space, has been discussed in my "The Characterization of Women in *Piers Plowman*," a paper read in May 1976, at the Eleventh Conference on Medieval Studies, The Medieval Institute, Western Michigan University.

4. William M. Ryan, *William Langland* (New York, 1968), p. 66.

5. In *Dante: Poet of the Secular World*, trans. Ralph Manheim (Chicago, 1929), pp. 173–74.

6. D. S. Brewer, "Courtesy and the *Gawain*-Poet," in *Patterns of Love and Courtesy: Essays in Memory of C. S. Lewis*, ed. John Lawlor (London, 1966), pp. 80–81.

7. Sr. Ritamary Bradley, "A Schema for the Study of the Characterization of Women in Medieval Literature," read at Midwest Modern Language Association in October 1972. See also her "Backgrounds of the Title *Speculum* in Medieval Literature," *Speculum*, 29 (1954), 100–15.

8. For a discussion of this concept, see Marcia Colish, *The Mirror of Language: A Study in the Medieval Theory of Knowledge* (New Haven, 1968).

9. The literature on Mariology is so voluminous as to be overwhelming. An extensive treatment of the medieval Marian tradition in English is Yrjo Hirn's *The Sacred Shrine* (1912; rpt. Boston, 1957), Part II.

10. For a summary and comment on the Eve/Mary analogy, see W. Staerk, "Eva-Maria. Ein Beitrag zur Den- und Sprechweise der altkirchlichen Christologie," *Zeitschrift für die neutestamentliche Wissenschaft*, 33 (1934), 97–104.

11. An exception is St. Ambrose, who sees Eve as a type of Sarah and Deborah as well as the Virgin: *De institutione virginis*, 3, 24, and 5, 32–39 (*PL* 16, 325, and 327–29); *De viduis*, 8, 49–59 (*PL* 16, 362–63). One of the fullest catalogues of biblical women as personifications of the Church is probably that of Isidore, *Allegoriae quaedam Sacrae Scripturae* (*PL* 83, 124–25), which adds not only Ruth and Esther, but even Mary and Martha to the list.

12. Joan Ferrante, *Woman as Image in Medieval Literature: From the Twelfth Century to Dante* (New York, 1975), p. 22, says, "anti-feminist attitudes are so prevalent in the *Glossa* that the commentator feels obliged to explain, when a woman is singled out to perform a good action instead of a man, why that should be." But for some "feminist" tendencies (at least in the early Fathers), cf. JoAnn McNamara, "Sexual Equality and the Cult of Virginity in Early Christian Thought," *Papers of the Berkshire Conference on the History of Women*, II (Cambridge, Mass., 1974).

13. See Helen Meredith Garth, *Saint Mary Magdalene in Medieval Literature*, Johns Hopkins University Studies in Historical and Political Science, Ser. 67, No. 3 (Baltimore, 1950), who cites, for instance, Peter Chrysologus as identifying Mary Magdalene as the New Eve (*PL* 52, 409). Also, Marjorie M. Malvern, *Venus in Sackcloth: The Magdalene's Origins and Metamorphoses* (Carbondale, Ill., 1975).

14. See Adolph Katzenellenbogen, *Allegories of the Virtues and Vices in Medieval Art: From Early Christian Times to the Thirteenth Century* (1939; rpt. New York, 1964); Morton Bloomfield, *The Seven Deadly Sins: An Introduction to the History of a Religious Concept, with Special Reference to Medieval English Literature* (East Lansing, Mich., 1952), passim; Rosemund Tuve, *Allegorical Imagery: Some Medieval Books and Their Posterity* (Princeton, 1966), Chap. 2; Ferrante, Chap. 2, "Allegory."

15. *Prudentius,* with *en face* trans. H. J. Thompson, Loeb Classical Library (Cambridge, Mass., 1949–53), pp. 274–383, lines 178ff., 109ff.

16. Katzenellenbogen, p. 7; Ferrante, p. 46.

17. See Frederick Goldin, *The Mirror of Narcissus in the Courtly Love Lyric* (Ithaca, 1967).
18. One hardly knows what to call it any more. See Donnell Van de Voort, "Love and Marriage in the English Medieval Romance," Diss. Vanderbilt, 1938; Margaret Lanham, "Chastity: A Study in the Sexual Morality of the Middle English Romance," Diss. Vanderbilt, 1948; Margaret Adlum Gist, *Love and War in the Middle English Romances* (Philadelphia, 1947); *The Meaning of Courtly Love*, ed. F. X. Newman (Albany, 1968); E. Talbot Donaldson, "The Myth of Courtly Love," in *Speaking of Chaucer* (London, 1970), pp. 154–63; and Francis L. Utley, "Must We Abandon the Concept of Courtly Love?" *Medievalia et Humanistica*, NS 2 (1972), 299–324. All of these disagree, to greater or lesser extent, with C. S. Lewis' influential *The Allegory of Love: A Study in Medieval Tradition* (1936; rpt. London, 1958). Numerous articles and books continue the argument. See Newman, pp. 97–102, for a bibliography. A recent discussion is Henry Ansgar Kelly's *Love and Marriage in the Age of Chaucer* (Ithaca, N. Y., 1975.
19. Goldin, p. 14.
20. Bradley, "Schema," p. 3.
21. See Francis L. Utley, *The Crooked Rib: An Analytical Index to the Argument About Women in English and Scots Literature to the End of the Year 1568* (Columbus, 1944). For medieval satire see, for example, Jill Mann, *Chaucer and Medieval Estates Satire: The Literature of Social Classes and the General Prologue to the Canterbury Tales* (Cambridge, 1973), pp. 121–27; Arthur Keister Moore, "Studies in a Mediaeval Prejudice: Antifeminism," Diss. Vanderbilt, 1945; G. R. Owst, *Literature and Pulpit in Medieval England*, 2d. ed. (Cambridge, 1961), passim.
22. Paul, I Timothy 2:11–14 (which may be pseudonymous, but belongs to the Pauline School); Augustine, Sermo 51, *De Concordia evangelistarum Matthaei et Lucae in Generationibus Domini*, 2 (*PL* 38, 334–35); Bonaventura, *Opera Omnia* (Quaracchi, Italy, 1882–1902), IV, *IV Sent.*, 760b. In spite of their differences on other matters, Bonaventura's views on women are surprisingly close to those of Aquinas, a view contested by Sr. Emma Thérèse Healy, *Woman According to Saint Bonaventure* (New York, 1955), p. ix and passim.
23. *Summa Theologica*, I, q. 92, a. 1; q. 99, a. 2 ad 1; q. 115, a. 2 ad. 3, and a. 3 ad. 4; *In III Sent.*, 3, 2.
24. Vern L. Bullough, "Medieval Medical and Scientific Views of Women," in *"Marriage in the Middle Ages,"* ed. John Leyerle, *Viator,* 4 (1973), 500. For scholarly contributions to stereotypes about women, see Robert A. Pratt, "Jankyn's Book of Wikked Wyves: Medieval Antimatrimonial Propaganda in the Universities," *Annuale Mediaevale,* 31 (1962), 5–27.
25. Odo, *S. Odonis Abbatis Cluniacensis Collationum*, 2, 9 (*PL* 133, 556). On Bromyard, see Owst, passim.

26. See Owst, passim; also *Medieval Handbooks of Penance, A Translation of the Principal libri poenitentiales and Selections from Relevant Documents*, ed. John T. McNeill and Helena M. Gamer (New York, 1938), passim; Bernard Lord Manning, *The People's Faith in the Time of Wyclif* (Cambridge, 1919), and W. A. Pantin, *The English Church in the Fourteenth Century* (Cambridge, 1955), both passim; *The Book of the Knight of La Tour-Landry, Compiled for the Instruction of His Daughters*, ed. Thomas Wright, rev. ed. EETS 33 (1906); Eileen Power, "The Ménagier's Wife, A Paris Housewife in the Fourteenth Century," in *Medieval People* (1924; rpt. New York, 1964), pp. 96–119; Andreas Capellanus, *The Art of Courtly Love*, trans. John Jay Parry (1941; rpt. New York, 1969), pp. 187–212.

27. Erich Auerbach, "Figura," in *Scenes from the Drama of European Literature: Six Essays* (New York, 1959); *Mimesis: The Representation of Reality in Western Literature*, trans. Willard R. Trask (1946; rpt. Princeton, 1968), passim.

28. Auerbach, *Mimesis,* p. 555.

29. Ibid., p. 202.

30. A good bibliography for recent historical sources which, however, neglects some older ones (as its editors admit) is that of Carolly Erickson and Kathleen Casey, "Women in the Middle Ages: A Working Bibliography," *Medieval Studies*, 37 (1975), 340–89.

31. See *Dictionnaire de droit canonique*, ed. R. Naz (Paris, 1934–65), s.v. "clandestinité," "mariage civil," "mariage en droit occidental," "mari," "mariage conditionale," "lien matrimonial," "divorce," "causes matrimoniale," etc.; William Blackstone, *Commentaries on the Laws of England*, ed. George Sharshwood (Philadelphia, 1839), I, Chap. 15.

32. One of the best accounts of the power of royal women is Henry Adams' "The Three Queens," in *Mont-Saint-Michel and Chartres* (1913; rpt. Garden City, N.Y., 1959), pp. 215–51.

33. *Paston Letters and Papers of the Fifteenth Century*, ed. Norman Davis, Part I (Oxford, 1971). Letter No. 36 describes Margaret Paston's spirited defense (with only twelve other persons) of a disputed manorhold against a thousand men in her husband's absence—a battle she not unexpectedly lost.

34. Eileen Power, "The Position of Women," in *The Legacy of the Middle Ages*, ed. C. G. Crump and E. F. Jacob (Oxford, 1926), pp. 408, 413–14. See also her *Medieval Women*, ed. M. M. Postan (Cambridge, 1975).

35. Owst, p. 404: "The English preachers' attitude to the question of fashions and finery in dress . . . proceeds generally on a much wider plane, and . . . includes both male and female in its indictment."

36. See *Before the Bawdy Court: Selections from Church Court and Other Records Relating to the Correction of Moral Offenses in England, Scotland, and New England, 1300–1800*, ed. Paul Hair (London, 1972).

37. *Morte Arthure*, or *The Death of Arthur*, ed. Edmund Brock, EETS 8 (1871; rpt. 1961); *The Alliterative Morte Arthure*, ed. Valerie Krishna, with In-

troduction by Rossell Hope Robbins (New York, 1976); *The Awyntyrs off Arthure at the Terne Wattelyne: A Critical Edition*, ed. Robert J. Gates (Philadelphia, 1969); and Ralph Hanna's edition, *The Awyntyrs off Arthur at the Terne Wathelyn* (New York, 1974); *Sir Gawain and the Green Knight*, ed. J. R. R. Tolkien and E. V. Gordon, 2d ed., rev. Norman Davis (Oxford, 1967).

38. William Matthews, *The Tragedy of Arthur: A Study of the Alliterative "Morte Arthure"* (Berkeley, 1960), p. 95.

39. See Gates, "Introduction," pp. 18–29; Ralph Hanna III, *"The Awyntyrs off Arthur," Modern Language Quarterly*, 31 (1970), 275–97; D. N. Klausner, *"Exempla* and the *Awyntyrs off Arthur," Medieval Studies*, 34 (1972), 307–25.

40. See especially, Lucy Paton, *Studies in the Fairy Mythology of Arthurian Romance* (1903; rpt. New York, 1960).

41. See Tolkien and Gordon, "Notes," p. 130, n. to 2460.

42. See B. J. Whiting, "Gawain: His Reputation, His Courtesy and His Appearance in Chaucer's Squire's Tale," *Medieval Studies*, 9 (1947), 189–239.

43. The most fervent advocate of this point of view is Mother Angela Carson, "Morgan la Fee as the Principle of Unity in *Sir Gawain and the Green Knight," Modern Language Quarterly*, 23 (1962), 3–16, but her arguments and those of others are easy to refute from the poem itself. See Albert B. Friedman, "Morgan le Fay in *Sir Gawain and the Green Knight," Speculum*, 35 (1960), 260–74.

44. See John A. Burrow, *A Reading of Sir Gawain and the Green Knight* (London, 1965), pp. 81–82.

45. J. F. Kiteley, "The *De arte honeste amandi* of Andreas Capellanus and the Concept of Courtesy in *Sir Gawain and the Green Knight," Anglia*, 79 (1961), 7–16.

46. See, among others, Peter J. Lucas, "Gawain's Anti-Feminism," *Notes and Queries*, 203 (1968), 324–25; P. C. B. Fletcher, "Sir Gawain's Anti-Feminism," *Theoria*, 36 (1971), 53–58; David Mills, "The Rhetorical Function of Gawain's Antifeminism," *Neuphilologische Mitteilungen*, 71 (1970), 635–40; and incidental references in D. S. Brewer, "Courtesy and the *Gawain*-Poet," in *Patterns of Love and Courtesy: Essays in Memory of C. S. Lewis*, ed. John Lawlor (London, 1966), pp. 77–78, and in Burrow, pp. 146–49.

47. Mary Dove, "Gawain and the *'Blasme des Femmes'* Tradition," *Medium Ævum*, 41 (1972), 20–26.

48. Gordon M. Shedd, "Knight in Tarnished Armour: The Meaning of *Sir Gawain and the Green Knight," Modern Language Review*, 62 (1967), 203.

49. For differences between the behavior of heroes and heroines in French and English romances, see Gist, passim; Lanham, passim; and Adelaide Harris,

The Heroine of the Middle English Romance (1928; rpt. Folcroft, Pa., 1969).

50. See, besides Carson and Friedman, Denver Ewing Baughan, "The Role of Morgan le Fay in *Sir Gawain and the Green Knight*," *Journal of English Literary History*, 17 (1950), 241–51; J. Eadie, "Morgan le Fay and the Conclusion of *Sir Gawain and the Green Knight*," *Neophilologus*, 52 (1968), 299–303; Douglas M. Moon, "The Role of Morgan la Fee in *Sir Gawain and the Green Knight*," *Neuphilologische Mitteilungen*, 67 (1966), 31–57; and Larry D. Benson, *Art and Tradition in Sir Gawain and the Green Knight* (New Brunswick, N.J., 1965), pp. 32–35.

51. *Pearl*, ed. E. V. Gordon (1953; rpt. Oxford, 1963).

52. A full treatment of *Pearl*, presented during the original reading of this paper, has here been omitted.

53. For specific references to the "realism" involved, see Marvin Alpheus Owings, *The Arts in the Middle English Romances* (New York, 1952), Chap. 2, "Castles," Chap. 3 ,"Architecture and Furnishings," which contain many citations from these poems.

54. Charles Moorman, "The Origins of the Alliterative Revival," *The Southern Quarterly*, 7 (1968–69), 345–67.

3

The Pardon Impugned by the Priest

RUTH M. AMES

LIKE the dreamer in Passus VII of *Piers Plowman,* we still puzzle over why the pardon given to Piers "alle the peple to conforte" was "impugned" by a priest "with two propre wordes" (VII.146–47).[1] Unlike the dreamer and the poet, commentators feel compelled to choose between Piers and priest and between one meaning of the pardon and the other. According to John Lawlor, the priest is "wholly right" in saying that the document shown him by Piers is not a pardon. It is, in fact, a statement "of rigour"; it is "no more than the moral law . . . which is written in all men's hearts."[2] Also agreeing implicitly with the priest, Rosemary Woolf feels called upon to justify the poet's "deception" in calling such a sentence of damnation (that is, the phrases of the Athanasian Creed that comprise the words read by the priest) a pardon.[3] R. W. Frank, Jr., on the contrary, says that these lines from the Creed do constitute a valid pardon; the priest denies the doctrine that to be saved men must do well, because he is a supporter of papal indulgences.[4] D. W. Robertson, Jr., and B. F. Huppé say that the priest is one with heretics and schismatics: because he lacks grace and faith, he sees "only the law" and not the invisible substance.[5] Mary Schroeder says that the priest is blind to the meaning of the document, as the Israelites were blind to the tables of the law brought from Sinai by Moses; the lines of the pardon taken from the Athanasian Creed

47

cannot be "spiritually inadequate," and the document is a
genuine pardon.[6]

Although the critical conclusions cannot all be correct, the
conflicting descriptions of the pardon are to be found in the text.
Indeed, an alliterative version of the yeas and nays of the critics
would sound rather like the dispute between Piers and priest—if
the redactor stopped short of the scholarly attempts to explain the
tearing of the pardon by explaining away the ambiguities of the
scene. The tearing itself will not be dealt with here because my
interest is in the meaning of the scene in the poem as a whole,
and I believe Langland deleted the act from the C-version because it did not fit into the large scheme. The ambiguities he left
in, however, must be meaningful. He seems to go out of his
way, for example, to tell us that the merciful pardon, as it is described at length by Piers, was given by Truth, and that the harsh
and brief lines construed by the priest were witnessed by Truth.
Perhaps Langland was implying (as do some of the critics) that
the differences are less in the document than in the eye of the
beholder, and that the dispute between Piers and priest propounds
a riddle. What is understood by some as justice and by others as
mercy? What is read by one as letter and by another as spirit? The
answer, I think, is the law of God, and the argument is over its
interpretation. Since both views are given by Truth, both must be
true; the difference in tone and emphasis of the viewers reflects
their different attitudes toward God and man.

There is no attempt to solve the riddle in Passus VII, and even
its terms are explained only gradually in the course of the poem.
Langland's slow and discursive revelation is not a trick or a deception, but an appropriate form for his complex meaning. His
vision of the law embraces the Old and New Laws both as historical periods and as timeless morality. He sees the reconciliation
of justice and mercy as accomplished by Christ but also as a perennial riddle, the answer to which must be sought by every man.
The allegory therefore slips back and forth in time, while characterization and versification indicate spiritual levels from the sublime to the ridiculous.

For a critical analysis of the questions raised by Passus VII, we need to know Langland's answers. I think it useful to look for them first in the later episodes. Langland's prophetic and transcendent concept of the fulfillment of the law is expressed unequivocally in the vision of the Good Samaritan. Faith-Abraham, Hope-Moses, and Charity-Christ represent the ideal by which all of the other characters who discuss the law must be measured. In the Dinner Party, in the Debate of the Four Daughters of God, and in the Debate between Christ and Satan, Langland portrays both various aspects of the law, and various levels of understanding and misunderstanding of the role of the law in the salvation of the individual and the race. In the light of these discussions, we can see that the argument in Passus VII also reveals different levels of perception, and that the priest can be both right and wrong. The clause he reads can be taken from the Athanasian Creed and yet be a rigorous statement, sound in its moral teaching, yet spiritually inadequate without Piers's message. The priest's blindness to that message is culpable not because he is a heretic or a supporter of papal indulgences, but because he is a literalist. Like the Doctor of Divinity at the Dinner Party, like Righteousness, like Satan, he does not wish to see the spirit of mercy in the letter. Like Moses and Patience and Peace, Piers prophesies the fulfillment of the law in love. The conflict between Piers and priest thus represents a conflict not between the Old and New Laws, both of which are true, but between the prophetic and priestly ways of interpreting the law of God in every age.

In the many discussions of the Pardon Scene, there is little agreement on Langland's attitude to the Old and New Laws. Some of the misapprehensions of his meaning result, I believe, from incorrect assumptions about either the prevailing views or Langland's use of them. Well versed in Scripture and commentary, the poet selected, rejected, and transformed the ordinary treatment of the subject. Morally simple, Langland's concept of the law is intellectually complex and spiritually profound.

Basic to Langland's handling of the theme is his belief in the lasting truth of the Old Law. Whatever the difficulty in determining the precise function of the law in a debate over the pardon, it

is safe to say that it serves God. The unfailing respect for the law
felt by Langland was derived from the traditional teaching of the
Church, which presupposed the immutability of God and the con-
sequent unity of the Scriptures. Church Fathers and medieval
apologists did not contrast Old and New Laws as good versus
bad, as forgiveness versus revenge; on the contrary, they insisted
that the essential law had not changed. They cited Old Testament
passages which taught love of God and neighbor, and which said
that revenge belonged to God alone; and they insisted that these
texts proved the concordance of the Scriptures and the unity of
Moses and Jesus.[7]

Even the manifest changes in the ceremonial law were explained as fulfillment rather than abrogation, although here something was conceded to time. It was said that the law given to
Moses was good: it was given to a sinful people to remind them
of God when they ate and drank, and to keep them separate from
the idolaters who surrounded them. The legal code, however, was
to remain in force only until the time of the greater prophet
foretold by Moses. Now that prophet had come and fulfilled the
letter of the law by his Passion, and thus opened the gates of
heaven which had been closed by the sin of Adam. And now that
the Gentiles had been called to the God of Israel, and Greek and
Jew were one in Christ, the time for the literal observances had
passed. Furthermore, the meaning of the old ceremonies had been
retained in the sacraments. Baptism, for example, was described
not as a new sacrament but as the spiritual fulfillment of carnal
circumcision. Finally, the Church claimed here, as in the moral
law, to be following the prophetic tradition of Judaism. Had not
the prophets thundered against those who thought to please God
by observing the sabbath and the sacrifices while exploiting the
poor? True religion, they said, consisted always in circumcizing
the heart, in loving justice and mercy, and walking humbly with
God (Micah 6:6–8).

While this was always the official theory, in practice Christians often slipped into their own legalism. Even in tracts demonstrating the fulfillment of the law, the emphasis frequently
shifts from the prophetic to the priestly. Perhaps because the

moral concordance needed little elaboration, writers devoted their energies to searching the Scriptures for prefigurations of the Church's sacraments, feast days, and fast days, in those of the Synagogue. They sometimes concluded by showing that baptism was now as essential as circumcision had once been.[8] More often than not, the comparisons turned into contrasts which demonstrated the superiority of the Church to the Synagogue.

Langland has little patience with this priestly preoccupation with ritual. Baptism "withoute more," says Lady Scripture, does not guarantee salvation (X.352). Deeply imbued with the prophetic spirit, Langland rages against those who observe forms while ignoring the essence of the law; and true observance of the law, Old and New, demands social justice and compassion. Like St. Paul, Langland believes that without the spirit of love, even the sacraments and the virtues do not lead men to God. Holy Church goes so far as to say that chastity without charity will be chained in hell (I.186). Similarly, justice, essential as it is in the life of individual and society, is insufficient without mercy. It is love that fulfills the law, and nothing less will serve.

As Langland tells the story of mankind, past and present, he consistently affirms this prophetic emphasis. It is no casual oversight that he, unlike most of his contemporaries, does not compare circumcision with baptism. His Abraham and Moses do not teach circumcision and sacrifice, as the heart of his allegory of the law is that the Old Law teaches the same faith, hope, and charity as the New. This is the law that Langland means when he says that it was written on stone, because it was to endure forever (XV.573): this "parfit Iewen law," he says is *"Dilige deum et proximum"* (XV.574). As God is and always has been love, so the law of God teaches and always has taught love, "longe er Crist were" (C.XV.38). When Langland's Abraham and Moses seek Christ, they are not seeking a new law, but the fulfillment of the spirit of the old in the perfect love of Christ.

On this point Langland's portrayal of the law might almost be a dramatization of the doctrine as it was expressed by Augustine and Robert Grosseteste. Grosseteste, the great English bishop who lived the life of Do-Best in the century before Langland, said that time is important to us but not to God. Following Augustine, he explained that while the Old and New Laws were given to men in different times, they are one with God in eternity.[9]

In *Piers*, the Old Law has been given to Moses before the New is given by Christ. But Moses and Jesus meet and are united in their teaching of the eternal law of love. Abraham and Moses personify the moral universalism that Langland teaches throughout the poem. As they are united with Christ, so all those who sincerely follow the law of love are united with Christ, however varied their earthly time or place. (So the pagan Trajan, who knew that law without love is not worth a bean, was saved by his goodness [XI.136ff.].) By the same reasoning, those who do not follow the law of love are separated from Christ whatever the accident of their time and place of birth. For this transcendent concept of the law, the dream that transcends time and space is a perfect vehicle. By bringing together persons and places of all times, the very anachronisms of the allegory dramatize the prophetic insistence on the universal justice and mercy of God and the unity and continuity of Revelation.

In Passus XVI and XVII the allegory of Faith, Hope, and Charity is so lucid, and the transcendence of time so in keeping with the lofty moral teaching, that we feel no incongruity in the mixture of past, present, and future, and of Old and New Laws. The dreamer, fourteenth-century Christian and everyman reliving salvation history, meets Abraham and Moses on the road to Jerusalem and they discuss the meaning of the law. It is "Mydlenten Sondaye" (XVI.172), the Sunday in the Church year on which the liturgy tells the story of Abraham; in the history of the world, Good Friday and Easter are soon to come. That is why Faith-Abraham, who has been Christ's herald here and in hell, now seeks that lord who will save us all and who comes "a newe lawe to make" (C.XIX.266). Next the dreamer meets Hope-Moses who is carrying a letter which, he explains, is the law given him on Sinai. "Is it asseled?" asks the dreamer. No, replies Moses; he now seeks him who has the seal in keeping, that is "Crosse and Crystenedome and Cryst there-on to honge"

(XVII.1–6). Carefully scrutinizing Moses' writ so that he may "the lawe knowe," the dreamer sees that the true text, on a piece of stone, consists of two "words," *"Dilige Deum et proximum tuum,"* and that to this is added a glorious gloss, *"In hiis duobus mandatis tota lex pendet et prophetia"* (XVI.9–13). The "gloss," of course, was spoken by Christ (Matthew 22:40). By putting Christ's words on Moses' table, Langland dramatizes the union of the two laws and in effect makes the New Law a glorious commentary on the Old.

The presumably Christian dreamer, however, is far behind the prophets in his spiritual understanding. Slow to see the point, he is rather anxious to argue it. Is this your lord's whole law? he demands. Yes, puts in Abraham; and whoever lives according to this writ shall never go to the devil. With this "charme" Hope has saved thousands. Your words are wonderful, retorts the dreamer, if they are true. But Abraham has already told me about a law of Trinity. What need for Moses' new and harder law of loving everybody, even shrews, if Abraham's was sufficient for salvation (XVII.15–46)? The new law here is that of Moses, but as the gloss and the journey to Jerusalem indicate, Langland was thinking also of the New Law of Christ, the necessity for which appears in the allegory of the Good Samaritan, which follows immediately.

According to the allegory, good as was the law, it could not bring pardon to the children of Adam. As in the works of the Fathers, the commentators, and the homilists, so here the man who fell among thieves is mankind wounded by the sin of Adam; the priest and Levite who helped him not are Abraham and Moses; the Good Samaritan is Jesus.[10] In Langland's telling, Christ himself takes great care to exonerate Abraham and Moses from blame. Let them be excused, he tells the dreamer. No medicine can heal that man without the blood of a babe born of a maiden. Most noteworthy, in *Piers*, Charity does not leave Faith and Hope behind. Faith-Abraham, he explains, will be forester and will show the way to Jerusalem. Hope-Moses will be the "hosterleres man" at the Inn called *Lex Christi* and lead the faint and feeble by the love his law commands. Still missing the point,

the dull dreamer asks the Samaritan whether he should believe
Abraham or Moses. Both, replies the Samaritan: be firm in faith
like Abraham, obey the commandments of Moses, and love your
fellow-Christians (XVII.87ff.). So the pardon of Christ is linked
forever with the law of Moses.

Small wonder that the dreamer, who had difficulty with this
transparent allegory, could make nothing of the dispute in Passus
VII! Or was he simply a foil in the earlier scene as he is here? In
both scenes he is recognizably the same slow-witted character.
Further, the subject in both is the pardon, and Moses in XVII
recalls Piers in VII in his concern for sinners. No one in the later
scene, however, reminds us of the priest, and there is no comparable disharmony.

The priest would be a more likely guest at the quarrelsome
Dinner Party. Less clear than Passus XVI and XVII but clearer
than VII, Passus XIII includes an allegory of the fulfillment of
the law, and seems designed to portray various degrees of perception of the meaning of the law. On the lowest level is the Doctor
of Divinity, a smugly hypocritical friar who is so lacking in the
spirit of God that he does not understand the letter of the law. At
the highest step is Patience, a Moses-Piers figure whose riddle is
a prophecy of the Passion and the New Law. Between these ex-
tremes are Clergy and Conscience, two lively personifications
which appear to have started on the way of salvation but still
have far to go.

The friar bows to Scripture but does not eat her food; he does
not practice what he preaches, and even what he preaches falls
far short of the doctrine of love expounded by Scripture who, in
Passus X, had said that since Christ "confermed the lawe,"
whoever wishes to rise with Christ must "the lawe fulfile" by
loving God above all things, by being kind both to Christians and
heathen, and by clothing the naked and feeding the hungry
(X.347ff.). Indeed, the friar's explanation of Do-wel as "Do non
yuel to thine euenecrystene" (XIII.104) is, as Professor
Goodridge points out, less positive than the law of Leviticus:
"thou shalt love thy neighbor as thyself" (19:18).[11] The quality

of the friar's mind is expressed in his precept to "do as clerkes techeth" (XIII.115).

What makes the scene perplexing is that although the other characters are not wicked like the friar, they do not seem to know that Christ has confirmed the law. They are apparently fourteenth-century Christians who are provided with the Evangelists and the Fathers, but as the conversation probes the meaning of Do-wel, they seem to be awaiting the coming of Christ and the New Law.

We know that the full Christian doctrine has not yet been revealed to Clergy and Conscience because they are waiting for the clarification of the hints of something new given by Piers. Clergy has heard that Piers has shrugged aside all except love, citing only two texts from the Old Testament, and proclaiming the infinity of love. Not only does this sound like a reference to Christ's fulfilling the Old Law in perfect love, but Conscience's remark that Piers would say nothing contrary to Scripture seems to allude to the teaching that the New Law did not abrogate the Old. One of Piers's "texts" is, in fact, taken from Psalm 15, the other is the "*dilige deum*" that will appear later on Moses' tablet (XIII.124–31). And when Conscience recommends that they leave the question until Piers comes to show them Do-wel, he seems to be prophesying the Crucifixion scene in Passus XVIII in which Christ will appear in the armor of Piers to "preue this in dede" (XIII.132). The merging of the medieval present with the Old Testament past is not accomplished here with the same polish as in the Good Samaritan scene, but the underlying concept is the same: in his spiritual development, every Christian must follow "the historical progression from the Old Law to the New."[12]

That timeless virtue, Patience, knows more than Conscience and Clergy because he was taught by a lady named Love to love his enemies, that is, to Do-best. Like Moses, he has confident foreknowledge, but because on the historical level of the allegory Christ has not yet come, Patience, for all that he quotes St. Paul, refers to the Passion only obliquely, in a riddle that is a prophecy. The words "*ex vi transitiones*" (which he carries) probably mean, as Professor Goodridge has suggested, "through the power of the passing-over," and refer to the Passover and the Passion. This would fit the calendar part of the riddle (XIII.153–54) which apparently refers to Holy Saturday, Easter, and the Wednesday of Easter week. The liturgy on these days teaches that the Passover was a prefiguration of the Eucharist and that all the sacrifices of the Old Law were fulfilled in the Passion of Christ.[13] Hidden inside these words, says Patience, is Do-wel, which protects the bearer against pain, poverty, fear, and fiends: *Caritas nichil timet* (XIII.157–71). Thus the perfect love of Christ is contained in the prophecy of the Passion.

The other persons present react to the message of Patience in accordance with their characters. Unwilling even to undo the bound words, the friar categorically denies the power of the riddle to make peace. He implies that Patience is a liar, his message a fiction like a minstrel's tale. Conscience is moved to become a pilgrim with Patience at once. Clergy sneers at the impulsiveness of Conscience and offers to bring a "bible a boke of the olde lawe" to teach him "the leest poynte to knowe," if riddle-solving is his motive (XIII.183–86). Conscience responds that he would rather have perfect patience than half of Clergy's books. The two are quickly reconciled, however. Conscience says that if Patience were friendly with both of them, together they could conquer evil, make peace, and bring Saracens and Jews to the faith. By way of agreement, Clergy says he will stay where he is, establishing children and novices in the faith while Patience proves Conscience to make him perfect (XIII.188–214).

Besides the obvious moral allegory, this exchange alludes to the fulfillment of the Old Law. His reference to the Old Law and to establishing novices in the Faith suggests that Clergy represents the work of preparation performed by the Old Law for the New.[14] Conscience's anxiety to join Patience, not only to be made perfect but also to carry the message of salvation throughout the world, may allude to the salvation of the Gentiles through the New Law of Christ. That they must await the working out of salvation history is indicated by the consistent use of the future tense.

The fulfillment of the law is also one of the themes of the parallel debates between the four daughters of God and between Christ and Satan. Taking place immediately before the victory over the devil is won in the depths of hell, the arguments raise the questions of the possibility of pardon for mankind and the justice of Christ's mercy, and Christ himself answers in word and deed.

The first debate, between the four daughters of God (XVIII.112ff.), appears at the outset to be a simple division of Old and New Laws defined as Justice and Mercy, but develops as another brief allegory of the union of the two laws in Christ. Mercy and Truth meet outside hell just before Christ's entry after the Crucifixion, and they wonder about the meaning of the noise and darkness and the radiance before the gates. Mercy says these are signs of great joy. After relating a brief summary of the life of Christ, she says that patriarchs and prophets preached that mankind would be saved. Truth, however, scolds her, calling her prophecy "a tale of Waltrot!" (XVIII.142). Truth angrily insists that once in hell, no man ever comes out again. Mercy mildly explains that this death, the Crucifixion, will destroy all that which Death through the devil destroyed before. Truth, however, wants to hear the opinion of Righteousness, who was alive before they were born. When Peace, dressed gaily in Patience, enters, she is more confident than Mercy, because Love has sent her a letter to say that she and Mercy are to save mankind. Righteousness, who comes from the North (probably an allusion to the fact that the northern part of a church building was symbolically allotted to the Synagogue),[15] rails at Peace, suggesting she is mad or drunk. The judgment of God against Adam and Eve can never be changed, she says; let them chew as they chose (XVIII.199)!

As their names indicate, Truth and Righteousness represent eternal virtues. Insofar as they want to isolate justice from mercy, however, they are wrong. They are wrong, not because the New Law of mercy supersedes the Old Law of justice, but because they interpret the Old Law in its harshest, narrowest sense. The other two sisters are closer to Moses in their interpretation. Mercy cites the patriarchs and prophets, and when Peace shows her "patent" of pardon received from Love, she quotes not the New Testament, as we might expect, but the fourth Psalm, apparently interpreted as a prophecy. And when, after the harrowing of hell later in the scene, Christ leads from hell all who loved him, there is no triumphing of one party over the other. Instead, the four daughters embrace and Peace says, Let no one perceive that we have quarreled (XVIII.417–23). In Christ, Truth and Righteousness, Mercy and Peace are united.

Before this joyous reconciliation, there is a similar debate between Christ and the devils. Lucifer confronts us with a view of the Old Law that seems as far from that of Moses as hell is from heaven. But justice, however bare of love and pardon, is the basis of the New as well as the Old Law, and the devil must be given his due.

Like Righteousness in the previous argument, legalistic Lucifer explains to Satan that since God said that if Adam ate the apple all would perish, therefore the "Law" will not allow the deliverance of mankind (XVIII.277–82). When shortly thereafter Jesus breaks the bars of hell, he stops to justify his action out of that law. He does not appeal to a New Law of mercy but to the Old Law of justice which, the devil says, Christ made himself (C.XXI.308). Christ concedes that Adam and Eve were condemned by the law of an eye for an eye, a tooth for a tooth, a life for a life. But he himself, as man, is rectifying all that man has misdone, member for member, life for life; and by that law he claims them. As man, he has paid for Adam's sin; as God he invokes the punishment of the same law against Lucifer, who robbed his palace, Paradise, against all justice. The devil won mankind by guile, and the Old Law says that he who deceives shall be deceived. And Christ quotes from the seventh Psalm that he who digged a ditch has fallen into it. Do not believe, he admonishes Lucifer, that I take Adam and his issue against the Law. *"Non veni solvere legem, sed adimplere"* (XVIII.332–59).

Christ's insistence here that he does not abrogate the eye for an eye precept is an extreme example of the exegetical tradition which proved that on every point the New Law fulfilled the Old.[16] It should be observed, however, that it is the devil who demands it; it is in keeping with his character and history that he can and will understand only the least elevated aspect of the doctrine. Such friends of God as Moses, Patience, Piers, Peace, and Mercy had long understood the law as love. Now Christ, after granting the claims of justice, carries the divine understanding of the infinity of mercy to the point of emptying hell of all but devils.

It was generally believed that at the Last Judgment, in the Vale of Jehoshaphat, Christ would separate the sheep from the goats for eternity. Langland's Christ, however, will save all. How could he refuse mercy to his brothers, all of whom are of one blood if not one baptism? None, he says, will be condemned to death without end. Since holy writ requires that he be wroth with sinners, he will send evildoers to Purgatory to be cleansed from their sins, and so he will grant mercy without offending justice. In the end, justice will rule over hell and Christ's mercy will be over all mankind in heaven (XVIII.363–401).

This all-embracing mercy would seem to cancel the clause in the pardon of Passus VII which declares that the devil will have the souls of evildoers. But in XVIII Christ explains that the mercy he will dispense at the end will be within the law because a king may lawfully pardon a felon (379–85). Langland apparently means that the king's privilege does not abolish the law or give men license to break it. When the pardon is granted again to Piers in Passus XIX, justice and mercy are carefully balanced and the condition of Passus VII is repeated. When, according to Conscience, Christ taught Do-best to the apostles after his Resurrection, he gave Piers power to pardon all manner of men "under covenant" that they acknowledge the pardon of Piers Plowman, and "*redde quod debes*" (XIX.178–82). Later in this same passage, Conscience says that at Doomsday, Christ will reward him who *reddit quod debet* and punish those who pay badly. And in much the same words of the sour priest who impugned Piers's pardon in Passus VII, he concludes that the good go to godhead and great joy, the wicked to dwell in woe without ending (XI.188–93).

Throughout the poem the enlightened understand the love and

mercy of God. This is not sentimental love, however, but the love of righteousness of the God of Israel, and in Langland's view love cannot exist without righteousness. When Piers sows the seeds of the cardinal virtues in men's souls, he harrows them with the Old and the New Laws so that love may flourish (XIX.306–8). At the end of the poem, the wicked are condemned by the Old Law and the New; and the dreamer, enlightened by Abraham and Moses and Jesus, and strengthened by the Eucharist, must fulfill the law in his own life in order to gain the pardon granted to Piers.

That pardon had been granted to Piers long before, but nobody seemed to know what to do with it then. As it is described at the opening of Passus VII, the pardon seems an eloquent but hardly controversial statement of the mercy of God. A priest, however, appears from nowhere to declare it is not a pardon but a warning; Do well and God will have your soul; do evil and "hop thow non other" but that the devil will have your soul (VII.112–15). In the B-text, but not in the C-text, Piers then tears up the pardon. An attack on bought indulgences or pardons is supported by the priest's view. The scene ends without giving the dreamer any reason to change his remark that he has pondered the meaning of Piers's pardon many times, but he has no "sauoure" in the interpretation of dreams (148).

No Joseph myself, I have the advantage of the dreamer in having read the rest of the poem, and I venture to see in this dream the same probing of the relation of pardon and law as in the later scenes. The allegory is neither sustained nor concluded, but in the light of the rest of the poem it seems that Piers's message is a prophecy of the New Law and that the words read by the priest represent a harsh interpretation of the Old Law. The quarrel of priest and Piers dramatizes the conflict between those interpreters of the law who deny and those who desire God's pardon for mankind.

Much is cloudy in this Passus, but it is clear that Piers's pardon represents the New Law. (Whether it is meant to be effective now or in the future *is* a question, to be taken up later.) The wordplay itself suggests that the pardon is the great indulgence of the New Law. "Bull" and "*a pena et a culpa*" are the language of papal indulgences. But ordinary indulgences remitted only punishment, not guilt. This pardon is extraordinary not only because it remits guilt, but because it was "purchased" by Truth, Truth being a frequent appellation in *Piers* for Christ. The statement, that with this pardon the heirs of Piers will be "felawes" in Paradise with "patriarkes and prophetes" (VII.1–12), is a rephrasing of the common dictum that Christ's death purchased man's forgiveness for the guilt incurred by Adam, thereby opening the gates of heaven to the patriarchs and prophets and all mankind.

If the first 105 lines describe the pardon of the New Law, the words read by the priest with no pardon in them would seem to be the Old Law, or one aspect of it. This identification raises two questions which I believe can be answered by referring to other parts of the poem. First, the references to judgment and an afterlife may seem inappropriate. It is assumed elsewhere, however, that although the Old Testament saints had to await the opening of the gates, there was no doubt that they were headed in the right direction precisely because they had done well. We are told emphatically in Passus XVII.15–16 that whoever lived according to the law of Hope-Moses would be saved; his law is a "charme" against the devil. Second, would Langland use phrases from the Athanasian Creed, which is the source of the words read by the priest, to represent the Old Law? The question implies a simple division between Old and New Laws, but as we have seen, Langland does not separate the Scriptures as we tend to. Indeed, Langland's Moses expresses a view of the Old Law that sounds more "Christian" than these words of the Creed. That does not mean that Langland was necessarily criticizing the Creed or identifying it as a whole with the Old Law. Free association divorced from chronology was Langland's common practice of quotation.[17] To take just one example, Abraham quotes from the Breviary a Latin commentary on himself (C.XIX.242).[18] The quotation was suitable because it was one that traditionally proved that Abraham had seen Christ. In Passus VII the quotation from the Creed lends itself to identification with the Old Law,

because of the traditional view that the basic moral law of the
Synagogue remained unchanged in the Church.

And although the lines read by the priest promise eternal life
to those who do well, the priest is correct, in one sense, in seeing
no pardon in them. If a man receives exactly what he deserves,
he receives justice, not mercy. The priest is also right in saying
that Christians neglect this justice at their peril. The indulgences
so bitterly condemned here are not worth a "pies hele" (VII.194)
precisely because they bypass the law of Do-well. Be not bold,
Langland warns, to break the Ten Commandments, because you
are rich enough to purchase pardons.

Piers's pardon, however, is not such an indulgence. It cannot
be bought and it specifically refuses mercy to dishonest lawyers
and beggars, while offering it to laborers who work honestly and
to kings and knights who rule justly. It does not differ in basic
morality from the priest's reading; it differs in its tone and in its
broad interpretation of the law. To individuals and to the race, it
offers hope of pardon through the love of Christ, and in its expansive interpretation of the Do-well of the priest, it is rather like
a commentary on the text. The fact that the words addressed to
the merchants are written in the margin, as glosses often were,
has been taken to mean that the pardon is such a commentary.[19]
Like the words of Christ which Moses called a glorious gloss on
the Old Law (XVIII.9–13), the words of the pardon stress love of
God and neighbor. If the merchants make amends by charity, if
they use their profits to help prisoners and those in hospitals, they
need not fear the devil at their death day. Safe, too, are those
lawyers who plead for the innocent and comfort the needy for the
love of God. In its emphasis on love as a cure, Piers's pardon
goes beyond the priest's precept of Do-well as Piers's new teaching in Passus XIII goes beyond the Do-well known to Clergy and
Conscience—as the pardon of the New Law goes beyond even
the Old Law of Moses.

Since in all of the later scenes we have looked at, the New
Law does not abrogate the Old, not even the eye-for-an-eye
clause, Piers ought not to tear up the Old Law—as he does in the
B-text. The much-discussed tearing has been called "irrevoca-

ble,''[20] but Langland revoked it in the C-version. Perhaps the poet could no more fit the dramatic gesture into the later development of the theme than can his commentators.[21] With the deletion, the scene fits the historical and moral pattern, though we could wish that, while he was revising, Langland had added a few lines to clarify or conclude the argument. Perhaps when he left Piers and priest jangling, he intended the inconclusive ending to suggest, again as in the later scenes, that the time was not ripe to settle the dispute. It would not, in fact, be ripe until Passus XIX: only after the Passion and the Resurrection could Christ grant mercy to men without offending the justice of God, and only then does he give Piers ''power'' (XIX.179) with the pardon.

If it is not time for the promulgation of the pardon, it must be the time of the Old Law, and Piers may be a prophet and his pardon a prophecy. There are too many ''ifs'' here, and I do not mean to suggest that the scene was conceived as part of the salvation history of the last five cantos, or even that figural allegory is more than incidental. But the underlying concept may well have been with Langland from the beginning, and it does seem that he was using the freedom of the dream here, as in the scenes of the Good Samaritan and the Dinner Party, to allude to the historical progression of the Old and New Laws. As in XIII, the characters in VII are Christians, but they do not seem to recognize the New Law. The failure of priest and dreamer to see Piers's pardon can be explained by their spiritual imperfections; they are not ready to ''see'' it. On the other hand, they are being asked to see something that is apparently not written in the document. The dreamer carefully reads the pardon over the priest's shoulder (as he later studies Moses' writ), and like the priest he can only see two lines. The earlier 105 lines of description are apparently a special revelation to Piers, like those received by Patience and Peace. So before the Incarnation, the New Law was hidden in the Old, and the prophecies were not clear until they were fulfilled. Perhaps it is because he realizes that he must await the fulfillment by Christ that Piers resolves to spend his time praying and doing penance like the prophets (VII.121).

The repetition of the seal image of Passus VII in Passus XVII also seems to connect the scene with the fulfillment of the law. In Passus VII the letter of pardon for the merchants is sent under Truth's secret seal (23). On the road to Jerusalem, Moses is also carrying a letter and he is seeking him who has the seal (XVII.5–8). In terms of salvation history, the Old Law would become a pardon for the human race when it was sealed with Christ's blood, "the blood of the new covenant," as the canon of the Mass phrases it. Perhaps the seal is "secret" in Passus VII because the private message would not become public until the Crucifixion, when the pardon cryptically prophesied would be made plain to all mankind.

It is doubtful, however, that the priest would be among those who welcomed it. If we review the other scenes, we see that the teaching of the New Law is constant; the gist of the message is that the devil will never harm those who help the poor and the needy for the love of God. And the proponents of the New Law—Piers, Patience, Moses, Peace—are alike in their visionary fervor. As Peace says, nothing is impossible to God, no wickedness so great that love could not bring it to laughter (XVIII.413–14). The characters who do not want to hear this news, however, are not all of a kind. Their negativism ranges from the cautious pharisaism of Clergy at the Dinner Party to the desperate denial of the devil in hell. What they have in common is that they cling to some portion of the letter of the law, and their nay-saying demonstrates that without the spirit that gives life, the letter kills. The daughters of God who deny mercy to the children of Adam and the devil who denies the right of Jesus to rescue mankind attempt to use the letter of the law as a means of excluding men from the mercy of God. And there is anger between these strict constructionists and those who believe that justice, however good in itself, is not enough without charity. In this latter company are Scripture, Imagination, Abraham, Moses, Piers, and Jesus, all of whom yearn for the pardon of all men.

In Passus VII the priest's advice to do well is sound, but his emphasis and tone are negative. The minatory phrase of the document is closer to the eye for an eye of Lucifer than to the "love God and neighbor" inscribed on Moses' tablets. Yet Christ did not deny the justice described by the devil, and in Passus VII the justice described in the words of the Creed must be observed. Moses sought the fulfillment of the law in love; but the priest will hear no more than the letter. Keenly aware of the need for justice in the affairs of men, Langland insists also on the need for mercy in the hearts of men. And the heart of the priest is wrong. He is like the scorner in the Proverbs of Solomon (VII.136–38);[22] he is a professional who looks down on Piers and condescendingly offers to translate the Latin into English. When Piers quotes from the Gospels, the priest jeers at his learning and implies that only priests should preach. He is akin to the Doctor of Divinity at the Dinner Party who sneers at the notion that Piers knows something more than he. Like Righteousness, this priest seems glad there is no pardon.

The dispute between the priestly priest and the prophetic Piers applies to both past and present, because their conflicting attitudes are perennial. They do not, however, represent a simple dichotomy of good versus bad. Surely Langland's heart is with Piers, as it is with Moses and Christ. The verse which describes the pardon as Piers sees it is fired with the thirst for justice and compassion for the poor, which we identify as the voice of the poet himself. And surely Langland deliberately portrayed the priest as sour and niggardly. But though the priest is no Moses, neither is he Meed; he does recognize justice. Neither disputant should win the argument in Passus VII because their views of justice and mercy, like those of the daughters of God, will be reconciled by Christ.

Passus VII lacks the clarity of the later scenes but it is clear that the priest's "two propre wordes," as well as the pardon he impugned with them, are essential to Langland's profound and profoundly poetic answer to the riddle of God's way of combining justice with mercy.

NOTES

1. William Langland, *The Vision of William concerning Piers the Plowman*, in *Three Parallel Texts*, ed. Walter W. Skeat (1886; rpt. Oxford, 1968). Unless otherwise noted, references are to the B-text by Passus and line.
2. John Lawlor, *Piers Plowman: An Essay in Criticism* (London, 1962), p. 77.
3. Rosemary Woolf, "The Tearing of the Pardon," *Piers Plowman: Critical Approaches*, ed. S. S. Hussey (London, 1969), pp. 53–54.
4. R. W. Frank, Jr., *Piers Plowman and the Scheme of Salvation* (New Haven, 1957), pp. 19–33.
5. D. W. Robertson, Jr., and Bernard F. Huppé, *Piers Plowman and Scriptural Tradition* (Princeton, 1951), p. 94.
6. Mary C. Schroeder, "*Piers Plowman*: The Tearing of the Pardon," *Philological Quarterly*, 49 (1970), 8–19, esp. 9–10.
7. In discussing the subject at some length in *The Fulfillment of the Scriptures: Abraham, Moses, and Piers* (Evanston, Ill., 1970), I have drawn heavily on St. Paul; on the Church Fathers, especially Justin Martyr, Tertullian, Irenaeus, Cyprian, Lactantius, Eusebius, and Augustine; on English commentators, especially Bede, Aelfric, and Grosseteste; and on such fiction as *A Stanzaic Life of Christ*, Lydgate's *Pilgrimage of the Life of Man*, and numerous plays.
8. See, for example: *The Miroure of Mans Salvacionne*, ed. Alfred H. Huth (London, 1888), pp. 47, 99; *Speculum Sacerdotale*, ed. Edward H. Weatherly, EETS 200 (1936), 52–63.
9. Robert Grosseteste, *De Cessatione Legalium, Parts 1 and 2: A Critical Edition from the Extant MSS.*, ed. Arthur M. Lee, Diss. Colorado, 1942, New York Public Library Microfilm, pp. 18–19.
10. Some of the Latin commentaries are conveniently cited in Ben H. Smith, Jr., *Traditional Imagery of Charity in Piers Plowman* (The Hague, 1966); see also *Old English Homilies*, ed. R. Morris, EETS 29, 34 (1868), 234; Adam of St. Victor, *Liturgical Poetry*, trans. Digby S. Wrangham (London, 1881), Vol. 1, Sequence viii.
11. J. F. Goodridge, "The Riddle of Patience," Appendix C, *Piers the Plowman*, Introduction J. F. Goodridge (Harmondsworth, 1966), p. 299.
12. St. Augustine, *De Diversis Quaestionibus* I, Q. lxvi.3, *PL* 40, 62, quoted by Schroeder, p. 16, in a discussion of the typology of Passus VII.
13. Goodridge, pp. 306–7.
14. In "Justice, Kingship, and the Good Life in Part II," *Piers Plowman: Critical Approaches*, p. 90, P. M. Kean remarks that Clergy "has only the Old Testament to offer the pilgrims. While they must go forward to the New, he still warns them that the Old, with its prophetic knowledge of Christ's coming, cannot be dispensed with." And E. Talbot Donaldson, in *Piers Plowman: The C-Text and Its Poet* (Hamden, Conn., 1966), p. 163, speaking of the substitution in the C-text of Piers for Patience (B.XIII; C.XVI),

suggests that Piers stands "for the prophets in the era before Christ's coming."

15. Emile Mâle, *The Gothic Image*, trans. Dora Nussey (1913; rpt. New York, 1958), p. 5.

16. There had been many pagan and a few Jewish opponents of Christianity who argued that the turn of the other cheek of the New Testament did in fact abrogate the eye for an eye of the Old. See Origen, *Against Celsus* VII, Ante-Nicene Library, Vols. X, XXIII (1869, 1872), and Nicolas de Lyra, *Biblia Sacra* (Lyons, 1545), VI.282ff. In Passus XVIII of *Piers*, when the devil, like the pagan or the Jew of the debates, insists on the law of punishment, Christ, like the apologists, must prove out of the Old Testament that he did not abrogate the law.

17. It was, indeed, the common practice of the time. Leclercq remarks that monks quoted from memory by means of "hook-words," and that the words belonged to the user who was perhaps not aware of their source. Jean Leclercq, *The Love of Learning and the Desire for God: A Study of Monastic Culture*, trans. Catherine Misrahi (New York, 1961), pp. 81–82.

18. *Breviarium ad Usum Insignis Ecclesiae Sarum*, ed. Francis Procter and Christopher Wordsworth (Cambridge, 1879–86), I: *Kalendarium et Temporale*, pp. 541, 546.

19. Woolf, pp. 53–54.

20. Lawlor, p. 316.

21. Lawlor, for example, mars his generally excellent interpretation of the law by forcing later episodes to fit the tearing of the pardon. He says that when Conscience leaves Clergy to go with Patience, "we leave aside the Old Law . . . as the Plowman has torn asunder his legal document" (p. 121). But so far from destroying the Old Law, Conscience agrees with Clergy that the day will come when they will be united. (See also n. 14.) Robertson and Huppé (pp. 93–94) relate the tearing of the pardon "atweyne" to the later scenes of the fulfillment of the Old Law in the New. They add that "Through his act Piers in sorrow indicates symbolically why not only a commandment but also a promise of pardon is contained in the New Law for those who have faith in it." I do not see how the destruction of the pardon can represent the fulfillment of the law or why Piers should have been sorrowful over the promise of pardon. Two other interesting interpretations of the tearing fail to take into account the high regard for the Old Law expressed so often by Langland. Professor Schroeder believes that the *Visio* is "figurally structured" to represent "fallen and graceless man" in the world of the Old Law, in which "there can be no progression towards goodness . . . no moral value" (p. 11). This dark picture ignores the luminous Abraham and Moses of Cantos XVI and XVII. Professor Woolf, referring to the traditional iconography of the Church and the Synagogue, remarks that there was "nothing doctrinally repugnant in demonstrating in artistic form the dispossession of the Old Law under the New Dispensa-

tion'' (p. 74). But the destruction of the law *was* doctrinally repugnant: not the law but the Synagogue was dispossessed; the tables of the law were presumably picked up by the triumphant Church, which was henceforth the guardian of the Scriptures. If, when Langland wrote the B version, he had the popular iconography in mind, he may have intended the priest to represent the Synagogue, Piers the Church. But if the document in the priest's hand is the Old Law, Piers ought not to destroy it; even in its most damnatory form, expressed by the devil in Passus XVIII, the law is not destroyed but fulfilled by Christ.

22. Speaking of such ''scorners,'' Chaucer's Parson remarks that ''they han joye whan the devel wynneth, and sorwe whan he leseth. / They have been adversaries of Jhesu Crist, for they haten that he loveth, that is to seyn, salvacioun of soule'' (*The Parson's Tale,* 637–38, *The Works of Geoffrey Chaucer,* ed. F. N. Robinson, 2d ed. [Boston, 1957], p. 248).

4

The Satiric Strategy of
Peres the Ploughmans Crede

DAVID LAMPE

AMONG the meager handful of Lollard verse extant, *Peres the Ploughmans Crede* is both the best known and the most successful.[1] Like *Piers Plowman*, of which it is the earliest imitation and from which it borrows both plot and title character, *Peres the Ploughmans Crede* is a polemical poem concerned with questions of religious authority, belief, and action.[2] Unlike *Piers Plowman*, however, this shorter and more neatly structured poem suggests a simpler and more coherent solution to these problems. It does so by juxtaposing the blatant hypocrisy and mean-spirited pettiness of the four orders of friars in the first half of the poem with the passionate, yet still humble, sincerity of Peres in the second half. Since the purpose of the poem is to explore and define the relationship between statement and action, the speeches of the characters *are* the vital action of the plot. Thus a careful consideration of the different language patterns, especially the contrasting usages of praise and blame and ethical appeal, will reveal the various layers of irony which allow for the poem's sharp satire.

After an initial trinitarian invocation, the poem introduces a conscientious unnamed narrator who, although he knows his alphabet, paternoster, and "*Aue marie* almost to þe ende," worries "for y can nohʒt my Crede."[3] Made painfully aware of this deficiency by his inability to perform the penance his parish priest will impose, and by Christ's own words "He þat leeueþ nouʒt on

me he leseþ þe blisse,'' (15) he searches for a teacher among
"many maner of men" who claim knowledge. This quest has
brought him in contact with the friars who tell him ''þat all þe
frute of þe fayþ was in here foure ordres'' (29). The first half of
the poem recounts his frustrating experience with representatives
of each of these orders.

Mentioning that a Carmelite has covenanted to teach him his
creed, the narrator asks a Franciscan for advice. Instead of a simple answer, what he gets is forty-six lines of slander. Carmelites
cannot teach him anything, he is told, since they know nothing of
God. Mere "jugulers and iapers" (43) who are neither in an
order nor out of one, Carmelites are a "faynt folk i-founded
vp-on iapes" (47). Since they are notorious lechers and gluttons,
it is a great sin to give them any gifts which permit them to
"lurken in her selles" where they wallow in worldly goods and
"wasten it in synne" (60–61). Instead of preaching like Paul and
moving people to penance they merely entertain with "gestes of
Rome" and long lying tales about the Virgin. They are, in fact,
the "enemyes of þe cros" that St. Paul warned of in Philippians.
Thus since "glotony is her God,'' the narrator is advised to
"Leue nouȝt on þo losels but let hem forþ pasen, / For þei ben
fals in her feiþ'' (96–97).

Apparently overwhelmed by this tirade, the narrator asks
where he can find someone reliable to teach him his creed. "Of
all men opon mold we Menures most scheweþ / Þe pure Apostel-
les life'' (103–4), the Franciscan answers, smoothly shifting
from blame of rivals to praise of his own order. All that is necessary, he assures the narrator, is that one contribute to the church
and chapel that our convent is building. The request for a creed is
summarily dismissed: "And, broþer, be þou nouȝt aferd; . . . /
Þouȝ þou conne nouȝt þi Crede kare þou no more. / I schal
asoilen þe'' (130–32).

Although he accepts this absolution, the narrator leaves the
friar "wiþ-outen any peine.'' The shift from vicious attack to
lavish self-praise has been too abrupt: "Þanne saide y to my-self
'here semeþ litel trewþe! / First to blamen his broþer and bac-

byten him foule' " (138–39). Though the narrator remains polite, his discontent grows with each encounter.

Indeed, the narrator has only seen what we also are expected to recognize. The Franciscan has insisted that Carmelites cannot teach pure doctrine because of their irregular lives, and because they are falsely founded: "þe foles foundeden hem-self" (65). Yet the only lesson he has for the anxious narrator is to pay his money, so that "seynt Fraunces him-self schall folden the in his cope, / And presente the to the trynitie" (126–27). Thus his denunciation of the Carmelites' preaching and penance also applies to his own perversions of those offices. Two additional kinds of irony qualify his statement that Carmelites are mere "jugulers" (43). St. Francis himself had called his followers *viellatores Dei* and *joculatores Domini*.[4] Lollards, however, complained that the followers of St. Francis had become "þe deuelis iogelours to blynde mennus gostly eiȝen."[5] The Franciscan's scornful sneering at the Carmelites' appearances at "feires & at ful ales" (73) has the very air of pietistic high seriousness and stubborn unsmiling arrogance that St. Francis had objected to and that, to Lollard critics of the friars, seemed the hypocrisy of modern Pharisees.[6]

Even if, like most English Franciscans, the Franciscan in the poem did not share the extreme spiritualist or *zelanti* belief in the virtue of absolute poverty, it is still ironic that he should accuse the Carmelites of that very vow: "And pride is in her pouerte" (76).[7] This same kind of irony continues in the burst of self-congratulation that follows. To prove that his order maintains the pure apostolic life, the Franciscan lists a series of their virtues (106–17). Poverty, the last of these, is, however, undercut in the next lines by the description of the elaborate church and chapel which the Franciscans are building and to which the narrator is encouraged to contribute (118–29). The Franciscans are thus shown to take a contradictory stance toward possessions and poverty; as a Lollard author observed, "þei bynden hem self to be dede to þe world & forsaken it & bysynesse, & on þe toþer side þei bynden hem to obedience for to take worldli bisynesse."[8]

Finally, as several later satiric poems show, the insistence on the words and preaching of St. Paul (80) also called forth that saint's example to critics of the mendicants. As a later friar manqué complains:

> Yf Y say hit longoþ not
> ffor prestis to worche where þei go,
> Þei leggen for hem holi writ,
> And sein þat seint polle did so.[9]

I have taken this much time with the first friar because both what he says and the ironic resonances of his statements suggest the satiric pattern that is used to present the other three. The fantastically fat Dominican (reminiscent of St. Dominic's vision of a threatening dragon)[10] attacks the Austins; their representative in turn slanders the Franciscans, till finally the Carmelite has his turn at the Dominicans. All the parties in this interlocking chain of satiric dialogue are obsessed with arguments about apostolic succession. Yet each is so preoccupied with strategies of self-praise and jealous blame of others that they lose sight completely of their prospective student, the poem's narrator. Although he offers each a chance to profess rather than merely protest true apostolic values, he is instead told not to worry, pay his fee, and leave it to them: "My soule y sette for þyn to asoile þe clene" (331). For the friars, penance has obviously lost all of its spiritual dimensions, and has become an empty act, a mere financial transaction. As with Langland and Chaucer it is this complete perversion of the office of penance that adds a bitter twist to the satire.

Yet, their squabbles are not without purpose, for on another level of irony, several charges each makes regarding rival orders hit the mark. The Franciscan accuses the Carmelites of drunkenness "At feires & at ful ales & fyllen þe cuppe" (73) for "glotony is her God wiþ gloppyng of drynk" (92). Later in a tavern the narrator finds "Two frere Karmes wiþ a full coppe" (340). The fat Dominican laughs at the Austin's claims of ancient antecedents and insists that they purchase their "pryuileges wiþ

penyes so rounde'' (246). This, he asserts, is ''pur pardoners
craft.'' Like a pardoner, the Austin later claims:

> We haue power of the pope purliche assoilen
> All þat helpen our hous in helpe of her soules,
> To dispensen hem wiþ in dedes of synne.
>
> (318–20)

To prove that the Franciscans are the ''image of ypocricie'' the
Austin describes their lavish accouterments (290–301). Their
hypocritical ''gile'' is apparent, he insists, in their prodigal
wealth; they have ''more good him-selue / Þan ten knyȝtes þat y
knowe'' (282–83) and ''more money hid þan marchantes of
wolle'' (289). The narrator is already aware of this pretended
poverty, for he has already been asked to contribute to an elaborate church and convent.

The Dominicans are castigated by the Carmelite, who twice
puns on their traditional iconography, *Domini canes*.[11] The
Carmelite contends that ''prechers'' are ''proude purlyche in
herte'' (381) and cites as evidence their role as royal confessors
and advisors. The dragon Dominican in his labyrinthine den
(London's Blackfriars, according to Doyle)[12] confirms this
charge. Dominicans, he proudly claims, are ''clerkes'' in schools
and courts; Dominicans are ''bichopes,'' ''seyntes,'' and finally
(for a Lollard the order is certainly anticlimactic) have been
''popes at Rome'' (250–57). The narrator, though initially awed
by the architectural splendor and immensity of the Dominican's
den, as much as by the bulk of the friar he finds in it, does not
allow him to begin his ''pitch'' but instead angrily reminds him
of the ideal of his order, ''pouernesse of spyrit'' (264).[13]

This outburst by the narrator is not an isolated instance either:
after the Franciscan attacks the Carmelites, the narrator leaves
him, thinking, appropriately enough, ''Whow myȝt-tou in thine
broþer eiȝe a bare mote loken, / And in þyn owen eiȝe nouȝt a
bem toten?'' (141–42). After the Austin has asserted his absurd
claim of ecclesiastic primacy (317), the narrator observes pri-

vately: "here is no bote; / Heere pride is þe *pater-noster* in preyinge of synne: / Here Crede is coueytise" (335–37). When the narrator admits to the Carmelite that he has "no peny in my palke" (399) he is dismissed as "a fol," for he has wasted the precious time of this busy man on his way to see "an houswife þe myddel-erde" (535; see verse 4). Neither do they "wepen for her no lenger lyven" (409–10, 417). As an appropriate summary observation on all four orders, the narrator turns away "and talked to my-selue / Of þe falshede of þis folk whou feiþles they weren" (418–19).

The second half of the poem, Peres's appearance and didactic diatribe against both mendicants and possessioners, may at first seem both diffuse and dull; yet it answers both the needs of the narrator and the poem. The description of Peres (421–41), "a sely man" that "opon þe plow hongen," not only echoes *Piers Plowman*, but also provides what H. S. Bennett calls "an unforgettable vignette of a side of medieval life Chaucer does not choose to depict in detail."[14] For the purposes of the poem it also provides the narrator with the source of his creed, and it is from statements in this section of the poem that the anonymous author has been judged a Lollard. Not only are both John Wycliff (528–32) and Walter Brute (657–63) cited as witnesses of "trewþe," but the doctrinal attitudes toward the eucharist (822–30) and the means of grace (818–19), together with numerous echoes of extant Lollard tracts, suggest that the author was a Lollard.

But more important than doctrinal delineations, at least for my purposes, is an awareness of the rhetorical pattern of Peres's argument in this portion of the poem. Not only does Peres's instruction lead to a "crede," but it does so by using quite different rhetorical strategies from those used by the friars in the earlier section. Put simply, Peres's preaching is an honest and ingenious usage of praise and blame, when compared to the devious manipulations of the friars. Though both Peres and the friars are engaged in polemics, the manner and matter of their usages of praise and blame are quite different. Since the proud friars believe that there is nothing to censure in their own order, because the only things to be blamed are the pretensions of their rival orders, they are content with piling up self-praise without the least hint of modesty or embarrassment. Though this self-congratulation uses some ecclesiastical references, the real criteria behind these trappings are those of the secular world: wealth, power, and prestige. Thus while they squabble, indeed because they are shown to be incapable of anything else, the very apostolic role that they debate eludes them. The narrator, after all, is asking for something as simple as the Apostle's Creed, which he finally gets from Peres who, I will argue, represents the apostolic succession as it was understood in Lollard terms.

Unlike the friars, Peres seems to be in touch with the ideas and spirit of the founders of the mendicant orders. On three separate occasions Peres recalls the "ordynaunce," "dedes," and practice of Augustine, Dominic, and Francis (464–67; 509–14; 775–78). In so doing, he underlines an important contrast between himself and the decadent descendants of these reformers. Peres does not live in the great halls of the fourteenth-century English Dominicans, and he thus has the true spirit of poverty and humility rather than their false pride. Like St. Francis, he is unencumbered by the offal weight of wealth, and thus has the *zelanti* virtue of true poverty. An ardent Lollard might even argue that Peres's wife *is* Dame Poverty who, with her three children, is shown to be fruitful and not sterile like the abandoned bride of the false Franciscans. Peres's insistence that mendicants "schulden deluen & diggen & dongen þe erþe" (785) shows that he both preaches and practices manual labor. Thus, since he practices what St. Augustine insisted upon in *De Opere Monachorum*, and unlike the friars he will not "Lat Austyn have his swynk to hym reserved," he can be seen as a truer heir of Augustine's rules than the Austins who claim to have been founded by that saint.

Additionally, I think it can be shown that Peres's polemic is not as random as it might at first seem to a modern reader. Peres's usage of the beatitudes provides an important clue to both the implicit structure and the meaning of this section of the poem. Following the Vulgate order of Matthew 5:3–10, the eight

beatitudes are used as a means of judging and condemning the
failures of the friars. All the orders fail to have the humility of
those "þat mene ben in soule" (520; see verse 3). "Proue hem
in proces," Peres notes, and "þei willn wexen pure wroþ" (523,
525). Their "proude wordes," fine clothes, elaborate dwellings,
and fondness for titles show that they are not among "þe meke of
þe myddel-erde" (535; see verse 4). Neither do they "wepen for
wykkednes" that they have done (612; see verse 5), nor "body-
liche hungreþ" for righteousness (619; see verse 6). They are not
merciful (629–36; see verse 7), and their hearts are far from
being "clene" (637–44; see verse 8); rather they are like "kurres
from kareyne þat is cast in dyches" (644). Waspish rather than
"pesible" (645–52; see verse 9), instead of being willing to suf-
fer persecution for truth, they are agents of persecution (653–63).
Peres's preaching follows a familiar homiletic pattern which also
allows him to engage in some Lollard hagiography. The first
beatitude is used to introduce Wycliff (528–32) while the last
calls forth the Lollard martyr Walter Brute (657–63). Thus, I
think it can be shown that Peres's presentation is not merely
slanderous and self-serving. Though he attacks the friars, it is not
simply to praise himself. Instead he speaks with the tones of a
reformer. His praise is for the ideals exemplified in the
beatitudes, and his blame is directed at those who fail to live up
to these ideals, though loudly professing them. Indeed, it is possible to argue that Peres not only announces but also himself
exemplifies the beatitudes.

The standard commentary on the beatitudes is St. Augustine's
De Sermo Domini in Monte. Augustine considers the individual
beatitudes not as separate categories of blessing, but, using the
analogy of the "seven gifts of the Spirit" and the seven petitions
of the pater noster, he insists that the "eighth maxim returns, as
it were, to the beginning." Thus, these seven maxims "constitute
perfection" which may be ascended step by step: "love of God,"
"piety," "knowledge," "fortitude," "counsel," "understanding," and finally "wisdom."[15] Peres's homily not only observes
this progression in expounding the beatitudes, but the manner of
Peres' presentation is itself an illustration of this progression.

But the poem's narrator does not immediately understand Peres. Having heard nothing but backbiting and slander from the friars, he questions Peres's motive. "Why dispisest þou þus þise sely pore freres" (672), he asks, and supplies his own answer:

> It semeþ þat þise sely men han somwhat þe greved
> Oþer wiþ word or wiþ werke & þerfore þou wilnest
> To schenden oþer schamen hem wiþ þi sharpe speche.
> (675–77)

Like the Lollard author of *Tractatus de Pseudo-Freris*, Peres dismisses this misunderstanding easily: " 'I praie þe,' quaþ Peres 'put þat out of þy mynde; / Certen for sowle hele y saie þe þis wordes' " (679–80).[16] That is, his motive is "love of God" and true rather than feigned "piety." Peres's "knowledge" is evident in his scriptural citations, and echoes that are as natural a part of his discourse as Langland's citations of the Vulgate. Peres's "fortitude" is evident in his endurance against all odds and in spite of the pitiful conditions that make him merely sigh sorely (442). His "counsel" and "understanding" are evident not only in his preaching, but also in the creed that he finally gives to the narrator, a creed designed to lead to the "wisdom of God."

As my title suggests, the purpose of this essay has been to trace some of the rhetorical strategies used by the speakers in the poem since these speeches are the primary action in the poem and thus the source of its sharp satire. As Maynard Mack notes, "Rhetorically considered, satire belongs to the category of *laus et vituperatio*, praise and blame."[17] The contrasting uses of these topics in the poem give rise to two different kinds of ethical appeal. The friars' only strategy seems to be to celebrate themselves at the expense of all rivals. Because of the ironies and contradiction in this mixture of encomium and *ad hominem* argument, their ethical appeal is entirely negative. Their character, as shown by their language, is that of those who live in an "up-so-doun" world where "word and deed," as Chaucer laments, "ben nothing lyk."

Like the friars, Peres does use emotional appeal, but he never

descends to their level of abusive name-calling, for his aim is to
provoke reform rather than to eliminate a rival. This motive, together with his use of a careful homiletic structure in which he
praises gospel ideals, creates a different and effective ethical appeal. The poem ends with this appeal paramount, for the narrator
addresses his reader in the same tone Peres has used in speaking
to him:

> But all þat euer I haue seyd soþ it me semeþ,
> And all þat euer I haue writen is soþ, as I trowe,
> And for amending of þise men is most þat I write;
> God wold hy wolden ben war & werchen þe better!
>   But, for y am a lewed man paraunter y miȝte
> Passen par auenture & in som poynt erren,
> Y will nouȝt þis matere maistrely auowen;
> But ȝif ich haue myssaid mercy ich aske,
> & praie all maner men þis matere amende,
> Iche a word by him-self & all, ȝif it nedeþ.
>   God of his grete myȝte & his good grace
> Saue all freres þat faiþfully lybben,
> And alle þo þat ben fals fayre hem amende,
> And ȝyue hem wijt & good will swiche dedes to werche
> Þat þei maie wynnen þe lif þat euer schal lesten!
>   (841–55)

After listening to Peres and learning his creed from him, the
narrator still portrays himself as a "lewed man" and disavows
any "maistrely" manner. Instead, his prayerful purpose is to
amend the errors of those who had ignored him as a naive fool.
Here is true humility, which has the ability to admit personal fal-
libility and at the same time balance this recognition with an absolute commitment to faith. Here is the new voice of a simple
Christian, the words and actions of real rather than feigned belief.

NOTES

1. Extant in two manuscripts (B. L. Royal 18 B. xvii; Trinity College Cambridge R. 3.15), the poem was printed by Reynold Wolfe in 1553. Alexander Pope wrote a paragraph summary of the poem in his copy which Thomas Warton quotes in his chapter-length appreciation, *History of English Poetry* (London, 1774), I, 287–308. The poem has been edited by T. Wright (1842; rpt. London, 1895) and by W. W. Skeat (London, 1867). It appears in A. S. Cook's *Literary Middle English Reader* (Boston, 1915) and in a modern translation in Loomis and Willard's *Medieval English Verse and Prose* (New York, 1948).

2. Modern evaluative assessments of the poem begin with George Saintsbury, who found it "an ill-tempered but vigorous Wyclifite lampoon," in his *Short History of English Literature* (1898; rpt. New York, 1929), p. 132. J. M. Manly terms it a "remarkable poem" for its author's "power of description," in *Cambridge History of English Literature* (Cambridge, 1908), II, 44. Wells also commends the "descriptive passages," in *A Manual of the Writings in Middle English* (New Haven, 1926), p. 269. J. P. Oakden says "the excellency of the dramatic satire is at once apparent," in *Alliterative Poetry in Middle English*, II (1935; rpt. New York, 1968), p. 59. John D. Peters is enthusiastic about the use of the beatitudes, "a tour de force unequalled anywhere else," and regards the verse as "racy, vivid, sometimes punning, always colloquial," in *Complaint and Satire in Early English Literature* (Oxford, 1956), pp. 54, 291. Recent bibliography in Rossell Hope Robbins, "Poems dealing with Contemporary Conditions," no. 109, in *A Manual of the Writings in Middle English 1050–1500*, gen. ed. Albert E. Hartung (New Haven, 1975), Vol. 5.

3. *Pierce the Ploughmans Crede*, ed. W. W. Skeat, EETS 30 (1867), lines 7–8. All subsequent citations are from this edition and line numbers follow each quotation in the text.

4. " . . . et post praedicationem omnes cantarent simul Laudes Domini tanquam joculatores Domini," *Speculum perfectionis*, ed. P. Sabatier (Paris, 1898), p. 198; and also St. Francis, *Regula*, Chap. 9. For discussion see D. L. Jeffrey, *The Early English Lyric and Franciscan Spirituality* (Lincoln, Nebr., 1975), pp. 121–23, 176.

5. "Of Prelates," in *English Works of Wyclif*, ed. F. D. Matthew, EETS 74 (1880), 99.

6. For St. Francis' suggestions regarding dealing with other orders see Thomas of Celano, *The Second Life of St. Francis*, trans. Placid Hermann, Part II, Chaps. 89–91, in *St. Francis of Assisi: Writings and Early Biographies*, ed. M. A. Habig (Chicago, 1972), pp. 466–68. The equation of Friars and Pharisees, a Lollard commonplace, can be found in "Leaven of Pharisees," and in "Tractatus de Pseudo-freris," *English Works of Wyclif*, pp. 2, 297.

7. David Knowles describes the Franciscan controversies over the concept of poverty, *The Religious Orders in England*, II (Cambridge, 1961), pp. 63–67, 90–91. For Lollard awareness of the controversy, see "The Rule and Testament of St. Francis," *English Works of Wyclif*, pp. 39–51.

8. "Of Clerks Possessioners," *English Works of Wyclif*, p. 126.

9. "The Fryers Complaynt," in *Cambridge Middle English Lyrics*, ed. H. A. Person (Seattle, 1962), 51b, 11. 17–20, p. 42. See also Poem 66 in *Historical Poems of the 14th and 15th Centuries*, ed. Rossell Hope Robbins (New York, 1959), p. 163. St. Paul's words are used against the Friars in *Piers Plowman*, ed. W. W. Skeat (London, 1886), B-Text, XIII.65–74, C-Text, XVI.68–79.

10. "Cum esset in Hispania, quibusdam sibi fratribus sociatis, apparuit ei per visum immanissimus draco quidam, qui fratres illos, qui secum erant, absorbere apertis faucibus nitebatur," in Jacobus de Voragine, *Legenda Aurea*, ed. Th. Graesse (1890; rpt. Osnabrück, 1965), p. 475.

11. They "deleþ in devynitie as dogges doþ bones" (357), and "þey ben digne as dich water þat dogges in bayteþ" (375). The source of this iconography is explained in *Legenda Aurea*: "Cujus mater ante ipsius ortum vidit in somniis se catulum gestantem in utero, ardentem in ore faculam bajulantem, qui egressus ex utero totam mundi machinam incendebat" (p. 466).

12. A. I. Doyle, "An Unrecognized Piece of *Piers the Ploughman's Creed*," *Speculum*, 34 (1959), 434.

13. Ironically enough, St. Dominic had, according to *Legenda Aurea*, refused election as Bishop of Conserano: "Electus aliquando in Cotoronensem, aliis Citaviensem episcopum, omnino renuit contestans se prius terram deserere, quam electioni alicui de se factae aliquatenus consentire" (p. 477). Knowles discusses the Dominican ideal of "poverty of spirit," *Religious Orders*, II, 92–93.

14. H. S. Bennett, *Chaucer and the Fifteenth Century* (New York, 1954), p. 72.

15. "Septem sunt ergo quae perficiunt: nam octava clarificat et quod perfectum est demonstrat, ut per hos gradus perficiantur et caeteri, tanquam a capite rursum exordiens. . . . Quapropter si gradatim tanquam ascendentes numeremus, primus ibi est timor Dei, secunda pietas, tertia scientia, quarta fortitudo, quintum consilium, sextus intellectus, septima sapientia." *De Sermone Domini in Monte*, I.iii.10–iv.11 (*PL* 34, 1234).

16. *English Works of Wyclif*, pp. 296–98.

17. "The Muse of Satire," *Yale Review*, 41 (1951–52), 83.

5

The Centuple Structure of the Pearl

JOHN V. FLEMING

Of all the qualities for which scholars and, indeed, general readers, have prized the poems of MS Nero A. x, none is more persistently pleasing than what might be called their Englishness. Sturdily *sui generis*, their stylistic uniqueness appropriately honored by the uniqueness of the manuscript itself, these poems have seemed to scholars to redeem a pledge of English poetry somehow forgotten since the time of the Exeter and Vercelli anthologies. The peculiar qualities of *Sir Gawain and the Green Knight* make it appear that, after all, the *matière de Bretagne* is just that, an island affair; Chrétien de Troyes, a talented and even brilliant foreign observer, is exposed as a mere writer of "Arthurian literature." The search for the "missing French source" of *Gawain*, Professor Kittredge's Lost Dutchman, may seem almost insulting to our own scholarly generation. Until Lancelot marches through the Wirral he will always have for his English readers a continental, faintly operatic, air of unreality. The religious poems, too—or perhaps the religious poems, especially—are inescapably and insistently English, monuments of the insular Gothic, despite the fact that one can hardly take a step to meet them without coming to the frontier of international Latin traditions.

It is by no means extraordinary under these circumstances that the Nero MS is often the central focus, or at any rate the silent arbiter, in discussions of the alleged English Alliterative Revival of the fourteenth century. To propose for these poems such a role, however, may be misleading if it inspires the critic to parochial expectation. The *Pearl*-poet is superficially akin to the author of *Richard the Redeless* in his prosodic principles; but he is much more like Hugh of Saint-Victor or Dante Alighieri in the way he thinks. The most remarkable thing about the poems of Nero A. x may turn out after all to be not so much their undisputed stylistic originality as their unique and happy wedding of tradition and the individual talent which we shall find so brilliantly fruitful nowhere else in medieval English literature unless it be in the best of Geoffrey Chaucer. In talking about certain formal aspects of *Pearl* which are more clearly connected with continental Latin traditions than with those specifically insular and vernacular, I do not for a moment mean to turn my back on its inescapable Englishness, nor of course do I mean to imply that the kind of concern which this essay will raise is the most appropriate, let alone the sole structural problem which the poem presents.

The truth of the matter is that the *Pearl* is one of the richest, most structurally complex of the great vernacular masterpieces of the later Middle Ages, and it is easy enough to identify at least three different kinds of interrelated "structures" in it. If the poem has the simple, unbroken, spherical unity of the gem which gives it its name, it has no less the multifaceted diversity of a finely cut diamond. One structure is defined by the complex of poetic images, largely of scriptural origin but invested with the privileged increment of exegetical tradition and the poet's own inventiveness, which gives the work its peculiarly satisfying density. Another kind of structure is articulated in its intellectual orchestration, the careful patterns of theological argument—never unambiguous but likewise never incoherent—through which it develops a consistent *sententia*. These two structures, or kinds of structure, have been the objects of what is without doubt the most fruitful work done on the *Pearl* in the last twenty years. My own essay is concerned with another and more limited "structure" in the poem—its external, almost calligraphic, structure, its one-hundred-and-oneness.

I may perhaps hope to be forgiven for writing about a quite mechanical aspect of the *Pearl*, a feature of its external artifice, if I remind my readers that there is not very much about the *internal* meaning of the poem which commands universal agreement. It has been called both an elegy and a *consolatio*; its theology exposed as arcane and even heretical, or expounded as catechistic and eventually rather boring. Who or what the pearl is, who the narrator is—such matters of presumably fundamental importance for any coherent exposition of the allegory are still matters very much under active discussion. There is, however, a basic narrative core to the poem, about which nearly all of its readers could join in at least tentative agreement. The *Pearl* is a poem about loss and consolation. What is lost is a pearl, "plesaunte to prynces paye"; its loss is stated explicitly and early, indeed in the first stanza of the poem: "Allas! I leste hyr in on erbere." Whatever else the pearl may be—and the fact that the Bible explicitly identifies a "pearl of great price" with "eternal life," together with the pearl's loss *in a garden*, has hardly constrained allegorists—it, or she, is a maiden, an innocent, a "daughter" to the narrator. The dynamic of the poem (quite apart from its specific allegorical meaning or meanings) is the process by which the uncomprehending narrator is gradually brought to a fuller and fuller understanding of his actual situation. What has rightly been called the "pattern of *consolatio*" in the *Pearl* is the classic kinesis of medieval visionary poetry, and it certainly has its proud counterparts elsewhere in the English Alliterative Traditions—in the "Dream of the Rood," for instance, and in *Piers Plowman*. The classic of the type in medieval literature, the true exemplar, is of course the *Consolation of Philosophy*.

The remarks which follow imply rather than argue a general interpretation of the poem. It is what might be called a compromise reading of the sort made notable by John Conley and others.[1] That is, I think that the poem is profoundly scriptural, as much in its expectations as its imagery, and that the language and style of Christ's parables are of particular relevance to it. Furthermore I do accept that the poem advances sophisticated, difficult, but coherent theological ideas. I might characterize the juxtaposition of these ideas as at times mildly eccentric, but I cannot go so far as to call them heretical. I do think that there is an obvious level of literary elegy in the *Pearl*: the pearl is among other things a dead young girl for whose loss the narrator is consoled by his own poem. The suggestion which I want to make about the structure of the *Pearl* is, I think, inclusive rather than exclusive. It is consistent with a good deal of the best recent work on the poem, but not partisan to any one particular interpretation.

At this point I must finally confess, as boldly as I can, that my structural suggestion is "numerological." It is of course somewhat embarrassing to do so, since in recent times the mysteries of numbers have largely been the province of sidewalk apocalyptics, pyramid buffs, Baconians, and Times Square pamphleteers. It would be too easy to forget that numerological practice has an ancient pedigree in the literary traditions which lie behind some of the most fundamental assumptions of medieval allegory—in Pythagorean harmonies, for example, and in the Jewish *midrash*. Yet what was to become the Christian science of numerology, such as it was, was unmistakably the work of the early Fathers, whose exegetical stance, though it shared more in common with ancient attitudes than has sometimes been realized, was in many respects strikingly original. Most scholars are now agreed that it was above all St. Augustine whose positively enthusiastic numerological speculations established a permanent authority of precedent for later medieval exegetes. Augustine found in the finality, inexorability, and pristine immateriality of mathematical operations the only human truths significantly analogous to God's truth. This attitude, still alive with Pascal, was quite common in the Middle Ages, and it was not without its consequences for medieval poetry.

Precisely what those implications are in any specific instance is of course a matter for close empirical analysis. The poetry of medieval England has received less attention from this point of view than that of the Renaissance, but in Europe, and especially in Germany, numerology has emerged as an identifiable school of literary study—perhaps with all that a school implies, including some excess of zeal, sectarian division, and immoderate reaction. Though in general terms the debate about the usefulness of number symbolism for the structural analysis of medieval German poetry remains in doubt, the controversy has at any rate exposed a very great deal of potentially valuable primary materials, particularly from the traditions of Augustinianism and of the "Carolingian renaissance."[2]

Of course certain of the numerological features of the *Pearl* are so insistent that they must claim the attention of any serious student of the poem's structure; they are perhaps too obvious to merit extended comment here, especially since they have been well explicated by other scholars. In particular A. Kent Hieatt has, in his illuminating essay on the numbers of *Sir Gawain*, succinctly identified the most important single numerological feature of the *Pearl* as well: the persistence of the number twelve.[3] The poem's basic element is the twelve-line stanza; its central anagogic mystery, specifically pointed to in the poet's explicit reference to the 144,000 "virgins" of Apocalypse 14:4 (867ff.), is the structure of the Celestial Jerusalem, whose duodecimal architecture is the mysterious subject of dozens of medieval scriptural commentaries. Hieatt further draws attention to the well-known fact that *Pearl*'s total number of lines, 1212, explicitly reduplicates the crucial number twelve when "read" in a linear fashion (just as the last line of the poem reduplicates elements of the first line, "perle" and "pay") and, as the mathematical product (twelve *times* twelve) it renders the 144 (thousand) maidens of the Lamb. Quite as obvious, though not quite so well explained, is the fact that the two most important poems in Nero A. x—*Sir Gawain* as well as the *Pearl*—both have exactly 101 stanzas each.

This 101 has been rather troublesome. It is easy enough to see how a round hundred could be a "perfect" number, especially given the decimal imagery of the scriptures and the arithmetic clichés of our own culture. One does not have to argue very strenuously in saying that Dante was right in putting one hundred cantos—not one more, and not one less—into his poem. One hundred and one is a different matter. The number is so unexpected—by virtue of being so close to what *is* expected—that it has more than once been suggested that the poet simply miscounted. "The natural supposition," says Charles Moorman, for example, "is, of course, that one stanza of the fifteenth group, probably either Stanza 72 or 76, is either spurious or was not canceled by the poet."[4] If so, he made the same mistake twice, unaccountably, so to speak, and Hieatt and others do not find it a winning suggestion. On the other hand, no very good reason has been suggested why there *should* be 101 stanzas. In this essay I want to suggest a possible reason, and to point to a literary tradition—or, if that is too grand a word, a pattern of literary precedent at any rate—which may link this very English masterpiece of the Alliterative Revival with some learned continental masterpieces which have little to do with *Pearl*'s time or place, but may have something to do with its subject or subjects.

Most of the significant numbers of medieval literature either come from the Bible in the first place, or can be ratified there; and I want to suggest that such is also the case with the *Pearl*-poet's 101. Simple recourse to a concordance is discouraging. There seem to be a hundred hundreds in Holy Writ, but not a single hundred and one. I should be falling short of my ceremonial duties as colloquy "Robertsonian," however, if I allowed the mere absence of a text to daunt me; "I shall fynde it in a maner glose." Specifically, I have come to believe that the scriptural source for the hundred and ones, which show up more frequently than one might suppose in the structural schemes of medieval books, will be found around the edges of a text which often was at the center of medieval discussions of Christian perfection: the nineteenth chapter of Matthew. So far as the themes of medieval literature are concerned, Matthew 19 is particularly dense. It contains, among other things, Christ's most explicit statement about the indissolubility of marriage and about spiritual and carnal eunuchry; the episode of the "little children" who are the types of the kingdom of heaven; and Christ's answer to the man (elsewhere called a ''ruler'') who asks the question *par excellence* of medieval spiritual literature, the question of *Piers Plowman*: ''What good thing shall I do, that I may have eternal life?''

Christ's answer to the man, that he must sell all he has and give it to the poor, was the beginning of every major medieval ascetic movement from the time of the desert anchorites to the bourgeois apostles of the mendicant orders. But it was also a ''hard saying,'' and one that sent this man, and no doubt many others like him in later centuries, away sad.

> Verily I say unto you, that a rich man shall hardly enter into the kingdom of heaven. And again I say unto you, it is easier for a camel to go through the eye of a needle than for a rich man to enter into the kingdom of God. When his disciples heard it, they were exceedingly amazed, saying Who then can be saved?

It was to this puzzled fearfulness which Christ addressed the consolation which became one of the most cherished texts of the medieval ascetic worlds: ''And every one that hath forsaken houses, or brethren, or sisters, or father, or mother, or wife, or children, or lands, for my name's sake, shall receive an hundredfold, and shall have everlasting life.'' The word here translated in the English as ''hundredfold'' is a rare one in the Vulgate, *centuplum*. ''Et omnis, qui reliquerit domum . . . centuplum accipiet, et vitam aeternam possidebit'' (Matthew 19:29).

There is a large enough range of usage in the Scriptures to see that *centuplum* is a term of financial and agricultural increase, as in the hundredfold increment of Isaac's sowing (Genesis 26:12) or in the parable of the sower (Luke 8:8). I suspect that the *centuplum* has not been brought into the discussion of the structure of *Pearl* because it may seem on the face of it one short; but the matter is more ambiguous. What does a hundredfold increase mean? The most obvious suggestion of the passage in Matthew 19 is a kind of adversary exchange. One gives up a home, a father, a son, a field, in order to find Christ; he finds as well a hundred other homes, fathers, sons, and fields. Such indeed seems to be the sense in which the passage is taken by some medieval commentators, particularly if they are concerned with the question of ascetic denial rather than with heavenly reward.[5] We should note, however, that the number 100 exists here only in the contingent relationship of ratio or proportion (100:1). Another exegetical approach construes the matter differently. In this reading, the spiritual *centuplum* of religious consolation does not involve a mystical transaction at an exchange rate of a hundred to one; it involves, rather, an *increase by a hundred*. This is particularly common among exegetes who take the *centuplum* in an immediately spiritual sense to mean "the kingdom of heaven" or "eternal life," that is, who take the terms *centuplum* and *vitam aeternam* in Matthew 19:29 as appositional alternatives. In this tradition, the *centuplum* is a factor to be added into a larger sum; it combines with the "gift" originally "denied" for Christ in hundredfold increase. The paradox involved in such an apprehension is of course closely related to that which takes up a good part of the narrator's education in the *Pearl*. The calculus which describes eternal life in terms of the functions of mortal life is inevitably startling. In either case—whether seen as a sum or as a proportional relationship—the number of religious consolation is not an isolated hundred, but one hundred and one.

As the number of religious consolation, 101 would have very felicitous overtones for the *Pearl*. (The possible implications for *Sir Gawain*, though not apt for this essay, are not inappropriate either.) But it is a large leap from the discovery of suggestive numerological possibilities in medieval exegesis to the demonstration that those traditions are at work in the formal structuring of medieval poems. What is needed, accordingly, is not so much an exegetical as an architectural history of the number 101. While I cannot pretend to answer that need fully in this essay, it will I hope be useful to draw attention to some of the ways in which this obtrusive number is used in the external structuring of a variety of medieval books. These would include one of the age's truly great masterpieces and several Italian works of the thirteenth and fourteenth centuries, molded by the same "Franciscan" aesthetic which is clearly reflected as well in some of the features of the poems of Nero A. x.

This is of course not the place for an extended discussion of the *Confessions* of St. Augustine. One hardly has to point out that there were few books written in the Middle Ages which had wider or more far-reaching literary influence. Pierre Courcelle has devoted more than seven hundred dense octavo pages merely to the external history of that influence, which was never greater, incidentally, than in the fourteenth century. The structure of the *Confessions, a* structure of it rather, is radically numerological though never slavishly so, and the work reveals in its architecture many of the numerical mysteries to which Augustine draws explicit attention elsewhere in his exegetical works. For example, its division into thirteen books, in two clear intellectual movements of ten and three, combines the two principal numbers of "spiritual structure": the ten is above all the explicit number of external morality in the Commandments, the three the radical number of the Godhead and of its dimly shadowed impress of *voluntas, memoria*, and *intellectus*. To the special importance of the final three books of the *Confessions* I shall return presently.

Furthermore, most of the *Confessions* are formally linked together in triads of books in a quite complicated way. The first three books, for example, deal with Augustine's first eighteen years, with his *infantia* and *adolescentia*. The first book has twenty chapters, the second ten, the third twelve. The total number of chapters in the three books is, accordingly, forty-two, an extremely significant number in patristic thought which pointed both to the mystery of redemption through the Exodus (from the forty-two stations of the pilgrimage) and to the eschatological certainty of the Judgment (from the forty-two "months" of the Apocalypse). The latter scriptural number of course had an enormous influence and currency in the later Middle Ages because of the part it played in popular Joachimism. Furthermore, the numerical ratio of the chapters in the first and second books of the *Confessions*, twenty to ten or two to one, is precisely the "ratio" of the nature of the incarnate Christ, developed explicitly and at length in one of the most famous passages of *De Trinitate*.[6] The twelve chapters of the third book, in addition to helping add up to forty-two, have multiple implications of their own (as in the *Pearl* itself) so far as the development of the spiritual argument of the *Confessions* is concerned.

It is, however, the final triad of books that reveal the *centuplum*. These three books are one of the murky problems of Augustinian studies. The tenth book of the *Confessions*, the work's most explicitly ascetic movement, examines Augustine's spiritual history beneath the topic of the "three temptations," and its sequence in the autobiographical structure, which it seems to complete, is clear. The final three books, however, an extraordinary, fragmentary commentary on the opening verses of Genesis, have been problematical. Their relevance to the rest of the *Confessions* was seriously doubted even by the editors of the famous Louvain edition, and there has been more than one issue of the work that excised them altogether. In fact the relationship between the two parts of the *Confessions*, though difficult, is clear enough. It is the relationship of life to death, of the vibrancy of trinitarian anthropology to the deadness of the old man condemned by the decalogue law. The eleventh book has thirty-one chapters, the twelfth thirty-two, the thirteenth thirty-eight. Its total number of chapters is a hundred and one, and the climax of its final book begins (XIII, 19, xxv) with a joyous hymn to the winners of the *centuplum*: "You, elect race, the world's weaklings, you who have abandoned all to follow the Lord, run after him and confound the mighty."[7]

The *Confessions* show how the "consolatory" one hundred and one could be used to structure a book, or at least a part of a book, through mechanical chapter divisions; but their witness is both partial and oblique. For a clearer analogue we must consider a book more obscure than the *Confessions*, though by no means so obscure as the single-copy poems of Nero A. x themselves. That book is the *Arbor vitae crucifixae Jesu* of the radical Franciscan Ubertino of Casale, completed in the opening years of the fourteenth century. This work is not widely known, even among medievalists; though it was much better known in the fourteenth century than now, it is by no means part of my argument to demonstrate its positive influence upon the author of the *Pearl*. What I seek to demonstrate, instead, is a generic pattern of thought which may be useful in an approach to the English poem. Ubertino was a profoundly controversial Franciscan— controversial as much in his being as in his thought or writing— intimately associated with the most sensational phase of the debate about apostolic poverty which rent the Franciscan Order in the thirteenth and fourteenth centuries. In the too casual categories of modern Franciscan history, Ubertino was a "spiritual," even "the leader of the Spirituals," who fanatically held out for the *arctus*, or strict interpretation of the Franciscan rule, both against the political leadership of his own order and the views of the papal commissions established to formulate policy on the question.

Ubertino wrote various apologetic and spiritual works—with him it would be difficult to draw a real distinction between the two—but the *Arbor vitae crucifixae* is by far his most ambitious and most brilliant work.[8] Indeed, there is nothing else very much like it in all of medieval literature. Though it takes its central structural metaphor of the tree from St. Bonaventure (who himself had hardly invented it), Ubertino's work goes far beyond the *Lignum vitae* in its scope and in its spiritual tone, even in those chapters which on superficial investigation would seem to come directly from it. Though its own form was to some extent imitated at the end of the fourteenth century in Barthelmy of Pisa's *Book of Conformities*, it too had in fact no very close heirs. This is not to say it was a book without marked influence. In spite of a concerted attempt to suppress important parts of the book which were overtly antipapal (Ubertino's attacks on Boniface VIII are particularly virulent), it enjoyed a wide circulation in the later Middle Ages, and it has left its clear impress on major schools of Catholic spirituality from Catherine of Siena to García Cisneros. Its ideas also penetrated the world of vernacular poetry. I claim to find its influence in *Piers Plowman* and in the "pilgrimage" poems of Guillaume de Deguilleville. As it is, Dante Alighieri is our most efficient and unambiguous witness to the poetic posterity of Ubertino, who is one of the living "characters" clearly alluded to in the *Commedia*. The allusion, which comes in the celebrated survey of Franciscan history in the twelfth canto of *Paradiso*, is neither flattering to Ubertino, nor very satisfactorily explained by the *dantisti*. It comes from the mouth of St. Bonaventure and nicely reflects the distaste for fanaticism which that great compromiser would almost certainly have had toward Ubertino. But the explicit allusion itself may well be a less accurate indication of Dante's own attitude to this uncompromising friar and to the ideas for which he stood, than are the overt borrowings from the *Arbor vitae* which have long since been convincingly demonstrated. Ubertino's work also entered the vernacular sphere through direct translations and adaptations, and we have forms of it, in part or in whole, in medieval Italian, Catalan, Castilian, and Low German.

The formal subject of the *Arbor vitae* is the life of Christ considered, in classical Franciscan fashion, as a mirror of asceticism. Its external structure is, in a very loose sense, chronological. There are five books. The first, eleven chapters long, begins with the preexistence of Christ and what might be called his career down to the time of his birth. A second book (only eight chapters long) deals with the childhood of Jesus. Book III (twenty-three chapters) begins with his contact with John the Baptist and ends just before the events of Palm Sunday. The fourth book is the longest. Its forty-one chapters dwell in lavish detail upon the events of the Passion and upon the spiritual mysteries of the Crucifixion. The eighteen chapters of the final book deal with the "eternal Jesus," particularly in relation to his association with the history of the Church in the "sixth age." The popular reputation of the *Arbor vitae crucifixae*, such as it is, is due almost entirely to several of the more remarkable chapters of the fifth book, particularly *Jesus vilificatus, Jesus Franciscum generans, Jesus falsificatus*, and *Jesus judex iratus*. It is in *Jesus falsificatus*, for example, that Ubertino makes his most explicit identification of Boniface VIII with the spiritual Antichrist.

It is probably needless to say that such a sketch of the book's external structure will reveal little about what is actually in it or why it was so admired by many of its early readers. The sketch is useful, however, as one possible model of what is in effect a long spiritual prose poem structured around a numerological convention which also informs the *Pearl*: the total number of chapters in the *Arbor vitae crucifixae* is indeed 101. I have counted them quite carefully since the only other scholar I know of who has been at all concerned with these matters in the last century—P. Godefroy in his influential article on Ubertino in the *Dictionnaire de théologie catholique*—actually mistook the right answer by ten.[9] Ubertino was fascinated by numbers and their mysteries; and it is too bad that even Frédégand Callaey, his most illuminating modern expositor, shunts this interest aside as an embarrassing intervention of the "gout de l'époque," for it can be a key to understanding his work.[10] So far as I know, Ubertino does not make an explicit statement about the meaning of the number 101 or explain how or why he has distributed the chapters of his book. He does, however, talk about the number 5—the number of its larger divisions—in a way that has clear meaning for us.

The seventeenth chapter of the third book (*Jesus panes multiplicans*) is an extended spiritual interpretation of the miracle of the loaves and fishes. John's account of the miracle (John 6:1ff) says that there were about five thousand people and five loaves to divide among them. Now 5, says Ubertino, is preeminently the number of humanity. With regard to all mankind, it is the number of the human senses. With special regard to the humanity of Christ, it is both the number of his wounds and of his separate effusions of blood (in the garden, at the flagellation, at the crowning with spines, at the Crucifixion, and at the piercing of his side). The line of thought is not very far from Gawain's much discussed catechism of the pentangle (*Gawain*, lines 640ff.), and no doubt reflects much of the same tradition. It seems to me extremely likely that in ordering the *Arbor vitae* in five books distributed among what is a strikingly original chronology of Christ's life, Ubertino has it in mind to make the very structure of his work focus upon the human person of Christ as the mirror for the ascetic reformation of carnal man. That is, the spiritual agenda of the *Arbor vitae* has much in common with the more

famous work by Ubertino's thirteenth-century Franciscan pred-
ecessor David of Augsburg, whose *De interioris et exterioris
hominis compositione* may well have been the novice manual by
which Ubertino prepared himself in the religious life. In the
commonplace ascetic tradition which Ubertino shares with David
of Augsburg, the "exterior man" is not so much fallen human
nature, the Pauline "old man," as it is the morally neutral (or
nearly so) edifice of human sensation, "animal man," the man
who knows things through his *fyve wyttes*. There is even a
suggestion, not schematically developed, that the ascetical intention of each of the five books is specifically directed toward the
discipline of a different sense. Certainly this scheme of organiza-
tion is common enough in other books of the sort. What seems
beyond question, however, after the elaborate exegesis of the
miracle of the loaves and fishes, is that Ubertino preeminently associated the number 5 with the phenomenon of human sensation,
whether in the sensory faculties of human nature generally or in
the specific and pathetic sensations of the human, redeeming
Christ.

The functional purpose of the religious life in the Middle
Ages was the taming, the edification, and the reformation of the
"exterior man." This aim was not the end of religious life, to be
sure, only a beginning, but it did represent something radical,
something fundamental, in the ascetic quest. For Ubertino's ascetic purposes, therefore, the numerological implications of the
larger divisions of the *Arbor vitae* are the right ones: they point
to the necessity of self-abnegation and voluntary abasement, the
leaving of father, and mother, and fields, and houses which is the
necessary prolegomenon to perfection. No less felicitous, poeti-
cally witty, is the numerological suggestion of the work's shorter
division, the 101 chapters. For if the number 5 points to a
theme of loss so painful to the "exterior man," the larger
number points to the theme of reward, of compensation or
consolation—to the hundred and one of the increase of the
centuplum—which are the wages of the "interior man."

Ubertino's numerological counterpoint is both more schematic
and more obvious than is Augustine's in the *Confessions*, written

with a much more personal spiritual program and before the ascetical *loci communes* of the Fathers had become the real commonplaces of the later Middle Ages. Augustine's line of thought, if I am correct, is to connect the idea of the spiritual consolation of the *centuplum* immediately with the contemplated mystery of the Trinity. To put this another way, the final three books of the *Confessions* are the spiritual reward of the first ten books; and it is probably for this reason that Augustine has left us with the two clear divisions: ten books redolent of the legislative imperative of reformatory and penitential conversion, the remaking of the "exterior man," three more pointing to the anthropological truth of the trinitarian impress longing to make itself visible on the brow of the "interior man."

Ubertino's own direct source of inspiration may well have been the famous *Meditations on the Life of Christ*, probably the most famous literary work of the later Middle Ages to reveal what I am here calling "centuple" structure. This book, one of the great masterpieces of the Italian *ducento,* was for centuries attributed to St. Bonaventure, though its actual author was probably a Tuscan friar named John of Caulibus. It has long been recognized as one of the truly seminal works of Gothic narrative and its stylistic influence on poetry, drama, and the visual arts was enormous. Its vernacular versions are rather better known to modern scholars than the Latin original, which, hidden within the maze of its own complex manuscript traditions, still waits for a complete critical edition. The textual complexities have also obscured the work's actual structure, since among the vast number of surviving manuscripts there are shorter and longer redactions, as well as what is in effect a discrete book containing thirteen meditations on the Passion. Furthermore, the different scholars who have tried to sort out its difficulties have divided its materials rather differently. It has most often been said that there are a hundred meditations, but that is not quite accurate. There are actually ninety-nine, ranging over the course of sacred history from the *Vorgeschichte* of the Incarnation to Pentecost and distributed unevenly through the seven days of the week. But there are two other clear rhetorical divisions at either end of the book, an introduction in which the author states his purposes, and a conclusion in which he summarizes them. The *Meditationes vitae Christi* is a book in 101 chapters.[11] I should add further that one of its chapters, the fortieth, is largely devoted to St. Bernard's allegorical interpretation of the *centuplum*. Like the *Pearl*-poet, Bernard finds an inspiration in the Apocalypse. He associates the *centuplum* with the "hidden manna" which goes "to the victor" (Apocalypse 2:17).

Such examples of the structural use of the *centuplum* to make up 101 formal parts of a large work are, I think, useful in suggesting something of a tradition in which the idea of penitential consolation was formalized through numerological convention. It would be easy enough to provide other examples, particularly of 101-line poems, but it may be more to the point to cite a more specific analogue to the *Pearl*, a poem made up not of 101 lines but of 101 rhymed stanzas. Such a poem has recently been published by Pasquale Tuscano from an Assisi manuscript. It is a stanzaic "life" of Mary Magdalene in *ottava rima*.[12] The poem is obviously "Franciscan" in a stylistic sense as well as in provenance, a fine example of the rich and varied body of pious Italian poetry written beneath the bright shadow of the *Meditationes vitae Christi*. The manuscript, like Nero A. x unique, dates from the fifteenth century, but the text itself is almost certainly older, probably in fact from the same vague "second half of the fourteenth century" to which we ascribe *Pearl*.[13] In *Santa Maria Maddalena* the idea of the *centuplum* is obvious but not explicit. The poem has two clear movements. The first, containing the scriptural life of the Magdalene, occupies forty-two stanzas. The other fifty-nine deal with her medieval legend as found in the *Legenda aurea* and elsewhere. The Franciscan emphasis on penitence is very marked, and the poem's major rhetorical emphasis, derived in part from the poetic *vitae* of St. Mary the Egyptian and other flamboyant penitents, is on the consolatory reward of eternal life for the radical abandonment of the world.

The fact that, so far as I know, no one has previously remarked upon the quite striking structural features of the books which I have just been discussing is not without its monitory significance. The question of numerological conventions in the *Pearl* or in any other work for that matter is one of strictly limited relevance to the larger concerns of literary criticism, and just as it is very easy to ignore numerological ornament in medieval books, it is very tempting to exaggerate its absolute importance when perceived. Acrostics, shaped poems, cryptic authorial signature, and so on are after all features of English poetry from Cynewulf to the Metaphysicals and beyond. When Herbert writes a poem called "The Altar," which is about an altar and some of the Christian associations an altar can have, the success or failure of the poem has little to do with the fact that the poem has been made by Herbert's wit and the compositor's manipulation to look vaguely like an altar on the printed page. Dante's *Commedia* is not a great poem because it has exactly 100 cantos distributed more or less evenly among three books, each of which ends with the word *stelle*. What one can say about such technical *features* of the poetry, as insistent, obvious, and perhaps as mechanical as they are, is that they reveal in quite unmistakable ways certain patterns of poetic intentionality which are in a general sense as relevant to the readers of these poems as to their writers. The intentions involved, at least in part, are those of the visible demonstration in incarnational verse of certain abstract and ideal truths. Since in a certain sense Dante's poetic vision, and Herbert's, would be incomplete without recourse to such devices, they may be regarded as a part, only that, of the data which must be examined by their scrupulous critics.

Pearl, to return finally to our English alliterative poem, is a poem for which no juster shape could be imagined than that of centuple consolation. A poem about worldly loss and heavenly gain, a poem fleshed out with scriptural language over a skeleton of scriptural narrative, it pursues its brilliant and unique Englishness even while it submits with dignity to a mysterious tradition, at once open and hidden, of continental, Latin learning. Its number is neither the first nor the most important part of it, but it is inescapably there, an implicit critical debt which only our fullest reading can repay.

NOTES

1. John Conley, *"Pearl* and a Lost Tradition" in *The Middle English Pearl: Critical Essays*, ed. John Conley (Notre Dame, 1970), pp. 50–72.
2. See in particular Ernst Hellgardt, *Zum Problem symbolbestimmter und formalästhetischer Zahlenkomposition in mittelalterlicher Literatur* (Munich, 1973), a skeptical survey with a rich bibliography. I am grateful to my friend and colleague Michael Curschmann for drawing my attention to the work of the German numerologists.
3. A. Kent Hieatt, *"Sir Gawain*: pentangle, *luf-lace*, numerical structure," in *Silent Poetry*, ed. Alastair Fowler (New York, 1970), pp. 116–40.
4. Charles Moorman, *The Pearl Poet* (New York, 1968), p. 50.
5. For a convenient anthology of patristic and medieval exegesis on the passage, see Cornelius a Lapide, *Commentarii in IV Evangelia* (Antwerp, 1712), I, 375ff.
6. *De Trinitate*, IV, iii.
7. *S. Aureli Augustini Confessionum Libri Tredecim*, ed. Martinus Skutella (Leipzig, 1934), p. 347.
8. The *Arbor vitae crucifixae Jesu* was printed in Venice in 1485; an offset reproduction of this edition, introduced by Charles T. Davis, was published in Turin in 1961.
9. "Ubertino da Casale," *Dictionnaire de théologie catholique,* XV, 2021ff.
10. Frédégand Callaey, *L'Idéalisme franciscain spirituel au XIVᵉ siècle* (Louvain, 1911), p. 84.
11. This assertion must be made somewhat tentatively, for the manuscript tradition of the *Meditationes vitae Christi* is very vexed. Columban Fischer, "Die 'Meditationes Vitae Christi': ihre handschriftliche Ueberlieferung und die Verfasserfrage," *Archivum Franciscanum Historicum,* 25 (1932), 312ff., describes the "longer text" as being composed of ninety-five chapters. This numeration is based on a fifteenth-century printed text, which is itself dependent upon a manuscript of the same century. I believe that the intended numerological structure is correctly reflected in the excellent translation of Paul Bayart, *Méditations sur la vie du Christ* (Paris, 1958).
12. *Cantari inediti umbri e altri testi*, ed. P. Tuscano (Bergamo, 1974).
13. Tuscano, pp. 18–19.

6

Figural Typology in the *Middle English* Patience

JOHN B. FRIEDMAN

THE book of Jonah had long exercised the imagination of biblical exegetes who produced some peculiar versions of the story by blending clarifying commentary on the text with ingenious narrative expansions. Many Latin writers, among them Tertullian, Jerome, pseudo-Cyprian, and Marbode, wrote—or had fathered upon them—works of this type.[1] Even medieval Judaism offered commentaries on the prophet. The eleventh-century rabbi Rashi of Troyes charmingly developed exegesis into narrative when he explained why in the Hebrew text the gender of the whale changes from one verse to the next. Actually, Rashi said, there were two whales, a male and a female. Jonah was first swallowed by a male and, finding his quarters pleasant, he was not penitent. God then commanded him to be spat up and swallowed by a pregnant female. Jonah now found himself so crowded and squeezed on every side by baby whales that he called out to the Lord for mercy.[2] Directly in line with such imaginative treatments of the Jonah story is the fourteenth-century English poem *Patience*. Displaying much of the artistry of its more famous manuscript companions, *Sir Gawain and the Green Knight* and *Pearl*, this poem made the Jonah legend available to a vernacular audience.

In reading *Patience* we are not, of course, dealing with relatively original plots like those of *Gawain* or *Pearl*, or even with a *catena* of biblical material like *Purity*, but with a work which at its simplest level is a translation. In so far as the *Patience*-poet's story is canonical, he cannot change the outcome of events, and as a result we see his hand most clearly in his additions, interpolations and expansions of an artistic or ornamental nature, like the beautiful storm scene, or in expansions and additions of a theological kind. I am concerned, however, primarily with the poet's theological additions to the story of Jonah as he found it in the Vulgate. In recent years, *Patience* has received a good deal of very competent attention, and the outlines of its structure and its purposes have become increasingly clear.[3] I do not think I misstate current opinions about the poem if I say that it was probably conceived by its author as a type of popular sermon, perhaps directed as an example of the genre to an audience of preachers, and that it embodies a good deal of medieval preaching technique and exegetical knowledge. Since scholarly interest in the poem has coincided with an increased awareness of biblical exegesis as an aid to the study of medieval secular poetry, it should not surprise us that recent critics of *Patience* have been concerned with the familiar patristic interpretation of Jonah as a type of Christ. As Malcom Andrew noted,

> Christian teaching . . . traditionally speaks of Jonah as a type of Christ, interpreting a number of events in the story of Jonah as symbolizing and foreshadowing events in the life of Christ. The poet makes use of these associations and interpretations to intensify and make more subtle the responses which *Patience* may elicit from a thoughtful and imaginative reader.[4]

I am afraid I must raise a dissenting voice here, for the character of the English Jonah has always struck me as notably un-Christlike. He is querulous, cowardly, argumentative, and devoted to *temporalia* far in excess of his biblical counterpart. Indeed, a student in a survey course in which I recently taught this poem remarked on his final examination: "I don't know if I ought to say this since he is a type of Christ and all that, but I simply don't *like* Jonah." I suspect a medieval audience's response would not have been a great deal different. Malcom Andrew's explanation of this difficulty is better than most. He suggests that the medieval penchant for interpreting events *in bono* and *in malo* allows "the poet to sustain a series of simultaneous parallels and contrasts between Jonah and Christ and this technique serves to deepen and intensify the relevance which his teaching could have in the lives of his audience." Andrew concludes that the poem emphasizes Christ's greatness and the weakness of even the best intentioned of mortal men.[5]

To be sure, this is an attractive and reasonable explanation, but in my opinion it presupposes a degree of sophistication in the audience not in keeping with the poem's purpose, style, and mood. There is, however, another way to look at the prophet, which more simply and satisfactorily accounts for the unattractive qualities of the Jonah presented by the *Patience*-poet. Homiletic and liturgical uses of the prophet's history often stressed the perfective aspects of the relationship between Jonah and Jesus, that is, the way in which Jesus fulfills and goes beyond what Jonah does unwillingly and imperfectly. Such a view is, of course, only a logical extension of the Christian doctrine that of the two testaments the Old was made to prepare for the New.

It is helpful at this point to remember Isidore's remark in the *Etymologiae* that "Vetus Testamentum ideo dicitur, quia veniente Novo cessavit," or Hervé of Bourgdieu's succinct statement that "Christ is the consummation of the Law."[6] Indeed, implicit in the very idea of the New Testament as *novissimus* or final is a judgment on the Old, which has been superseded; and this is how a medieval audience understood Christ's comparison of himself with the Old Testament prophet in Matthew 12:38–41:

An evil and adulterous generation seeketh after a sign; and there shall no sign be given to it, but the sign of the prophet Jonas: For as Jonas was three days and three nights in the whale's belly; so shall the Son of man be three days and

three nights in the heart of the earth. The men of
Nineveh . . . repented at the preaching of Jonas; and, be-
hold, a greater than Jonas is here.

If I am correct in my argument thus far, not only this passage, but the whole Gospel of Matthew in which it appears, seems
to have shaped the *Patience*-poet's approach to his story. For it
was Matthew, we recall, who more than the other evangelists
stressed the fulfillment of the Old Testament by the New. From
Matthew the *Patience*-poet took the Beatitudes, which he grafted
onto the opening of his Old Testament story. From him also
came the whale—since the Vulgate says merely that the prophet
was swallowed by a great fish. And most importantly, Matthew
provided the poet with scriptural authority for parallels to be
drawn between the careers of Jonah and Christ.

Elaborations of Christ's comparison of himself with Jonah
were very common, of course, among all sorts of early Christian
and medieval writers on scriptural subjects, but one place where
they are of special interest for the study of *Patience* is in the
liturgy and in homiletic texts intended for the use of preachers.

Since the poet addresses a vernacular audience, we may assume that he will use storytelling techniques and interpretations
of his material familiar to his listeners from their parish worship.
A few examples from the poem will suffice to make this point
clear. He begins the work in the characteristic manner of the
homilist or preacher taking as his text an abstract theme: "Pa-
cience is a poynt, þaȝ hit displese oft" (1).[7] He interpolates material on monotheism at the end of the storm scene, and stresses
Jonah's Old Law Jewishness beyond the Vulgate's simple declaration, "Hebraeus ego sum." But most important, he proceeds at
once to graft Matthew's account of the eight beatitudes onto his
Old Testament story.

Moreover, the *Patience*-poet introduces this material in a
manner which suggests the expositor within the confines of a
church. "I herde on a halyday, at a hyȝe masse" (9), he says,
the story of the beatitudes, apparently alluding to the gospel of
the Mass for the feast of All Hallows in the use of Sarum. To be

sure, this sort of tag is common in Middle English poetry and generally has no particular liturgical significance. Yet it is striking that the poet later introduces the story of Jonah in much the same way: "Wyl ȝe tary a lyttel tyne and tent me a whyle, / I schal wysse yow þer-wyth as holy wryt telles" (59–60).

Several liturgical and homiletic texts emphasize the typological nature of the Jonah story and especially those qualities which make the prophet representative of the Old Law. In the York and Sarum Missals, which contain the liturgy for the English mass at the time the poet wrote, the story of Jonah appears in a sequence by Adam of St. Victor in the mass for Easter Monday.[8] The first line of the sequence is a paraphrase of I Corinthians 5:7 "Zima vetus expurgetur"; the "old leaven" is in effect purged by the perfective nature of the New Law. Adam of St. Victor's triumphant poem places Jonah among other Old Testament types, Isaac, Joseph, Moses, and Samson, whose histories prophesy resurrection. In this use of the Jonah story, Adam is simply following expansions of Matthew such as that of Raoul Ardens (fl. 1190), who explained that the "throwing of Jonah into the sea openly prefigures Christ's passion, his being taken into the belly of the whale, his entombment, and his being returned alive on the beach, his resurrection."[9]

Adam of St. Victor's synopsis of the book of Jonah is brief and incisive, focusing on the episode of the whale to the exclusion of the preaching to the Ninevites:

> In the story of the whale
> Jonah fugitive
> Figures forth the True Jonah;
> After three days he came live
> From the whale's narrow belly.
> The flower of Synagoga withers
> And that of Ecclesia blooms.[10]

The pattern here is a familiar one: Ecclesia, the Church of the New Law, replaces the Synagogue, symbolizing the Old, just as the fugitive Jonah, trying to shirk his mission and flee to Tarsus, is replaced by Christ, the "True Jonah," who accepted his mission and, facing its dangers, conquered death.

At this point we may pause to ask how this traditional presentation compares with that in *Patience*. An examination of the poem will, I believe, reveal a wealth of material which gives form to or elaborates the perfective view expressed by Adam of St. Victor. Consider, for example, the passage early in the story where God tells Jonah to preach repentance to the Ninevites. Here, the *Patience*-poet tells us, Jonah's first thought is for his own safety, lest

> . . . wyth þose typþynges, þay ta me bylyue,
> Pyneȝ me in a prysoun, put me in stokkes,
> Wryþe me in a warlok, wrast out myn yȝen.
>
> (78–80)

Once Jonah decides to flee to Tarsus and sets out on the road to "port Japh," he again rejects the idea of suffering in God's behalf—"he nolde þole for no þyng non of þose pynes"—and remarks that God would be disinterested in his pains if he be "nummen in Nunniue and naked dispoyled, / On rode rwly torent with rybaudes mony" (91, 95–96). His specific reference to the rood or cross in this context is more than a naive Christianizing anachronism. Jonah's rejection both of the mission and the cross indicate clearly that we are to see the prophet failing at being Christ rather than merely prefiguring him.

A more complex and subtle comparison of Jonah with Christ is embodied in the justly famous whale episode of *Patience*, a scene sixty lines long developing from a single verse of the Vulgate: "Now the Lord prepared a great fish to swallow up Jonah. And Jonah was in the belly of the fish three days and three nights."

Interestingly, the poet presents first what seems to be an "official" version, and then, in a new section, returns to dwell in greater detail on the swallowing of Jonah. The scene at the end of Section I—small blue initials mark these divisions in the manuscript—in which Jonah is tossed overboard, moves quickly and follows the Vulgate closely, though with slight amplification.

> Tyd by top and bi to þay token hym synne;
> In-to þat lodlych loȝe þay luche hym sone.
> He watȝ no tytter out-tulde þat tempest ne sessed;
> Þe se saȝtled þer-with as sone as ho moȝt.
>
> (229–32)

Here the author specifies the manner in which the sailors seized the prophet, qualifies the sort of sea it was, in order to heighten the drama of events, and stresses God's power in the two-line amplification of the Vulgate's spare "stetit a fervore suo." The conclusion of Section I, therefore, with its praise of monotheism and its attention to the fate of the sailors who achieve a safe harbor for their correct action, logically completes this aspect of the story.

In Section II, however, the poet returns to the scene of Jonah's capture, and offers his personal rendition of the last events of Section I, for he recapitulates: "Now is Jonas þe jwe jugged to drowne; / Of þat schended schyp men schowued hym sone" (245–46). Few readers of *Patience* can fail to notice how the contact between Jonah and the "wylde walterande whal, [that] wyrde þen schaped" (247) comes with startling rapidity after the somewhat leisurely introduction: "Þe folk ȝet haldande his fete, þe fysch hym tyd hentes" (251). This voracious seizure of Jonah by the whale, much as a fish rises to and seizes a baited hook, is the poet's own contribution, carefully distinguished from the Vulgate account in Section I. Critics have been puzzled by the scene but have not fully explored the implications of its restatement. For example, A. C. Spearing notes that Jonah is "seized by the fish with a rapidity which seems symbolic or parodic, it is imagined so graphically and enacted in a line of such packed action."[11]

Now I should like to suggest that, while much has been written about Jonah's role as a type of Christ, very little has been

said about the whale's part in this comparison. The whale is, of
course, a "type" or figure for something too, and while I do not
wish to overstate the obvious, I think that a brief examination of
just what the whale represents will repay us with a better understanding of the passage mentioned earlier, as well as of later
scenes in *Patience* in which Jonah is compared with Christ.

Adam of St. Victor had spoken in the liturgical sequence
"Zima vetus expurgetur" of another of the "True Jonah's" great
acts, when he remarked that "Christ with hook and loop pierces
the dragon's jaws."[12] This image relies on a conflation of two
biblical texts in exegesis and the visual arts: the prophecy in
Isaiah 27:1 that the Lord would punish "Leviathan, the twisted
serpent, and kill the whale which is in the sea," and the query of
God to Job in Job 40:20, "Canst thou draw up Leviathan with a
hook?" Commentators associated both of these images of
Leviathan with hell and with Satan as well as with Jonah. The
thirteenth-century exegete, Hugh of St. Cher, commenting on the
Jonah story, explained that the "cetus" of Isaiah was the devil.[13]
A pseudo-Augustinian sermon noted that by the whale of Jonah
we ought to understand hell.[14] And we are all familiar with the
doom scenes, stage settings, and manuscript illustrations which
show the mouth of hell as a whale or as the gaping jaws of
Leviathan.[15] The poet elsewhere shows an awareness of this tradition, in *Purity,* where through sin "þroly into þe deueleȝ þrote
man þryngeȝ bylyue."[16]

It should not surprise us, then, if the Old Testament idea that
God would kill Leviathan with a hook was quickly adapted to the
story of Christ's passion and triumph over death. In Rufinus'
Latin version of Origen's homily on Leviticus, for instance, we
learn that

> . . . the Lord foretold in the Gospel of Matthew of the great
> whale which would be slain; its type was the type of Jonah.
> Jesus, who would kill this whale, this devil, compared his
> stay of three days and nights in the heart of the earth with
> Jonah's stay in the whale's belly.[17]

By the sixth century, such imagery was incorporated into Gregory's *Moralia in Job*. Commenting on Job 40:20, Gregory explained that

> Leviathan is taken by the hook of Job because when he took the bait of our redeemer's body, he was punctured by the point of his divinity. The hook was marvelously suspended for the death of this whale in the murky depths of water. The line of the hook is the genealogy of the Patriarchs recorded in the Gospel, like a knotted line at whose end the incarnation of Christ, that is, this hook, is tied, which, suspended in the water of mankind, is swallowed up by the open mouth of this whale. And that this whale, lying in ambush for mankind, might no longer devour whom he wished, this hook held firm the jaws of the spoiler and wounded him that bit it.[18]

As the metaphor developed in the Middle Ages, it took the particular form of a hook, manipulated by God and baited with the body of Christ. Jerome's commentary on the book of Jonah has Christ say, "Death wants to devour me, but does not see that just as a bait is taken on a hook, my death will be the death of Death."[19] In the "Letter to Heliodorus," Jerome turns again to this metaphor in an ironic apostrophe to Death: "You were drawn to the bait of that body and thought it a meal for your fierce jaws, but your guts were pierced by the point of that hook."[20] Illustrators of this idea rendered it with varying degrees of literalness. It seems to have been especially popular in Germany, perhaps owing to Honorius of Regensburg's widely known amplification of Gregory's allegory.[21] A manuscript in the Cistercian monastery at Wilhering near Linz gives us some fifteenth-century *tituli* for certain Romanesque wall paintings once in the church of St. Emmeram at Regensburg. Apparently high in the wall of the western part of the nave at the transept was a representation of the "piscacio saluatoris de Leviathan." A distich follows, summarizing the fishing scene: "Piscatore deo leviathan captus ab hamo. Reddit aduncatus raptum rapto spoliatus."[22] A late fourteenth-century wall painting, from the cloister of Brixen, now Bressanone in the south Tirol (Figure I), shows the hand of God emerging from the heavens and catching Leviathan with a hook; the other hand cuts open the body, allowing the souls swallowed by the beast to emerge.[23] A variation of this painting occurs in a miniature from a twelfth-century Swabish choir book from Zweifalten and now in the Württemburger Landesbibliothek of Stuttgart (Figure II). The legends come from Honorius of Regensburg.[24] Herrad of Landsburg, in her illustrated spiritual encyclopedia, the *Hortus Deliciarum* (1180), renders the allegory very literally (Figure III). Here we see the patriarchs forming a cord between the fishing pole of God the Father and the crucified Christ, who descends as a bait on the hook of the cross for the whale below.[25]

Two French artists adapted the fishing of Leviathan to include the story of Jonah. The Alton Towers triptych in the Victoria and Albert Museum is a Mosan enamel done about 1150 (Figure IV). The left panel, containing three registers (Figure V, detail), depicts at the top Jonah emerging from the whale, Abraham and Isaac in the middle, and Christ angling for Leviathan at the bottom. An inscription top and bottom reads, "As the whale renders up Jonah, so in the same way the earth renders up the one who has been put in the tomb." And "the flesh of Christ becomes a hook to Leviathan."[26] One more example will suffice. The connection of Jonah, Christ, and Leviathan is made at greater length by Joinville and his illustrators in his popular version of the Nicene Creed, done in the middle of the thirteenth century. And he, like Adam of St. Victor, stresses the perfective aspect of the connection between Christ and Jonah. In the *Credo*, Joinville takes the story of Jonah as an exemplum for the fourth article, on the Entombment and the Harrowing of Hell. In the Old French text, he cites Job 40:20:

You know that when a fisherman wishes to take a fish on his hook, he covers the iron with a bait; the fish seizes the bait and is taken. Now we see that in order to take the devil also with a hook, God covers his deity with our humanity.[27]

The miniature representing this idea in the Leningrad Breviary sequence of illustrations for the *Credo* (Figure VI) shows in the upper registers, left, the story of Jonah thrown to the whale, and right, Christ answering the Pharisees in Matthew by comparing himself with Jonah. In the lower register, left, a figure holds a phylactery reading "nunquid capiet Leviathan hamo." This is probably Job.[28] On the right side, we have the prophecy of Hosea 13:14: "ero mors tua, o mors tuus ero, inferne." Hosea's wordplay on "death" and "bite" makes him peculiarly appropriate for a scene of Jonah and the whale; as a resurrection figure generally he is sometimes juxtaposed with a reluctant Jonah in the *processio patrum*, as in the choir screen relief from the choir of St. George, Bamberg Cathedral (Figure VII), where he seems to admonish the prophet.[29]

Returning briefly to the miniature from Joinville's *Credo* (Figure VIII, detail), we can see the way that these disparate motifs are woven together as Christ and Job float in a boat over a winged Satan in the water, while Christ lowers a fishing pole over the side.

Though few would deny that illustrations of this kind are germane to our understanding of *Patience*, only one critic, David Williams, has noted that the poet's sources for the whale scene may have been manuscript illustration; he seems to have had in mind, however, only the illustrations for the book of Jonah or the psalter. Certainly, Bible illustration provided a precedent for one of the features of this scene in *Patience*, and that is the lowering of Jonah into the water head first. Most of the extant Romanesque miniatures that depict Jonah being taken by the whale show him held by the legs or ankles and dangled overboard, or in some cases, being virtually stuffed into the whale's mouth by the sailors.[30] A well-known Carolingian psalter from Stuttgart (of French provenance) shows this scene with the twisted Leviathan whale of Isaiah 27 (Figure IX) as an illustration for Psalm 68.

Fig. I. Fishing of Leviathan, cloister fresco, Bressanone, 14th century. *Photo courtesy Nona C. Flores.*

Fig. II. Fishing of Leviathan, choir book from Zweifalten. Württemburger Landesbibliothek, Stuttgart, Cod. Hist. 2, 415, fol. 87, 12th century. *By permission of Württemburger Landesbibliothek, Stuttgart.*

Fig. III. Fishing of Leviathan, Herrad of Landsburg, *Hortus Deliciarum, c.* 1180, fol. 84ʳ, MS now destroyed.

Fig. IV. Fishing of Leviathan, Alton Towers triptych, Mosan enamel, *c.* 1150, Victoria and Albert Museum, London. *By permission of the Trustees of the Victoria and Albert Museum, London.*

Fig. V. Detail of Alton Towers triptych.

Fig. VI. Scenes from Joinville's *Credo*, Missal of St. Niçaise of Reims, Leningrad, Hermitage, MS Q.v.I. 78(BN 546) fol. 59, before 1297. *Photo courtesy of Lionel J. Friedman.*

Fig. VII. Hosea and Jonah, choir screen relief of choir of St. George, Bamberg Cathedral, 1220–30.

Fig. VIII. Detail of scenes from Joinville's *Credo*.

Fig. IX. Jonah thrown to the whale, psalter, Württemburger Landesbibliothek MS 23, fol. 797, *c*. 9th century. *By permission of the Württemburger Landesbibliothek.*

Fig. X. Jonah thrown to the whale, *Patience*, British Library MS Cotton Nero A. x, fol. 82, 14th century. *By permission of the Trustees of the British Library.*

Fig. XI. Jonah, illustration for Psalm 68, by William de Brailles, Oxford, MS New College 322, fol. 67, mid-13th century. *By permission, Bodleian Library, Oxford.*

The whale is understood here as Leviathan. His horns connote his diabolical nature, and the curly flame-forked tail harks back to early Christian sarcophagi representing this scene. Clearly fearful of displeasing God by killing Jonah, as in the text, amplifying Jonah 1:14, one sailor piously covers his eyes at the moment Jonah is thrown overboard. Not the least interesting feature of this miniature is the connection made between the Leviathan whale and the sea of *temporalia*, through the siren who blows her horn as a lure to mariners. The artist probably alludes to Ambrose's comment in the *Explanatio super Psalmos* that the sirens are young maidens who tempt mariners to shipwreck on the rocks, for "they symbolize lust and flattery. Just so does the lust of the world delight us with flattering flesh in order to deceive us."[31]

Evidently the miniature depicting the whale episode from the manuscript of *Patience* itself (Figure X) was inspired by Bible illustrations like these, though it does not reproduce the events of the poem in all particulars, and treats them statically rather than with the drama the poet strives for.

Students of this poem know that the illustrations in Cotton Nero A. x are few and crude, and seem to have been conceived by a mind not as sophisticated as that of the poet.[32] The illustration of the whale scene on folio 82 is especially stylized and simple. Though the poet stresses the large number of sailors, indicates the precise type of boat, and develops the idea that it is a sailing ship with the utmost attention to nautical jargon and detail, most of this material is absent from the miniature. The sailors are reduced to two, the boat is powered only by the oars referred to in the Vulgate, and Jonah, from the position of his hands and body, seems to have been modeled on some earlier illustration showing him emerging from the whale in the posture of an *orans*.

One illustration for the *incipit* of Psalm 68, however—in which David in his tribulations cries out to God—many have influenced the *Patience*-poet's writing of the whale scene (Figure XI). This miniature appears in an English psalter at New College, Oxford, and is the work of William de Brailles, the well-known head of an Oxford atelier of five other illustrators during the mid-thirteenth century.[33] In the lower compartment of the letter S, Jonah's presentation to the whale is dramatically depicted and Jonah, the bait, is the center of interest. Much as the *Patience*-poet had made the Vulgate's "gubernator" of the ship into the "Lodesman" and the undifferentiated "vir" of the Vulgate who suggests the idea of the lots, into the "spakest" or cleverest of the sailors, so the illustrator distinguishes the steersman and the man holding Jonah's feet from the other members of the crew clustered on the right. And, as in the poem, the fish seizes Jonah while "the folk yet held his feet."

Although the poet's positioning of Jonah is supported by the English painter's treatment of this subject, it is tempting to see in this detail yet another comparison of Jonah with Christ. Again, it would be a comparison unfavorable to Jonah, whose ignominious entry into the whale is in sharp contrast with Christ's descent from the cross, feet first, in the Herrad of Landsburg miniature. Without wishing to conjecture too far what the poet had in mind, we can at least note that it would be wholly in keeping with the perfective view of Jonah to see his entrance into the whale in *Patience* as a parody or inversion of a traditional motif, drawn not from Jonah illustrations but from scenes of Christ as a bait on a hook. Evidence that the English Jonah in the whale is to be understood in this way comes from a number of details in Sections II and III of the poem which are quite foreign to the account of Jonah in the Vulgate.

The poet tells us, for example, that "euer walteres þis whal . . . þurȝ ronk of his wylle; / For þat mote in his mawe mad hym, I trowe, / Þaȝ hit lyttel were hym wyth, to wamel at his hert" (297–300). That the Leviathan is sick at heart and belly as a result of what he has swallowed is an idea developed by Jerome and others; it seems likely that this detail is intended to remind the audience of the whale's figurative identity as the Satan wounded by Christ. After Jonah repents in the Vulgate, God acts quickly: "et dixit dominus pisci; et evomuit Jonam in aridam." But the poet's rendition of this scene is far closer to commentary tradition than to his source, for he heightens the idea

of Leviathan as conquered by Christ in the way he has God speak
"sternly" to him and has him spit Jonah up "quickly." So, too,
the remark that the whale goes at God's will seems carefully
placed by the author to be read in contrast to the earlier statement
that the whale went at his own will.

Statements of God's perfect power over Leviathan are not rare
in medieval homiletic writing. In the words of the homilist
known to the period as "Eusebius Gallicanus":

> The whale seized Jonah in the water but did not defile the
> thing he ate . . . marvellously, nothing he ate was his own.
> Who is this who may be taken in a greedy gullet but not
> consumed. . . . Who is this that can go safely through that
> vast throat? . . . I consider that this is our Lord Jesus
> Christ, whom savage death seized as a bait like an insatiable
> beast and who trembled at the instant of capturing his
> meal. . . .[34]

But the heart of any comparison between Christ and Jonah is,
of course, the three days and nights that each of them spends in
the depths. How, then, does the *Patience*-poet treat this subject?
First, in case we do not immediately recognize the parallel between the whale's belly and hell, the poet enforces it for us.
Jonah is described as in the "warlowes gutteʒ" (258) and the
belly stinks like the "deuel" and "helle." Finally he makes
Jonah describe himself as being in "hellen wombe" (306).

It cannot be accidental, moreover, that the contents of the
whale's stomach are made so vividly unpleasant as to suggest
some meaning beyond the purely naturalistic. The generalized
"saym" and "sorʒe þat sauoured as helle" (275) may be alliterative tags, but a little later the poet tells us that Jonah was surrounded by "ramel ande myre" (279). These words recall the
complaint of David in Psalm 68, "infixus sum in limo pro-
fundi," and his later request to God, "eripe me de luto." *Limus*
and *lutum* correspond well enough to the "muck and mire" of
the whale's belly, and as we have seen from the Stuttgart and
de Brailles miniatures, Psalm 68 was occasionally illustrated by

the story of Jonah.[35] Another English example is the miniature of
the psalter of Henry Bohun in the Vienna National Library,
painted about 1370.[36]

Latin psalters from very early times often had, at the head of
each psalm, *tituli* designed to give the poem a Christian direction,
and these *tituli* later served as the cores of commentaries on the
psalter during the patristic period.[37] Psalm 68 was interpreted as
an illustration of Christ's passion as early as Irenaeus, and Hilary
of Poitiers says that the psalms announce Christ's advent, incarnation, passion, and resurrection.[38] As early as the sixth century,
these *tituli* had related Psalm 68 to the Easter liturgy and to
Christ's passion: "legendus ad lectionem Jonae pro-
phetae . . . Vox Christi cum pateretur" reads one such
titulus.[39] A commentary on this psalm by Richard Rolle, contemporary with *Patience*, explains that "Salvum me fac" is the voice
of Christ saying, "Let me not remain in death," and that "it is
the voice of Christ in his passion."[40]

Just as David had cried out from the depths in Psalm 68, so
Jonah calls out to his maker in his torment. One of the highlights
of the Vulgate Jonah is the canticum in which the prophet prays
to God and is delivered. It is rendered very literally in *Patience*
with nothing of the author's point of view. But somewhat before
the canticum in *Patience*, Jonah offers up another prayer. From
lines 282 to 288 Jonah calls upon God in imagery which evokes
the familiar contrast between the Old and the New Law, the one
represented by a wrathful Jehovah, the other by a merciful God.
Jonah asks, "Now, prynce, of þy prophete pite þou haue," and
implores God "De-woyde now þy vengaunce, þurȝ vertu of
rauthe. . . . Haf now mercy of þy man and his mys-dedes"
(282–87). Undoubtedly, such a stress on mercy in these New
Testament ideas inserted into the poem encourages us to see that
the Old Law prophet metaphorically turns to the values of the
New in his trouble, and generalizes the contrast of mercy and
wrath.

Lest it seem that I have looked to a limited spectrum of
medieval exegesis for these perfective interpretations of Jonah's
legend, I should like to conclude by glancing at the *Glossa Or-*

dinaria, the greatest standard collection of exegetical materials in the Middle Ages. Once associated with the name of Walafrid Strabo, it is now connected with the circle of Anselm of Laon.[41] While the *Glossa Ordinaria* does not comment on the book of Jonah as such, it does make a number of interesting points about the prophet in the Gospels of Matthew and Luke; these glosses were probably contributed by Ralph of Laon. The glosses on Luke 11:31, for example, make a number of striking contrasts between Jonah and Jesus. Jonah preached but briefly to the Ninevites, while Christ preached a long time. Jonah wandered among aliens, while Christ preached to his fellows. Jonah made no miracles, but Christ made many. Jonah was a prophet and a servant, Christ was Messiah and Lord. Jonah went living into the whale, while Christ went dead into the tomb but came forth living. Jonah was a reluctant prophet, while Christ preached spontaneously. And finally, Jonah preached of destruction, and Christ of heaven.[42] Enough of these points and those discussed earlier are made in the *Patience*-poet's characterization of Jonah to account, I maintain, for the prophet's unappealing personality in the poem and to provide a medieval audience with a constant homiletic contrast between the English prophet and the "True Jonah."

NOTES

1. The most thorough study is that of Yves-Marie Duval, *Le Livre de Jonas dans la littérature chrétienne grecque et latine* (Paris, 1973).
2. *R. Salomonis Jarchi Commentarius Hebraicus in Prophetas Maiores et Minores*, trans. J. F. Breithaupt (Gotha, 1713), III, Chap. 2, p. 899.
3. A helpful bibliography to 1969 is given by J. J. Anderson, ed., *Patience* (Manchester, 1969), pp. 24–29. Later articles include Jay Schleusener, "*Patience*, lines 35–40," *Modern Philology*, 67 (1969), 64–66; David Williams, "The Point of *Patience*," *Modern Philology*, 68 (1970), 127–36; Jay Schleusener, "History and Action in *Patience*," *PMLA*, 86 (1971), 959–65; William Vantuono, "The Structure and Sources of *Patience*," *Mediaeval Studies*, 34 (1972), 401–21; and Malcom Andrew, "Jonah and Christ in *Patience*," *Modern Philology*, 70 (1973), 230–33.
4. Andrew, p. 233. To be sure, many medieval works, both Latin and vernacular, make this identification. For liturgical examples, see M. Ferotin,

ed., Liber Ordinum (Paris, 1904), item LIII, col. 255 (eleventh century). A typical example from Middle English drama occurs in Harley 2124, the Holmes MS of the Chester plays. Expositor says: "Right as Jonas was dayes three / in wombe of whall, so shall he [Christ] be / in earth lyinge— as was he—/ and rise the third daye." R. M. Lumiansky and David Mills, eds., *The Chester Mystery Cycle,* EETS SS 3 (1974), Appendix Ib, 478, ll. 357–60.

5. Andrew, pp. 231, 233.
6. *Isidori Hispalensis Etymologiarum Libri,* ed. W. M. Lindsay (Oxford, 1957), Book VI, Chap. 1. Hervé of Bourgdieu, *In Rom., PL* 181, 740. On this subject generally, see Henri de Lubac, *Exégèse médiévale,* I, 1 (Paris, 1959), pp. 309ff.
7. All quotations from the text of Anderson, cited above.
8. See J. W. Legg, ed., *The Sarum Missal* (Oxford, 1916), and W. G. Henderson, ed., *Missale ad usum insignis Ecclesiae eboracensis,* Surtees Society 59 (Durham, 1874), 133–34.
9. *Homiliae,* II, 24, *PL* 155, 2028. See Bernhard Geyer, "Radulphus ardeus und das *Speculum Universale,*" *Theologische Quartalschrift,* 93 (1911), 63–89.
10. I translate from the Latin text of E. Misset and P. Aubry, *Les Proses d'Adam de St.-Victor, texte et musique* (Paris, 1900), XVII, 188, stanza XI. On the history of this sequence, see J. Julian, *A Dictionary of Hymnology* (New York, 1907), 1305–6, 1729, and C. Blume and H. Bannister, eds., *Liturgische Prosen des Übergangsstiles und der zweiten Epoche* (Leipzig, 1915), pp. 228ff. an interesting analogue to the "Zima vetus" idea occurs in an elaborate metaphoric poem by the *Patience*-poet's contemporary, Richard Ledrede, in which Mary bakes "bread" with the mystical fire of her own womb. See Edmund Colledge, ed., *The Latin Poems of Richard Ledrede, OFM* (Toronto, 1974), no. 52, pp. 128–30.
11. A. C. Spearing, "*Patience* and the *Gawain*-Poet," *Anglia,* 84 (1966), 311.
12. Misset and Aubry, *Les Proses,* p. 188, stanza VII.
13. Hugh of St. Cher, *Opera Omnia in Vniversum Vetus et Novum Testamentum* (Venice, 1732), II, fol. 231v.
14. Pseudo-Augustine, *Sermo* 1, 36, c. 4, *PLS* 2, 981.
15. For a thorough study of the medieval hell-mouth convention, see Ernst Guldon, "Das Monster-Portal an Palazzi Zuccari in Rom. Wandlungen eines Motius vom Mittelalter zur Manierismus," *Zeitschrift für Kunstgeschichte,* 32 (1969), 229–61.
16. J. J. Anderson, ed., *Cleanness* (New York, 1977), line 180.
17. W. A. Baehrens, ed., *Die Homilien zu Genesis, Exodus, und Levitikus,* GCS 29 (Leipzig, 1920) *Hom*. VIII, 3. See on this homily Henri Crouzel, *Bibliographie critique d'Origène, Instrumenta Patristica* VII (Steenbrugge, 1971), p. 652.

18. Gregory, *Moralia in Job*, 33, 9, *PL* 76, 682–83.

19. Paul Antin, ed. and trans., *Saint Jérôme, sur Jonas*, Sources Chrétiennes 43, (Paris, 1956), I, 12, p. 71 and II, 1, p. 75.

20. Jérôme Labourt, ed. and trans., *Saint Jérôme Lettres* (Paris, 1953), III, lx, c. 2, p. 91. See a similar passage in Chromatius of Aquileia, *Tractatus* 54 on Matthew, with the addition of a first and second Adam parallel. The Latin is given in Duval II, p. 505, n. 67. A simplified form of the idea had a wide currency in medieval hymnody and song. See, for example, F. J. Mone, ed., *Lateinische Hymnen des Mittelalters* (Freiburg, 1883), I, no. 142, p. 192, stanza 5, fourteenth century: "Christe . . . Leviathan perforans / maxillam hamo armilla," and G. M. Dreves, ed., *Lieder und Motetten des Mittelalters*, Analecta Hymnica Medii Aevii XX (Leipzig, 1895), I, no. 10, p. 43, stanza 4: "Ut Satan perforetur / Hamus in esca latuit, / Ut homo liberetur, / Hominem Deus induit. . . ."

21. Honorius of Regensburg, *Speculum Ecclesiae, PL* 172, 937.

22. J. A. Endres, "Romanische Deckenmalereien und ihre Tituli zu St. Emmeram in Regensburg," *Zeitschrift für Christliche Kunst*, 7 (1902), Part I, p. 208, and 8 (1903), Part II, p. 238. An interpretative gloss on such fishing scenes is offered by pseudo-Hildebert (Peter Riga?) commenting on Job 41:1: "Piscator pater est; mare mundus; Filius hamus; esca, caro; Deitas, ferrum; generatio Christi, linea. Leviathan piscis dum devorat escam occidens carnem, captus Deitate tenetur." *PL* 171, 1270.

23. I am grateful to Nona C. Flores for photographs of this fresco.

24. On this miniature see K. Loeffler, *Die Schwäbische Buchmalerei in romanischen Zeit* (Augsburg, 1928), p. 57. The foot of the cross itself serves as the hook for Leviathan in a miniature from the *Liber Matutinalis* of Conrad of Scheyern, Munich CLM 17401, fol. 14^v, thirteenth century.

25. Published in A. Straub and G. Keller, eds., *Herrade de Landsberg, Hortus deliciarum* (Strasbourg, 1879–99), fol. 84^r. See J. Zellinger, "Der geköderte Leviathan im *Hortus deliciarum* der Herrad von Landsberg," *Historisches Jahrbuch*, 45 (1925), 161–77, and Gérard Cames, *Allégories et symboles dans l'Hortus deliciarum* (Leiden, 1971), pp. 40–42.

26. The Alton Towers triptych is discussed and published by Marie-Madeleine Gauthier, *Emaux du moyen âge occidental* (Fribourg, 1972), p. 141, pl. 97, and pp. 352–53.

27. See Lionel J. Friedman, ed., *Text and Iconography for Joinville's Credo* (Cambridge, Mass., 1958), p. 38.

28. Missal of Saint-Niçaise de Reims, Hermitage, Leningrad, MS Q. v. I. 78 (BN 546), fol. 59, before 1297. I am grateful to Lionel Friedman for supplying me with a photograph of this miniature and information about the MS.

29. See Wilhelm Pinder, *Der Bamberger Dom* (Berlin, 1927), pl. 53. Jonah appears with Hosea on the west façade of Amiens Cathedral; the prophet

program seems to have been drawn from Isidore's [*Librum*] *de ortu et obitu Patrum*, *PL* 83, 129–56.

30. For well-known examples, see the Roda Bible, BN Lat. 6, fol. 83^v; the Souvigny Bible, Moulins MS I, fol. 196^v; and the Bourges Bible, MS 3, f. 246^r.
31. *Explanatica Psalmorvm*, 43. 75, ed. M. Petschenig, CSEL 64 (Vienna, 1919), p. 315. On this subject see Hugo Rahner, *Greek Myths and Christian Mystery* (London, 1963), pp. 350ff.
32. See Jennifer A. Lee, "MS Cotton Nero A. x: A Study of the Illustrator and Translator as Primary Critics of the Middle English *Pearl, Cleanness, Patience*, and *Sir Gawain and the Green Knight*," Diss. Stony Brook, 1974, *DAI* 35:407 A.
33. See Graham Pollard, "William de Brailles," *Bodleian Library Record*, 5 (1955), 202–9.
34. J. Leroy and F. Glorie, eds., *Evsebivs 'Gallicanvs' Collectio Homiliarum*, CCL, 101 (Turnhout, 1970) *Hom.* XIII, 8, p. 159. On the complex textual history of these homilies and possible authorship by Faustus of Riez, see Introduction, pp. vii–xxiii.
35. See V. Leroquais, *Les psautiers manuscrits latins des bibliothèques publiques de France* (Mâcon, 1940–41), I, 99.
36. This is MS 1826, fol. 57^b. (See M. R. James and E. G. Millar, *The Bohun Manuscripts* (Oxford, 1936), pl. XLV, and p. 38.
37. See Pierre Salmon, *Les "Tituli Psalmorum" des manuscrits latins* (Rome, 1959), pp. 9–12.
38. Irenaeus, *Adversus Haereticos* IV. 21.3, *PG* 7, 1046, and A. Zingerle, ed., *S. Hilari Episcopi Pictaviensis Tractatus super Psalmos*, CSEL 22 (Vienna, 1891), *Instructio psalmorum* 5, p. 6.
39. Salmon, Series I, p. 65.
40. *Tractatus super Psalmum vicesimum*, University of Illinois Library MS, fol. 85 (De Ricci, *Suppl.* 106) "deus ne in morte remaneam. Vox Christi in passione."
41. See Beryl Smalley, *The Study of the Bible in the Middle Ages* (Oxford, 1952), pp. 56–66.
42. *PL* 114, 292.

7

The Structures of Clannesse

EARL G. SCHREIBER

LIKE the unfortunate guest in the poem's prologue, *Clannesse* has frequently been cast out of the critical wedding feast into the dark dungeon of critical disfavor. Many critics find the poem to be like the guest's foul and tattered garments—a loosely structured work, lacking clear focus in its design and stressing the evils of *fylþe* rather than the virtues of *clannesse*. All in all, such readers claim, the poem is (again like the guest) a rather sorry intrusion into the otherwise seemly works of the *Gawain*-poet. Consequently, the poem has received little critical attention, with the notable exception of articles by Charlotte C. Morse and A. C. Spearing.[1] But even these two perceptive readers generally overlook the major structures of the poem, and my purpose is to suggest that the poem is more fully unified and coherent than most readers realize. In simplest structural terms, the poem follows the common preaching technique of moral principle and amplifying exempla: the prologue narrating the parable of the wedding feast is the moral principle, and the remainder of the poem is the amplification. But just as much medieval preaching and commentary assume and operate through complex analogies and draw implications for all of human endeavor, so too does the poem possess interlocked metaphors, and structures are initiated in the prologue and amplified throughout the poem.

I

The poet begins the prologue by singling out hypocritical priests, the "renkez of relygioun" (7).[2] They are particularly debased because they are "honest utwyth, and inwith alle fylþez" (14). Their sin is especially great because they approach God's temple and handle his body in the Eucharist, and consequently their reward will be God's wrath. God, the archetypal king presiding over a court of resplendent angels, stands in direct contrast to such foul persons:

> He is so clene in his corte, þe Kyng þat al weldez,
> And honeste in his housholde and hagherlych served,
> With angelez enorled in alle þat is clene,
> Boþe wythinne and wythouten, in wedez ful bryȝt. . . .
>
> (17–20)

The points of comparison are clear: God and his angels both possess and are surrounded by cleanness, but the perverse priests have filth; God's true servants have "wedez ful bryȝt," but the sinful are whited sepulchers; the angels in their purity serve God, but the unclean "loþe God and his gere" (16); those clothed in cleanness "cleche grete mede" (12), but those who are polluted "hym to greme cachen" (16). This description of God's court in contrast with the filthy is surely apocalyptic and probably alludes to Apocalypse 5:9–10 wherein the twenty-four elders surrounding the Lamb prostrate themselves in praise:

> And they sing a new canticle, saying, "Worthy art thou to take the scroll and to open its seals; for thou wast slain, and hast redeemed us for God with thy blood, out of every tribe and tongue and people and nations, and hast made them for our God a kingdom and priests, and they shall reign over the earth." [Douay-Rheims translation]

Hence, all men are called to be proper "renkez of relygioun." Moreover, all Christian men handle God's body in the Eucharist, either as literal priests in the consecration or as metaphoric priests receiving Christ within the temple of the body in communion. And just as the Church Militant is the earthly analogue of the Church Triumphant, so too is human society the analogue of the society of the New Jerusalem. The emphasis in the beginning of the prologue is that the poet is beginning with the metaphoric association of men as priests in the service of God: all men must serve God in cleanness within the earthly kingdom if they wish to serve God forever in the kingdom of Heaven.

The reward for proper service is the beatific vision, and in the prologue the poet reminds his audience of the sixth beatitude:

> Þe haþel clene of his hert hapenez ful fayre,
> For he schal loke on oure Lorde wyth a bone chere.
>
> (27–28)

But the poet has made two important additions to the biblical text, and these resound throughout the poem. First, the person clean of heart is not simply blessed, but he also "hapenez ful fayre," that is, he fares very well. The second addition is equally significant: the person who is clean of heart shall not simply see God but shall see him "wyth a bone chere," that is, with joy. In the later narratives, the horror and fear of the drowning persons, of the Sodomites and Gomorrahans, and of Belshazzar's court well attest to the terrible rather than the joyful vision of God that awaits the unclean. In fact, the wicked do not actually see God but only the effects of his wrath. Thus, the poet advises, no one with any stain of uncleanness will ever have the beatific vision:

> . . . to þat syȝt seche schal he never
> Þat any unclannesse hatz on, auwhere abowte . . .
>
> (29–30)

Just prior to his narrative of the wedding feast, the poet gives a prefatory epitome of the parable and initiates a major metaphoric pattern:

Forþy hyȝ not to heven in haterez totorne,
Ne in þe harlatez hod and handez unwaschen.
For what urþly haþel þat hyȝ honor haldez
Wolde lyke if a ladde com lyþerly attyred,
When he were sette solempnely in a sete ryche,
Abof dukez on dece, wyth dayntys served—
Þen þe harlot wyth haste helded to þe table
Wyth rent cokres at þe kne, and his clutte traschez,
And his tabarde totorne, and his totez oute,
Oþer ani on of alle þyse, he schulde be halden utter,
With mony blame, ful bygge a boffet, peraunter,
Hurled to þe halle-dore and harde þeroute showved,
And be forboden þat borȝe to bowe þider never,
On payne of enprysonment and puttyng in stokkez;
And þus schal he be schent for his schrowde feble,
Þaȝ never in talle ne in tuch he trespas more.

                                                    (33–48)

Clothes indicate morality, much like the conventional medieval interpretation of physical disease as a manifestation of spiritual illness. Just as this man's exterior is disordered, so too is his interior in disarray, as the term "harlot" suggests.[3] Clothing, however, is only one type of garb in the poem, and as the poem progresses, the poet expands metaphoric clothing to include a diversity of vessels: the pure soul (much like the angels who are "enorled in alle þat is clene" [19]) is arrayed with the luminescent clothing of faith and good works; the body is the raiment of the soul; the womb enwraps the body; Heaven enwraps the souls of the saved; the Church mystically subsumes all the faithful; and human society surrounds the individual.[4] An imbalance in any term of this analogy often distorts and perverts all of the other terms.

    It is important to remember that the celebration in the parable is a wedding feast, because in the medieval scheme of analogies many bonds are metaphoric marriages: the union of Christ and the Church, the bond between king and kingdom, the conjunction of body and soul, the relationship of reason and passion, and so on. But this wedding feast is totally gratuitous (like salvation, which it represents), and we have no clear indication of the social status of the first group of invited guests. The narrator, however, in keeping with his developing metaphor of clothing as morality adds to the biblical account that all the guests are to come "in comly quoyntis" (54) to a feast that by any standard is sumptuous. In their refusals, the little group of invited guests anticipates the major moral failings of those who later exemplify *unclannesse*: they are more concerned with temporality, physical possessions, and the flesh than with social obligation. In this respect, the lord's reply takes on special significance:

> "Now for her owne sorȝe þay forsaken habbez,
> More to wyte is her wrange þen any wylle gentyl."
> (75–76)

"Gentyl" should not be glossed as "gentile" (as do most editors) but as "genteel" or "gentle" (in the sense of "gentleman"): the king is complaining that the guests' refusal is an error greater than any mere social incivility—in the context of the expanded parable, the invited guests reject the king, just as in the later biblical narratives of the poem the wicked reject the kingship and society of God. Moreover, the poet's use of the parable of the wedding feast strengthens and extends his initial allusion to the royal wedding feast of the Lamb in the heavenly Jerusalem.

The king resolves, however, to fill his hall and orders his servants to seek new guests, just as God will replenish Creation twice in salvation history and in the poem: first after the fall of Lucifer when he creates Adam and Eve and then after the Flood when Noah and his family must replenish the earth. And just as salvation is open to anyone without regard to social position, so too does the king send his servants to search even in the lowliest of places for a sufficient number of guests to fill his hall:

> Thenne þe sergauntez, at þat sawe, swengen þeroute,
> And diden þe dede þat [is] demed, as he devised hade,
> And wyth peple of all plytez þe palays þay fyllen—

Hit weren not alle on wyvez sune, wonen wyth on fader.

(109–12)

Even though few are immaculate, all are seated hierarchically (in a manner reminiscent of the *Pearl*-maiden's description of Heaven), and all are fully served:

Wheþer þay wern worþy oþer wers, wel wern þay stowed,
Ay þe best byfore and bryӡtest atyred,
Þe derrest at þe hyӡe dese þat dubbed wer fayrest;
And syþen on lenþe bilooghe ledez inogh,
And ay a segge soerly semed by her wedez.
So with marschal at her mete mensked þay were. . . .

(113–18)

In the middle of the feast the king appears to greet his guests, but as he passes in an orderly fashion from guest to guest, he notices the man in foul clothing:

Bot as he ferked over þe flor, he fande wyth his yӡe—
Hit watz not for a halyday honestly arrayed—
A þral þryӡt in þe þrong unþryvandely cloþed,
Ne no festival frok, bot fyled with werkkez;
Þe gome watz ungarnyst wyth god men to dele.

(133–37)

The issue here is clearly not that the man is lacking finery, because a few lines earlier the narrator has observed that few of the guests are immaculately or stylishly attired: "And ay a segge soerly semed by her wedez" (117). Rather, the guest is improper because his clothes are "fyled with werkkez," that is, they are not sufficiently cleansed. The king's diction in his denunciation of the filthy guest clearly underscores the clothing-morality metaphor: the raiment does not befit the "halyday" (with a pun on holy-day, holiday). The guest is therefore a "gome ungoderly" (with a possible pun: ungoodly, ungodly), and he demeans the king's order by attempting "to aproche my presens hereinne"

(147), an echo of the poet's earlier line about the wicked priests who dare to approach God's presence in a defiled condition. Just as the king notices the one filthy person among all the guests, so too God will always see the true condition of one's soul even if it is, like the hypocritical priests' garments, covered over with false finery.

The guest's terror corresponds to the king's anger:

> Þat oþer burne watz abayst of his broþe wordez,
> And hurkelez doun with his hed, þe urþe he biholdez;
> He watz so scoumfit of his scylle, lest he skaþe hent,
> Þat he ne wyst on worde what he warp schulde.
>
> (149–52)

The guest's speechlessness anticipates the loss of speech and misuse of language by the wicked persons of the later narratives. The king, however, has no such linguistic problem, and he orders the filthy guest to be bound and cast not into the outer darkness of the biblical account but into his dungeon:

> "Takez hym," he biddez,
> "Byndez byhynde, at his bak, boþe two his handez,
> And felle fetterez to his fete festenez bylyve;
> Stik hym stifly in stokez, and stekez hym þerafter
> Depe in my doungoun þer doel ever dwellez,
> Greving and gretyng and gryspyng harde
> Of teþe tenfully togeder, to teche hym be quoynt."
>
> (154–60)

The purpose of the king's command—"to teche hym be quoynt"—is an ironic echo of the king's original invitation: the guests are "in comly quoyntis to com to his feste" (54). As I have suggested, this clothing-morality metaphor (here expressed in a pun) is a major metaphor of the poem. Moreover, the poet's substitution of the dungeon for the biblical outer darkness both utilizes the common medieval metaphor for hell (as, for example, in *Piers Plowman* and the morality plays) and initiates a spatial displacement of the wicked from the pure which pervades the poem.

The narrator draws the obvious conclusion from his expanded parable of the wedding feast: the parable tells of the eternal feast in the New Jerusalem to which all persons, both "þe luþer and þe better" (163), are invited. But one must first be cleansed with baptism and also be clothed properly with the weeds of good works and with "þe lykyng þat lyȝe in þyn herte" (172), if he wishes to see God; there must be a harmony between inner and outer, between container and contained. In contrast, those who have pursued *unclannesse* will not see God but will be cast directly into "þe develez þrote" (180)—another analogue to the hell-mouth of the morality plays. Moreover, the sins of *fylþe* are both personal and social:

> For fele fautez may a freke forfete his blysse,
> Þat he þe Soverayn ne se—þen for slauþe one,
> As for bobaunce and bost, and bolnande pryde,
> Þroly into þe develez þrote man þrynges bylyve;
> For covetyse, and colwarde and croked dedez,
> For mon-sworne, and men-sclaȝt, and to much drynk,
> For þefte, and for þrepyng, unþonk may mon have;
> For roborrye, and riboudrye, and resounez untrwe,
> And dysheriete and depryve dowrie of wydoez,
> For marryng of maryagez, and mayntnaunce of schrewez,
> For traysoun and trichcherye, and tyrauntyre boþe,
> And for fals famacions and fayned lawez—
> Man may mysse þe myrþe þat much is to prayse. . . .
>
> (177–89)

The poet significantly has placed "marryng of maryagez" prominently in his catalogue, for, as I have suggested, the poet sees marriage and the marriage feast both literally and metaphorically, and all the other sins which the poet names come from the rupture of the bond of literal or metaphoric marriage. Those who do not follow God's laws and accept the gratuitous invitation to salvation will merit the antifeast of hell:

> Man may mysse þe myrþe þat much is to prayse
> For such unþewes as þise, and þole much payne,
> And in þe Creatores cort com never more,
> Ne never see hym with syʒt for such sour tornez.
>
> (189–92)

Just as the marriage feast in the prologue is a type of the heavenly feast, so the feasts of Adam and Belshazzar are types of the infernal antifeast presided over by anti-priests, and at the anti-feast of damnation one wears "fele fetterez" rather than resplendent robes and has only "greving and gretyng and gryspyng harde / Of teþe tenfully togeder" rather than "myrþe." And, of course, it is then too late to learn "to be . . . quoynt."

By the end of the prologue, the poet has initiated the major thematic and metaphoric concerns of the poem: priests, feasts, clothing, marriage, vessels, spatial descents, deformity, and perversion in contrast to beauty and cleanness; and estrangement, destruction, and sorrow in contrast to union, eternal life, and joy. Moreover, the poet's emphasis on sight and vision throughout the prologue suggests that he intends his poem to be apocalyptic in the double sense of the word: it is both a description of the destruction attendant upon sin and a medium for showing others this vision of moral order.

II

Throughout the poem the association of the good man with the proper priest and feast is clear. When Noah leaves the ark, he immediately offers a proper sacrifice to God:

> Bot Noe of uche honest kynde nem out an odde,
> And hevened up an auter and halʒed hit fayre,
> And sette a sakerfyse þeron of uch a ser kynde
> Þat watz comly and clene—God kepez non oþer.
>
> (505–8)

When the angels appear to Abraham and Lot, the latter im-

mediately begin to prepare the proper feast, a direct analogue to
the Mass. As Spearing has noted, Abraham's proper service for
the three messengers of God has overtones of the English picnic:

> Þe burne to be bare-heved buskez hym þenne,
> Clechez to a clene cloþe and kestez on þe grene,
> Þrwe þryftyly þerone þo þre þerve kakez,
> And bryngez butter wythal, and by þe bred settez;
> Mete messez of mylke he merkkez bytwene,
> Syþen potage and polment in plater honest.
> As sewer in a god assys᷈ he served hem fayre,
> Wyth sadde semblaunt and swete, of such as he hade.
>
> (633–40)

Lot's banquet is similarly appropriate and deferential:

> Þe wyȝez wern welcom as þe wyf couþe;
> His two dere doȝterez devoutly hem haylsed,
> Þat wer maydenez ful meke, maryed not ȝet,
> And þay wer semly and swete, and swyþe wel arayed.
> Loth þenne ful lyȝtly lokez hym aboute,
> And his men amonestes mete for to dyȝt:
> "Bot þenkkez on hit be þrefte, what þynk so ȝe make,
> For wyth no sour ne no salt servez hym never."
>
> (813–20)

All these men humbly accept God's will and participate in
proper and fruitful marriage and receive a fitting reward; to use
the poet's addition to the sixth beatitude, each "hapenez ful
fayre" (27). Noah is the medium of replenishing the earth, as
God commands him:

> "Bot waxez now and wendez forth and worþez to monye,
> Multyplyez on þis molde, and menske yow bytyde." .
>
> (521–22)

The three angels tell Abraham that he is to be the father of "þe worþely peple, / Þat schal halde in heritage þat I haf men ʒark[ed]'' (651–52). Lot and his family escape the destruction of Sodom and Gomorrah by obeying the angels' commandment. Daniel does not participate in marriage, but he implies true service to God and proper marriage by denouncing Belshazzar's "bobaunce" and perverted marriage.

Although marriage is a common medieval metaphor for many types of relationships, the parable of the wedding feast in the prologue is a narrative set specifically within a larger social context. As the poem progresses, it becomes increasingly concerned with the body politic, the spirit which informs human society, and the *clannesse* or *fylþe* it contains, as well as with the individual body and soul. Just as the court of the parable is the narrative norm for the poem, so "Þe Creatores cort" (191) which is "comlych" and ruled by the "Kyng . . . of blysse" (546) should be the norm for human society. In the narratives after the prologue, we discover the antisociety of Lucifer, the proto-society of Adam, the world of Noah, the twin cities of Sodom and Gomorrah, Zedechiah's Jerusalem, Nebuchadnezzar's court, and Belshazzar's kingdom, the most fully realized society within the poem. All of these societies fall through pride, which leads them to break the laws of God and nature and to commit more specific sins. Lucifer "seʒ noʒt bot hymself how semly he were," and "his Soverayn he forsoke" (209–10). Adam fell because he "fayled in trawþe" (236). Noah's neighbors "controeved agayn kynde contrare werkez" (266) and brought forth giants and evils which "multyplyed monyfolde inmongez mankynde" (278). Sodom and Gomorrah rejected God's "ordenaunce" (698) and "scorned natwre" (709) for "usage unclene" (710). Zedechiah "of leaute . . . watz lat to his Lorde hende" and "used abominaciones of idolatrye" (1172–73). Nebuchadnezzar had "pryde / For his lordeschyp so large and his lyf ryche" (1657–58). Belshazzar "trawed / Þat nauþer in heven ne [on] erþe [he] hade no pere" (1335–36). His ripping of "his wedes" (1583) when he sees the handwriting on the wall is the most graphic expression of his complete rending of all structure through his pride: he has violated the temple of God and of his own body, destroyed marriage by taking concubines,

and perverted ordered society. Thus, *fylþe* and *unclannesse* are
not merely sins of the flesh; rather, they are any offense against
God's law, and these offenses come primarily from pride, as the
poet has specifically argued at the conclusion of the prologue
(177–92).

The anguish of the man in foul clothing who trembled and
"ne wyst on worde what he warp schulde" (152) anticipates the
reaction and linguistic confusion of those destroyed in the later
narratives. The drowning persons of Noah's world cry out to God
for mercy:

> And alle cryed for care to þe Kyng of heven,
> Recoverer of þe Creator þay cryed uch one,
> Þat amounted þe mase—his mercy watz passed,
> And alle his pyte departed fro peple þat he hated.
>
> (393–96)

The inhabitants of Sodom and Gomorrah similarly petition Christ:

> Rydelles wern þo grete rowtes of renkkes wythinne,
> When þay wern war of þe wrake þat no wyȝe achaped;
> Such a ȝomerly ȝarm of ȝellyng þer rysed,
> Þerof clatered þe cloudes þat Kryst myȝt haf rawþe.
>
> (969–72)

And Belshazzar cannot control himself in his terror:

> When þat bolde Baltazar blusched to þat neve,
> Such a dasande dred dusched to his hert,
> Þat al falewed his face and fayled þe chere;
> Þe stronge strok of þe stonde strayned his joyntes,
> His cnes cachches to close, and cluchches his hommes,
> And he wyth plattyng his paumes displayes his lers,
> And romyes as a rad ryth þat rorez for drede,
> Ay biholdand þe honde til hit hade al graven,
> And rasped on þe roȝ woȝe runisch sauez.
>
> (1537–45)

Again, like the filthy guest cast "depe in . . . doungoun þer doel ever dwellez" (158), the wicked societies literally fall into horrible punishment. Satan and his followers "fellen fro þe fyrmament" (221) into chaos; Adam fell from paradise and merited "þe deþe þat drepez uus alle" (246); Noah's neighbors endured terrible agonies and "fellen in fere and faþmed togeder" (399); Sodom and Gomorrah "sunkken to helle" (968); Nebuchadnezzar was reduced to the level of a beast and "fare[d] forth on alle faure" (1683); and Belshazzar became mad and was bludgeoned to death, most fully displaying this descent:

> He watz corsed for his unclannes, and cached þerinne,
> Done doun of his dyngnete for dedez unfayre,
> And of þyse worldes worchyp wrast out for ever,
> And ȝet of lykynges on lofte letted, I trowe,
> To loke on our lofly Lorde late bitydes.
>
> (1800–4)

The chaotic and rapid descent of these wicked persons is the inevitable, final and external correlative of their chaotic and debased moral natures.

But ironically, although the king in the parable thought he had separated himself from those who reject him, there is nonetheless still one man in foul clothing. Theologically, this is an important issue because it implies that evil cannot be excised but will always continue. Similarly, evil continually reasserts itself in the other biblical narratives of the poem. God creates Adam to fill the void left by the rebellious and fallen angels, but Adam also rebels and falls. God attempts to cleanse the earth with a flood, but the black raven released by Noah flies immediately to carrion and does not return to the ark. God decides to spare Lot's family, but Lot's wife rebels against God's commandment and must be punished. Nebuchadnezzar suffers punishment and purgation and becomes regenerate, but his son Belshazzar learns nothing from this incident and is horribly murdered.

III

No amount of delineating thematic and metaphoric structures and continuities, however, will necessarily establish the unity of the poem or effectively counter readers who find the poem obsessed with *fylþe* rather than *clannesse* or who, like Dorothy Everett, find the poem poorly structured and its central virtue and sin defined too expansively:

> *Patience* is simpler in conception than *Purity* and therefore neater and more unified in construction. . . . In *Purity* the homiletic element is more important, for the poet attempts to use the argument as a framework to link together a number of Biblical stories, including the three main ones. . . . This more ambitious scheme is not entirely successful, for, in order to include the story of Belshazzar's Feast, the poet has to juggle with his interpretation of "uncleanness" and make it cover the defiling of what belongs to God as well as unchastity. Moreover, since he is still mainly interested in narrative, he tends to tell his stories at disproportionate length.[5]

Perhaps human nature disposes us to dwell upon and remember the scandalous lives and grisly deaths of those who pursue *fylþe*, but to see the poem as concerned exclusively with *unclannesse* and urging *clannesse* only by negative example is simply a misreading, because, as I have argued, Noah, Abraham, Lot, and Daniel as examples of purity in every way contrast with Lucifer, Adam, Noah's neighbors, Sodom and Gomorrah, Zedechiah, Nebuchadnezzar, and Belshazzar. Moreover, *unclannesse* is not simply "unchastity" (as Everett would define the term), but any prideful attempt to contravene God's order.

God's punishment of these *unclene* people is from our perspective surely just, but a central consideration of the poem and a major element of its unity is that perspective. The poet can quickly dismiss in half a line God's dispassionate punishment of Lucifer—"And ȝet wrathed not þe Wyȝ" (230)—because as a purely spiritual being Lucifer had knowledge of his act and its consequences. Adam, however, is of a lower order, and although his punishment is just, there is the promise of future reconciliation:

Al in mesure and meþe watz mad þe veng[a]unce,
And efte amended wyth a mayden þat make had never.

(247–48)

With the Fall, man loses Adam's preternatural gifts, and man's only moral guide is his contemplation of the law of "kynde" in the dim perspective of fallen reason. Hence, although justice must prevail, it must be tempered, as God says to Noah:

"Now, Noe, no more nel I never wary
Alle þe mukel mayny [on] molde for no mannez synnez,
For I se wel þat hit is sothe, þat alle mannez wyttez
To unþryfte arn alle þrawen wyth þoȝt of her herttez,
And ay hatz ben, and wyl be ȝet, fro her barnage;
Al is þe mynde of þe man to malyce enclyned;
Forþy schal I never schende so schortly at ones
As dysstrye al for manez [dedes], dayez of þis erþe."

(513–20)

Paradoxically, man must shun *fylþe* and pursue *clannesse*, but he lacks a model for this moral process. Without such a model, human history is virtually a repetition of Adam's life, as the poet suggests by concluding his narrative of Sodom and Gomorrah with a description of the trees around the Dead Sea bearing fruit superficially pleasing, but only ashes within:

And þe fayrest fryt þat may on folde growe,
As orenge and oþer fryt and apple garnade,
Also red and so ripe and rychely hwed
As any dom myȝt device of dayntyez oute;
Bot quen hit is brused, oþer broken, oþer byten in twynne,
No worldez goud hit wythinne, bot wyndowande askes.

(1043–48)

The moral paradigm is, of course, Christ, and between the narratives of Lot and Belshazzar is the narration of the birth of Christ. This section is not a digression (as many readers claim) but rather a major unifying element of the poem, because through the Incarnation God's relationship with man is most fully established and affirmed. Christ is the sublime *perle* born of a spotless maiden, who together are the fullness of the vessel and clothing metaphors, the absolutely pure union of container and contained. Celestial music and "solace and songe" (1080) rather than the chaotic noise of sin attend his birth, and the law of "kynde" is reaffirmed, for the animals "knewe hym by his clannes for Kyng of nature" (1087). Christ is also the "ful cortays" king, the archetypal "Cortayse" (1097), the essence of *clannesse* made incarnate, and even though he scorns all *fylþe*, he cures the deformed and diseased who come to him:

> ȝet comen lodly to þat Lede, as lazares monye,
> Summe lepre, summe lome, and lomerande blynde,
> Poysened, and parlatyk, and pyned in fyres,
> Drye folk, and ydropike, and dede, at þe laste—
> Alle called on þat Cortayse and claymed his grace.
> He heled hem with hynde speche of þat þay ask after,
> For what so he towched, also tyd torned to hele,
> Wel clanner þen any crafte cowþe devyse.
>
> (1093–1100)

The importance here is twofold: Christ's efficacy in word and deed turns physical disease and deformity into health and beauty and, more important, he bestows his cures gratuitously on all who ask. Moreover, this principle continues spiritually throughout all time for those who will seek shrift and penance:

> ȝis, þat Mayster is mercyable, þaȝ þou be man fenny
> And al tomarred in myre, whyl þou on molde lyvyes;
> Þou may schyne þurȝ schryfte, þaȝ þou haf schome served,
> And pure þe with penaunce tyl þou a perle worþe.
>
> (1113–16)

Unlike the old dispensation of justice, the new dispensation of mercy both requires and enables man to be purified, polished "bryȝter þen þe beryl oþer browden perles" (1132), and "waschen wyth water of schryfte" (1133). But such an option also carries greater responsibility, and once man is cleansed, he is all the more loathsome should he revert to *fylþe* and befoul his vessel:

> War þe þenne for þe wrake; his wrath is achaufed
> For þat þat ones watz his schulde efte be unclene,
> Þaȝ hit be bot a bassyn, a bolle, oþer a scole,
> A dysche, oþer a dobler, þat Dryȝtyn onez served,
> To defowle hit ever upon folde fast he forbedes,
> So is he scoymous of scaþe þat scylful is ever.
>
> (1143–48)

This principle, the poet asserts, is shown in the story of Belshazzar, who learned nothing from the experience of his father Nebuchadnezzar. Like Belshazzar, those who seek filth reject the love of the purifying Christ and are hence subject to the law of justice.

One might, however, object that the story of Belshazzar is inappropriate, because his immoral life and gruesome death occurred before the Incarnation, and further that such a conclusion to the poem is the most persuasive evidence of its unsatisfactory structure. But such a view neglects the central function of Daniel, the good man, the prophet of God and, as Belshazzar's queen explains, the master of words who can unlock their secrets:

> "His sawle is ful of syence, saȝes to schawe,
> To open uch a hide þyng of aunteres uncowþe.
> Þat is he þat ful ofte hatz hevened þy fader
> Of mony anger ful hote wyth his holy speche.
> When Nabugodenozar watz nyed in stoundes,
> He devysed his dremes to þe dere trawþe,
> He kevered hym wyth his counsayl of caytyf wyrdes;
> Alle þat he spured hym in space he expowned clene,

Þurȝ þe sped of þe spyryt þat sprad hym wythinne
Of the godelest goddez þat gaynes aywhere.''

                                          (1599–1608)

But ironically, the secrets of which the queen speaks are not mysteries at all because, as Daniel explains, Belshazzar has simply
neglected the clear and well-known example of his father:

"Bot þou, Baltazar, his barne and his bolde ayre,
Seȝ þese syngnes wyth syȝt, and set hem at lyttel,
Bot ay hatz hofen þy hert agaynes þe hyȝe Dryȝt[y]n,
Wyth bobaunce and wyth blasfayme bost at hym kest,
And now his vessayles avyled in vanyte unclene,
Þat in his hows hym to honor were hevened of fyrst. . . ."

                                          (1709–14)

Thus God "hatz sende into þis sale þise syȝtes uncowþe" (1722).
Although Daniel can foretell the specific nature of Belshazzar's
death, the king should have known, by remembering his father,
that "froþande fylþe" (1721) inevitably leads to destruction.
Daniel teaches Belshazzar what should be obvious, but Belshazzar, like most men, constantly needs such instruction. Daniel's
function in the narrative of Belshazzar suggests what I find to be
the primary unifying element of the poem: the poet as guide and
teacher, the shaper of the vessel of truth, and the master of words
who unlocks their secret meanings which ironically are not secret
meanings at all.

    The poet implies this function in the first four lines of the
poem:

Clannesse who so kyndly cowþe comende,
And rekken up alle þe resounz þat ho by riȝt askez,
Fayre formez myȝt he fynde in for[þ]ering his speche,
And in þe contrare, kark and combraunce huge.

                                          (1–4)

Those who praise *clannesse*, presumably by being clean and obeying God's order, have fair speech; those who pursue *fylþe*, as do the well-known examples later in the poem, lack such "fayre formes," an obvious pun on body and word suggesting both physical and verbal debasement. The parable of the man in foul clothes comes from Christ, who "kydde hit hymself" (23) and through Matthew's writings "Þat þus of clannesse unclosez a ful cler speche" (26). And although the poet freely expands his sources, he reminds us of his unnamed verbal sources at the beginning of his narrative of Lucifer:

> Bot I have herkned and herde of mony hyȝe clerkez,
> And als in resounez of ryȝt red hit myselven. . . .
>
> (193–94)

And:

> Bot never ȝet in no boke breved I herde. . . .
>
> (197)

After the narrative of Noah, he warns us that God sees and hears everything and that we must beware of "tales" (presumably not his poem) that say otherwise:

> Bot sa[v]or, mon, in þyself, þaȝ þou a sotte lyvie,
> Þaȝ þou bere þyself babel, byþenk þe sumtym
> Wheþer he þat stykked uche a stare in uche steppe yȝe,
> ȝif hymself be bore blynde, hit is a brod wonder;
> And he þat fetly in face fettled alle eres,
> If he hatz losed þe lysten hit lyftez mervayle;
> Traue þou never þat tale, untrwe þou hit fyndez.
>
> (581–87)

Having recounted the destruction of Sodom and Gomorrah, the poet clearly states that his narratives thus far are instructional figures:

Alle þyse ar teches and tokenes to trow upon ȝet,
And wittnesse of þat wykked werk, and þe wrake after
Þat oure Fader forferde for fylþe of þose ledes.

(1049–51)

With a touch of author's pride and a sure grasp of his own function, he notes that all men must not only be "waschen wyth
water of schryfte" (itself an obvious pun) but also "polysed as
playn as parchmen schaven" (1133, 1134). And with deadpan
self-irony he prefaces his story of Belshazzar, the longest narrative:

Ȝif ȝe wolde tyȝt me a tom, telle hit I wolde,
Hou charged more watz his chaunce þat hem cherych nolde
Þen his fader forloyne þat feched hem wyth strenþe,
And robbed þe relygioun of relykes alle.[6]

(1153–56)

The implications of this preface are the strongest rejoinder to
Everett's claim that the story of Belshazzar is a serious flaw. Belshazzar's sin was especially grievous and his "chaunce" was
"charged more," because he neglected the wise and holy Daniel,
and he had the immediate and human example of his father, who
safeguarded the holy relics, fell through pride, but ultimately
acknowledged God. For those living in the New Dispensation and
having the example of the incarnate Christ and the instruction of
the Bible, the "chaunce" is charged even more. The story of
Belshazzar following the poet's narration of the coming of Christ
is not a chronological imperfection, but an apocalyptic warning to
those who would reject the perfect example of *clannesse*, and the
medium of this warning is the poet, the analogue to Daniel.

The poet draws his poem to a close in the first person by
reaffirming his function as a teacher who has restated the Lord's
hatred of *fylþe* and love of *clannesse*:

Þus upon þrynne wyses I haf yow þro schewed,
Þat unclannes tocleves in corage dere

Of þat wynnelych Lorde þat wonyes in heven,
Entyses hym to be tene, tel[des] up his wrake;
Ande clannes is his comfort, and coyntyse he lovyes,
And þose þat seme arn and swete schyn se his face.

(1805–10)

And perhaps lest he err through pride, he rejoins the community
of men and concludes in the plural:

Þat we gon gay in oure gere þat grace he uus sende,
Þat we may serve in his syȝt þer solace never blynnez. Amen.

(1811–12)

Thus the poet is a vessel filled with wisdom drawn from the
words of other men, and his poem is likewise a vessel filled with
his wisdom and shaped by his function as teacher and discloser of
truth. The reader similarly must draw wisdom from the poem so
that he may make his own vessel more pure and pleasing to God.
Like Christ who "heled . . . with hynde speche," the poet can
cure, but the bitterest irony is that the poet teaches us nothing
new and that even in the New Dispensation men all too often
neglect the teachings of the holiest of books and the examples of
their fellow men. And if, as Professor Spearing has warned us,
we insist on approaching the poem with Aristotelian standards,
then we shall surely find it poorly shaped and its vision unclear,
but if we take the poem on its own structural terms, then we shall
find it indeed a well-wrought vessel.

NOTES

1. Charlotte C. Morse, "The Image of the Vessel in *Cleanness*," *University of Toronto Quarterly*, 40 (1971), 202–16; A. C. Spearing, *The Gawain Poet* (Cambridge, 1970), Chap. 2.
2. All quotations are from *Purity*, ed. Robert J. Menner (1920; rpt. Hamden, Conn., 1970), hereafter cited by line numbers parenthetically within the text.
3. See *Middle English Dictionary*, s. v. "harlot" and "harlotrie."

4. I draw on Morse's analysis, which is an important study, but from my point of view, it does not pursue the fullest implications of the vessel image.

5. Dorothy Everett, *Essays on Middle English Literature*, ed. Patricia Kean (Oxford, 1955), p. 70.

6. The key word in this passage is *tom*, which Menner glosses as "time, opportunity," and Mabel Day (who supplied the glossary for Gollancz's text) glosses as "opportunity." Both cite ON *tom*. But given the poet's frequent references to books and writing, the word also (and, I think, primarily) suggests "tome" or "book," a derivation from medieval Latin *tomus*, which Latham glosses as "tome, book, or letter" (1362) and perhaps as "literary flourish" (1359).

8

Willfulness and Wonders: Boethian Tragedy in the Alliterative Morte Arthure

RUSSELL A. PECK

> "Be war of wylffulnesse . lest wondris arise."
> —*Mum and the Sothsegger*

THE latter part of the fourteenth century was marked by disenchantment with virtually every institution invented by man. Like so much of the literature of this chaotic period, the alliterative *Morte Arthure* is imbued with a deep concern about what constitutes virtuous behavior. God "schelde vs fro schamesdede and synfull werkes" (3), says its opening prayer, "and gyffe vs grace to gye and governe vs here" (4).[1] The poet would study government, but rather than attack institutions, he directs his attention to personal behavior, the government of ourselves. In this regard he is typical of his age, where moral positions tend to be introspective and self-critical. Like Gower, Chaucer, Langland, and the political moralists at the end of the century, he espouses the idea that the chaos man sees about him is caused by man himself. As Gower puts it in the *Confessio Amantis*:

> man is overal
> His oghne cause of wel and wo.
> That we fortune clepe so
> Out of the man himself it groweth.[2]

Like other writers of his day, the poet of the *Morte Arthure* singles out the will as the faculty which most determines an individual's life. His poem is a masterful study of willfulness and the wonders it can conjure.

For fourteenth-century literary men, Boethius is the principal spokesman on matters of the will. A brief review of his ideas proves helpful in establishing some of the premises within our poem. The *Consolation of Philosophy* is a treatise on personal government in which a person is likened to a king who has sovereign rights over the kingdom of his soul. If he rules that kingdom well, he enjoys happiness and steadfastness.[3] Good rule is partly a matter of self-knowledge (the remembering of who you are) and partly a keeping of balanced perspective on one's own good and the greater good, supremely embodied in God Himself.[4] Paradoxically, then, man's power over his kingdom is not exclusively his own, but is contingent upon God's power. The sovereignty is his own only through his own right choices which enable him to participate in the *summum bonum*. Good rule requires an awareness of discrete boundaries between what is one's own and not one's own.

Intimately tied up with these Boethian ideas of good rule are two subtopics, fate and tragedy, which likewise figure largely in literature dealing with the will. Gower, for example, follows Boethius when he asserts in the *Vox Clamantis*:

> Each man shapes for himself his own destiny, incurs his own lot according to his desire, and creates his own fate. And thus a free mind voluntarily claims what it does for its various deserts in the name of fate. In truth, fate ought always to be handmaiden to the mind, from which the name itself which will be its own is chosen.[5]

If fate is what one chooses, then tragedy is that condition when the will, through wrong choices, isolates the soul from its proper good, so that it feels wretched and lost. The will may rationalize its misery, placing the blame elsewhere (on Fortune, perhaps), but that very rationalization is symptomatic of its own indiscretion which is the efficient cause of its misery.

A dramatic moment near the beginning of the *Consolation* poses this configuration of ideas with admirable brevity. Lady Philosophy has just heard Boethius' lament about his imprisonment and the unjust charges brought against him. Fortune, it seems, has been his malicious enemy. Lady Philosophy replies:

> Whan I saugh the . . . sorwful and wepynge, I wiste anoon that thow were a wrecche and exiled; but I wyste nevere how fer thyn exil was yif thy tale ne hadde schewid it me. But certes, al be thow fer fro thy cuntre, thou n'art nat put out of it, but thow hast fayled of thi weye and gon amys. And yif thou hast levere for to wene that thow be put out of thy cuntre, thanne hastow put out thyselve rather than ony other wyght hath. For no wyght but thyselve myghte nevere han doon that to the.[6]

Several points here have bearing upon the alliterative *Morte Arthure*: (1) The soul, in governing itself, must know and maintain its true residence. (2) Fortune has no power over man's true country. The only way a man may be exiled is by his own willful departing. (3) Such a departure, not Fortune, is the cause of wretchedness. (When Fortune subsequently offers her famous *de casibus* definition of tragedy, she is describing an effect, not a cause.[7]) (4) Exile is largely a matter of disorientation, a forgetting of what is properly one's own, or a misidentification of rightful possessions. Seeking to possess something which is not rightly its own, the will dispossesses itself. (5) When the will makes its misidentifications, it substitutes its own fantasies for true realities. These are the "wondris" which the Sothsegger speaks of when he warns young rulers to beware of "wylfful-nesse."[8] By approaching the *Morte Arthure* as a study of willful behavior we come close to its heart and its author's intention.[9] Such an approach, moreover, exemplifies one of the later fourteenth-century's major topics, the dangers of willfulness.[10]

I

The poet takes his story from the chronicles of Wace and
Layamon, rather than the later, more popular romances.[11]
Perhaps his reason is that he wants the story to seem more like
history. He develops his plot as a sequence of events, each of
which requires decisions of Arthur or his knights and imposes
consequences on that which follows. It is noteworthy that the
poem's opening announcement of its subject (12–25) speaks of
the glorious deeds of Arthur, his war with Lucius, and the conquest of Rome, but makes no mention of the poem's disastrous
outcome. Perhaps the point of that omission is to avoid making
the plot seem fated from the beginning. The fate of each character and the outcome of the poem will be determined by the characters themselves, who as the plot progresses, will get "what
them likes." I mention the familiar tag because it occurs in various forms over a hundred times in the poem and is one of the
poet's principal devices for focusing attention on willfulness.
(The second most common tag, the reflexive pronoun in its inten-
sive form—himselven, themselven, myselven, etc.—has something of the same effect and is often used in conjunction with the
"as him likes" tag.)

Because the plot is designed to unfold as Arthur shapes his
fate, I shall conduct my analysis according to the sequence of
events as the poet introduces them. But first I would call attention to one other plotting device which the poet uses to create
irony and a heightened sense of impending tragedy. The plot of
the poem falls into two main parts of about the same length: (1)
the events leading up to the Battle of Sessoine and the defeat of
Lucius; and (2) the events which follow that victory. The main
difference between the parts lies in Arthur's motive for fighting.
In the first half he is primarily concerned with defending his
lands, title, and people from a usurper. After the victory his motive becomes personal revenge. Revenge, as John Finlayson has
noted, is not (according to chivalric manuals) a lawful reason for
war.[12] More important for our purposes, in Boethian psychology,
revenge, like any form of tyranny or aggression, stems from a

willful misunderstanding of what is rightfully one's own. Consequently, the actions of the second half of the poem tend to reflect deluded judgment and to parody the more rationally oriented events of the first part. William Matthews and others have noted the rising and falling action of the poem as Fortune turns away from Arthur.[13] But the plotting is more intricate than that. The poet has arranged situations within the two parts geometrically in a hysteron proteron fashion, where the first event ties up with the last (which is a reverse of the first), the second with the next to the last, the third with third to last, and so on:

1. Arthur at his Christmas banquet, surrounded by joyous knights.

2. The council of Arthur and his knights.

3. Dream of the dragon, which bodes well, and the crossing of the channel to France.

4. Arthur's holy battle with the Giant of Gene, who despoils the land, devours Christians, and rapes women. Arthur founds a church on the crag.

5. Gawain's purposeful embassy to Lucius.

6. Presumptuous Sir Cador risks lives to win glory. Gets scolded by king.

13. Dying Arthur, surrounded by his dead knights.

12. Arthur's refusal to call a council at the request of Sir Wichere.

11. Dream of Fortune, which bodes ill, and the crossing of the Channel to England.

10. Arthur despoils Italy, torments the people, makes widows aplenty, and destroys churches.

9. Gawain passes time somewhat idly in the Priamus interlude.

8. Presumptuous Arthur works "naked" beside the walls of Metz. Gets scolded by Sir Ferrer.

7. The Battle of Sessoine. Arthur's victory, and the beginning of his defeat.

These structural antitheses are not absolutely symmetrical, but
they are sufficiently parallel to call attention to themselves and
create ironies which resound throughout the second part, as Arthur's behavior becomes progressively more arbitrary. The hysteron proteron structure, where acts parody former acts, focuses
attention on the crucial central scene, where Arthur's motives become clouded and, instead of returning home with victory, he
turns to seek revenge for the death of Sir Kay.

II

The *Morte Arthure* begins, as we have noted, with an elaborate prayer which defines the poet's intent to help men learn to
govern themselves. In emphasizing the need for right governance
"in this wrechyd werld" (5), the prayer directs our attention to
the poem's central motif, and by presenting God as a king beyond history who maintains his feudal court in "the kyngdom of
Hevyne" (6), it establishes a model of kingship which is beyond
fortune. The poet stresses God's glory and graciousness. The reflexive pronoun tag occurs three times in the prayer, not to indicate God's willfulness but his gracious self-possession and shared
self as he shields men "thurgh grace of Hymseluen" (1) and
calls men "Ewyre . . . to byde in blysse wyth Hym seluen"
(8). The idea seems to be that God knows his own place and
through his generosity enables men to know and govern theirs. In
Boethian terms, self-possession is the antithesis of exile, where a
man's will drives him away from what is truly his own.

The opening scene is designed to show Arthur as a powerful
and wise king. There can be no question of his kingliness, if
kingliness is measured by success. In one swift catalogue of con-
quests he recovers all the lost lands of his ancestors (26–47).
Having secured lands "ynowe" (45), he rests for a season "to
solace hym seluen . . . as hym beste lykes" (54–55). But he is
more than a conqueror. He founds the city of Caerleon. In the
chronicle sources Caerleon is a well-established city to which Arthur retires to enjoy its splendor.[14] Perhaps the *Morte Arthure*
uses the founding of the city as a sign of Arthur's generative

behavior. In his treatise *On Kingship* St. Thomas Aquinas designates city-building as the principal duty of a creative king.[15] Arthur would seem to be such a ruler. At his Christmas feast he shares his magnificence in high style with his great company of dukes, earls, doucepeers, archbishops, "and oþer ynowe" (67) at Carlisle. In addition to restressing his having plenty "ynowe" (45, 67), the poet, by use of other recurring tags, emphasizes Arthur's having accomplished his will—he rules "as hym lykys" (32), sojourns "as hym best lykes" (55), assembles his courtiers "to see whenn hym lykyde" (63) while they bow and "buske when hym lykys" (69). He won his lands "at hys will" (33), "by drede of hym seluyn" (46), "fre til him seluyn" (34), so that now he may surround himself with the courtiers he "commaundez hym seluyn" (71). As if to allay any doubts we might have of the completeness of Arthur's satisfaction, the poet says there "whas neuer syche noblay in no manys tym / Mad in mydwynter in þa weste marchys" (76–77). The greater the magnificence here, of course, the more stark the contrast at the end of the poem, where, hysteron proteron, Arthur stands desolate among his dead knights, with nothing "as hym beste lykes." Our study will be to discover how he got from one state to the other.

Certainly, if a king is to rule, he must have his own will. The success of his rule will depend largely, however, upon his personal ability to govern that will. One recalls the Sothsegger's advice to young rulers to "be war of wylffulnesse . lest wondris arise." It is precisely when one has his will that he is most likely to be challenged. The splendor of the scene at Carlisle is comparable to the Christmas feast in *Sir Gawain and the Green Knight*, where amidst all its plenty that court is confronted with wonders. In the chronicle sources of the *Morte Arthure*, the embassy from Lucius comes at Whitsunday.[16] Perhaps our poet chose the midwinter season to suggest a time of pending, a time when the court's blessings stand out against an otherwise barren scene. The challenge from without comes as a jolt to Arthur and his court. As the first course of their banquet is being served, the Romans appear "sodanly" (80) and boldly assert their demands. Arthur meets the challenge as a good king should, with balance and courtesy. He entertains the Roman senator well, allows him seven days to see England's glories, and sees to it that his desires are satisfied. He gives him an allowance to "spende what þe lykys" (162) and wines "ynow" to try "whoso lykes" (205). Assured that the senator has all he wants "for solauce of hym seluen" (239) in "thees barayne landez" (224), Arthur calls his own counselors to him, thus showing further his wisdom as ruler. Christine de Pisan observes that a prince may take up arms to obtain justice for himself once he has consulted impartial counselors.[17] Though Arthur's counselors are far from impartial, he himself shows good judgment as he weighs their advice carefully, warning them against haste and headlong action. When the impetuous Sir Cador "lughe on hym luffly with lykande lates" (248) at the prospect of getting back to war instead of lying around like "losels," Arthur warns him:

> . . . thy concell es noble;
> Bot þou arte a meruailous man with thi mery wordez;
> For thow countez no caas, ne castes no forthire,
> Bot hurles furthe appon heuede, as thi herte thynkes.
>
> (259–62)

Arthur shows balanced judgment. Instead of leaping after the words of the "meruailous man," he would "trette of a trew towchande þise nedes" (263). He measures his rights against those of Lucius, observing that if ancient titles are the issue he has as much claim to the title of Rome as Lucius. Rather than succumb to Lucius' demands, Arthur will meet him in the field to defend his own. After the council, Arthur pays tribute to his knights for their support and acts decisively with the embassy. In fact, his kingly presence is so overwhelming that, even after they have returned to Rome to report to Lucius, the Romans are terrified and spontaneously praise him.

This initial image of Arthur as king is altogether positive. He is awesome in power, magnanimity, counsel, and firm decision. The next situation in which his judgment is tested is more subtle.

Since he must travel abroad he must choose a lieutenant to look after the realm in his absence. This is an important moment,[18] especially in a literature dealing with Boethian ideas of self-possession (home) and willful wandering (exile). The mere fact that a king travels abroad does not mean, of course, that he is a willful wanderer. That Melibee disported in the fields, for example, is less important than his carelessness in leaving his castle unguarded. There are many examples of kings in medieval literature who govern so well that their authority is in no way diminished by their physical absence.[19] Nevertheless, there is always the possibility that in setting off to seek wonders abroad one will discover the greatest wonder of all, the loss of his homeland.

The *Morte Arthure* explores Arthur's choice of Mordred as lieutenant in much greater detail than the chronicle sources. The poet carefully obscures any hints that Mordred might be a poor choice. In Layamon, with the first mention of Mordred, the poet curses him as "forcuþest monnen," noting that "treouþe nafde he nane . to nauer nane monne."[20] Our poet's Mordred is a good man, mild of speech and conscientious. He is loyal to Arthur and worried about his ability to bear the burden of so large a responsibility, wondering if Arthur might not be wiser to choose some more warlike man. If there is an identifiable fault in the choice it lies in Arthur's insistence that Mordred take the job, want it or not. Aquinas, in keeping with Boethius' notion of right rule and proper domain, warns that the tyrant who seeks his own private good at the expense of his citizens is the worst of all rulers.[21] Similarly, Dante argues that a good king is one who guarantees the free choices of his people, mankind being at its best when it is most free.[22] Arthur is careless of Mordred's prerogatives, announcing publicly his choice of "me sybb, my syster son, Sir Mordrede hym seluen, / Sall be my leuetenaunte" (645–46), even before speaking to Mordred. Arthur presumes upon his kinship. The sources avoid mentioning Mordred's kinship to Arthur at this point. They would obscure the blood tie, if possible, for it seems embarrassing. Our poet stresses it, for it seems honorable.

Mordred addresses Arthur as "my sybbe lorde" (681), and Arthur replies:

> Thowe arte my neuewe full nere, my nurrée of olde,
> That I haue chastyede and chosen, a childe of my chambyre;
> (689–90)

and "for the sybredyn of me" (691) insists that Mordred undertake the task. Mordred's desire to be excused of the charge should not be taken as hypocrisy. Arthur's insistence demands scrutiny, however, for his threats leave Mordred no choice:

> . . . foresake noghte þis offyce;
> That thow ne wyrk my will, thow watte whatte it menes.
> (691–92)

It is the first time Arthur has acted arbitrarily in the poem or been willfully highhanded. But although Arthur's aggressiveness might be disturbing in an assessment of his personal wisdom, it seems in keeping with his regal power, and the poet does not question it here. There will be other acts more willful before we learn the shortcomings of this present judgment. Though Arthur's insistence is arbitrary, from the evidence the poet offers we must conclude at this point that Arthur's choice of his kinsman was sound.

On behalf of Arthur's judgment, we might note the explicitness with which he instructs his lieutenant in his powers and obligations (none of these details occurs in the chronicles): Mordred is to have complete authority throughout Arthur's lands. He must also look after Gaynor to see that she lacks nothing "þat hire lykes" (653). He must attend the king's personal estates, keep his castles well equipped, and make appointments ("ordayne thy seluen") of chancellors, chamberlains, auditors, judges, and other officers according to his own judgment—"chaunge as þe lykes" (660). He should act justly under God, he should look after the treasury, and in the event of Arthur's death, he should be king. Or, if Arthur should return safely, then Arthur will make Mordred his heir,

When I to contré come, if Cryste will it thole;
And thow haue grace gudly to gouerne thy seluen,
I sall coroune þe, knyghte, kyng with my handez.

(676–78)

These are powerful promises by Arthur. He is to be commended for his guidelines, though his constraint of Mordred's will to the office, then the giving him such unrestrained liberties within that office, are perhaps questionable.

A portion of the departure scene is devoted to Arthur's farewell to Gaynor. It also is original with our author and contributes to our perception of Arthur's governance. Gaynor is presented as a loving person, but one who is fearful and generally weak. Arthur reassures her by reminding her that she has in the past "mekyll praysede" (711) Mordred and that he "sall be thy dictour . . . to doo whatte the lykes" (711–12). The dramatic irony of the passage is poignant, not only for Arthur, but Mordred and Gaynor as well. At this crucial moment the poet gives the first hint that all may not be well. As Arthur leaves, Gaynor swoons, and we are told: "cho sees hym no more" (720). The half-line's closed syntax creates a disconcerting sense of finality and leaves us wondering what wonders might arise to prevent Arthur's happy return.

The next hint which calls into question Arthur's decision occurs as he sleeps in his boat and dreams of the dragon and the bear. The philosophers who accompany Arthur assure him that the dragon signifies himself and that he will destroy the bear, that is, some tyrant or giant, who torments his people. They ignore, however, that part of the dream which says that the dragon "come dryfande ouer þe depe to drenschen hys pople" (761). The dream seems to suggest the possibility that Arthur might destroy his own. We tend to forget the phrase, however, for even though Arthur seems momentarily in the hands of fortune as his boat floats on the water, he soon lands safely and the meaning of the dream as the philosophers glossed it unfolds. "A grett geaunte of Geen, engenderde of fendez" (843) torments Arthur's people, and he rescues them.

The poet takes pains to present Arthur as a model Christian king in the encounter with the giant. He heightens the religious implications of the conquest, by making the giant specialize in devouring "fawntekyns" and Christian maidens. In the chronicles the giant is simply a rapist who is swiftly dispensed with by a combined effort of Sir Bedevere, Sir Kay, and Arthur. The issues in the *Morte Arthure* are entirely different. As Arthur undertakes the task "by my selfe one" (937) and "for rewthe of þe pople" (888), his quest has overtones of a religious mission. He arms himself ceremonially[23] and sets Sir Bedevere and Sir Kay to pray. The giant, with his kirtle "bordyrde with the berdez of bur-lyche kyngez" (1002), is the epitome of willful usurpation. The "wafull wedowe" (950), who tells Arthur of the giant's crimes, typifies those bereft by the usurper. The giant wants Arthur's beard, and, to pass the time until he gets it, sups on "seuen knaue childre, / Choppid in a chargour . . . with pekill and powdyre of precious spycez, / And pyment full plenteuous of Portyngale wynes" (1025–28), then rapes to death the serving girls. He does not even have enough manners to sit up when he eats, but luxuri-ously lolls "lenand on lang" (1045), warming his bare backside at the fire as he crunches on a man's thigh.

The ensuing battle is a *tour de force* of alliterative excitement and comic grotesquerie. The giant lands the first blow, striking Arthur on the crest. The king is undaunted, however, for his strength lies not in earthly symbols but in "þe crafte of Cryste" (1107). He uses his wits, gets under the monster's guard, and stabs him through the brain. Unfortunately, the brain seems to be no vital organ in this fiend, for the blow scarcely fazes him. Ar-thur's next blow is more lethal as he hits "Iust to þe genitales and jaggede þam in sondre" (1123). That makes the sex-fiend roar and thrash fiercely. So Arthur stays in close and

Swappez in with the swerde þat it þe swang brystedd;
Bothe þe guttez and the gor guschez owte at ones,
Þat all englaymes þe gresse one grounde þer he standez.
(1129–31)

This provokes the giant to throw away his club, embrace Arthur in his deadly grip, and wrestle him all the way down the hill onto the flood marshes. Arthur finally slays him with his dagger, which, as Finlayson observes, probably signifies "trust in God,"[24] while the not yet raped (and thus still living) maidens pray that Christ keep Arthur from sorrow. Though Sir Kay and Sir Bedevere fear the king is lost, when they finally pry him from the monster's death grip he has only three broken ribs.

None of these details is found in the chronicles.[25] The point of their invention (besides their comic violence, so artfully maintained throughout the passage) is perhaps twofold. First, they dramatize the ideal Christian prince in his struggle to defend his people against the willful aggression of evil tyrants. Arthur has fought alone, but not on his own:

"it was [he says] neuer manns dede, bot myghte of Hym selfen,
Or myracle of Hys Modyr, þat mylde es till all."

(1210–11)

He shares the glory of the event with the people as he "Cristenly carpez" with them, distributes the giant's treasure to the "comouns of the countré" (1215), keeping only the kirtle for himself, and commands a church to be built on the crag to commemorate the martyred duchess. There is a second effect produced by the passage, however, which cannot be recognized until the later part of the poem when Arthur himself becomes a tyrant and "turmentez þe pople" (3153), "wroghte wedewes full wlonke wrotherayle synges" (3154), "stroyene for evere" their cities (3127), and "spoylles dispetouslye" 3159) the countryside. There Arthur's activities remind us of the giant of Gene, and we wonder if Arthur has not, after all, added his beard to the usurper's aegis. Perhaps the one relic he claimed after the battle reflects even so soon in the poem an incipient overreaching. Likewise, the giant's first blow to his crest, though incidental in the battle, perhaps anticipated the blow Arthur's truly kingly nature suffers when he gives way to willfulness. The image of Arthur locked in the

monster's death grip perhaps prefigures what is in store for Arthur should he stop fighting to defend the innocent in the name of
God in order to seek revenge by his "awen strenghe" (2472).
Then he becomes victim of his own tyrannical acts and ends up
comparing himself to the "wafull wedowe" (4285) rather than
the saintlike victor.

But those events are far away from the scene where Arthur,
with good Christian intent, slays the Giant of Gene. That he himself might become tyrannical has been scarcely suggested. Certainly he is guilty of no actions which would qualify as "shames-
dedes." During the early conduct of the war Arthur continues to
behave like a responsible leader. The question of right judgment
and just cause as opposed to willful action the poet centers
around the headstrong Sir Cador. Charged with the responsibility
of conveying prisoners to Arthur in Paris, Sir Cador sidesteps his
mission in order to win glory against unfavorable odds. His recklessness costs him several of his best knights. When he reports
to Arthur, the king is grieved:

> Sir Cador, thi corage confundez vs all!
> Kowardely thow castez owtte all my beste knyghttez.
>
> (1922–23)

Sir Cador defends himself boldly against the scolding—"Karpe
whatte ʒow lykys" (1929)—and reprimands Arthur for criticizing
him after he has faced danger doing his "delygens todaye"
(1934) on the king's behalf.

Arthur does not emerge from the dispute very well. His authority seems shaken, and he himself confused about what constitutes virtuous behavior. One of Arthur's most attractive qualities
is his great love and loyalty to his men. But it is also his point of
weakness. When Cador questions that love, Arthur reverses his
position and gives him complete endorsement. He goes even further. In a flood of affection he names Cador and his children to
be his heir. In his loving outburst Arthur seems to forget his
larger office. In promising the kingdom to Cador, he

thoughtlessly breaks his pledge to his forgotten kinsman Mordred. Arthur has no reason to believe that Mordred is not performing his "delygens" at home. If he did suspect infidelity he would be obliged to return home to set the matter straight. In his eagerness to appease Sir Cador, he breaks faith with his lieutenant. War deeds matter more than peaceful commitments. The battlefield usurps the rights of home.

Though Arthur's judgment as king has been seriously compromised at this juncture, his greatness as conqueror grows more luminous. The poet delights in showing what a clever military leader the king is. Arthur tricks Lucius into attacking him from a disadvantageous position. When his own men need support he backs them vigorously, nobly confronting the giant Golopas, whom he cuts down to size by lopping off his legs. Arthur's personal entrance into the fray sets the Romans to flight. But it is here that the turning point of the poem occurs. Here, at the poem's exact center, Sir Kay receives his deathblow: "At þe turnyng that tym the traytoure hym hitte" (2173). Kay is the first of the men really close to the king to be slain. The poet takes what had been a passing reference in the chronicles and turns it into his crux. The "turnyng that tym" makes all the difference to Arthur. Mortally wounded, Sir Kay "weyndes to þe wyese kyng and wynly hym gretes" (2185). He asks for fitting burial and requests that he be remembered to the queen, the "burliche birdes" of court, and his "worthily weife, þat wrethide me neuer" (2191). His recollection of the English court adds a domestic poignancy, reminding us of the homeland which they are theoretically defending. Arthur, in his great love of his men, is enraged over Kay's death, and thinks more of revenging the dead man than heeding his dying words. He swiftly defeats Lucius (though not without losing Sir Bedevere, his cup-bearer), and gives vent to his wrath by refusing ransom to his enemies, whom he mercilessly slaughters so that "Sir Kayous dede be cruelly vengede" (2264). He ships the corpses of Lucius and his senators to Rome in lieu of the tribute they had demanded—"assaye how hym likes!" (2347)—along with an announcement that the war the

Romans wanted will now come to Rome—"be ware ȝif ȝow
lykes" (2370). In his anger, Arthur would ram their willfulness
down their throats.[26]

It is noteworthy that the poet interrupts his narrative at this
point to announce the date of the victory:

> In the kalendez of Maye this caas es befallen;
> The roy ryalle renownde, with his Rownde Table,
> One the coste of Costantyne, by þe clere strandez,
> Has þe Romaynes ryche rebuykede for euer.
>
> (2371–74)

Arthur has his victory.[27] The rhetorical finality of the passage
demarcates a major section of the plot. From this juncture Arthur
fights in what he chooses to think of as his own cause. That
cause is not a return home, but a seeking of revenge.

The second half of the poem differs from the first in subtle
shifts in tone and kind of events. Where in the first we had a
series of episodes in which Arthur exercised judgment, we now
have a sequence of progressively vain actions marked by lack of
judgment. After his victory over Lucius, instead of returning with
his kingdom intact, Arthur calls a war council. This council contrasts sharply with the council at Carlisle when he began his
foreign campaign. Here, instead of listening to his counselors and
weighing what they say against his own understanding of causes,
he "karpes in the concell" and "comandez them" what to think
(2392ff.). He says he has heard of a knight "that I haue cowayte
to knawe" (2397), whose lovely lands he would like for himself:
"I will that ducherye devyse and dele as me lykes" (2400). His
motive seems more like that of the tyrant Lucius than a just ruler.

In the first half of the poem, when knights became reckless,
Arthur cautioned them. Now the situation is reversed: Arthur becomes the reckless one, to the consternation of his knights. In the
siege of Metz, Sir Ferrer cautions Arthur against the "foly"
(2432) of fighting without armor so near the walls. Arthur's
nakedness before the wall might be interpreted in several ways:
first, as a sign of his recklessness;[28] second, as a sign of his ne-

glecting to put on God's armor as he had done when he fought the Giant of Gene; and third, as an indication of his lack of regard for his own men, whom he now slightingly calls "gadlynges" (2443). Outraged at Sir Ferrer's suggestion, Arthur mocks him as a "fawntkyn" who will be "flayede for a flye þat on thy flesche lyghttes" (2441). There was a time when Arthur defended "fawntekyns." Now that term becomes one of derision. Scorning Sir Ferrer as a coward, he boasts his own fearlessness—"I am nothyng agaste" (2442). Ironically, it is just now that Arthur begins to have something to fear. His greatest recklessness lies not in his prancing before the wall "sengely in thy surcotte" (2434), but in his attitude toward himself. His crown, instead of signifying his reverence, constancy, good name, and common domain,[29] becomes an excuse, a privilege which he thinks sets him apart from the common lot. "Sall neuer harlotte haue happe . . . to kyll a corownde kyng with krysom enoynttede!" (2446–47), he boasts. That is one bit of political philosophy which fourteenth-century Englishmen knew to be patently false. Fortune is no respecter of vaunted anointments.

As the Battle of Metz gets underway, Arthur, for the first time in the poem, fails to accomplish his will. In contrast to the fight with the Giant of Gene, where Arthur fought with the strength of God, he tries to win this one on his own. Though his army breaks down the gate and almost secures a garrison "be theire awen strenghe" (2472), they are forced to retreat. Instead of victory they settle for a siege. The battle at Metz is not mentioned in the chronicles, which direct Arthur south through Burgundy. By having Arthur turn east to conquer lands along the way, the poet emphasizes Arthur's growing ambition. The episode becomes a symbol of vanity, as Arthur lays siege to the cities of the world while neglecting his own land.

As commentary on the emptiness of Arthur's aggression, the poet inserts into the middle of the episode the interlude of Gawain and Priamus. Finlayson has noted that the interlude has the markings of a *chanson d'aventure*, as Gawain, to pass the time during the siege, sets out "wondyrs to seke" (2514).[30] The *chanson d'aventure* formula was popular among fourteenth-century English writers who, in their concern over disintegration of social and political values, found the blame in the willful behavior of men seeking their fortune.[31] Like other poems of this kind, the Priamus interlude calls attention to the will wandering in Fortune's domain, and suggests the need for behavior accountable to truths beyond Fortune. Both Priamus and Gawain are fortune hunters. After wounding each other, they discover that they must rely on each other's help if either is to recover. The cure is dramatically ironic as we think ahead to Arthur's wound by his kinsman, a wound for which he finds no cure.

Following this vignette of mutual dependence, the poet shifts back to the capture of Metz, emphasizing the satisfaction Arthur gets in his victory:

> Thus in Lorayne he lenges, as lorde in his awen,
> Settez lawes in the land, as hym leefe thoghte.
> And one þe Lammese Day to Lucerne he wendez,
> Lengez thare at laysere with lykyng inowe.
>
> (3092–95)

Arthur's actions have become a kind of idleness, a self-indulgent lingering. He thinks he is increasing his possessions, but in truth he is calling things by their wrong names. As he sets laws according to his pleasure, what he is really changing is his own definition of king. In becoming a tyrant, he dispossesses himself. With his true country abandoned, he is less "lorde in his awen" than he imagines. Nor can he expect much love from the woeful widows.

With each new conquest Arthur *thinks* he is greater, though his actions prove increasingly vain. The poet dramatizes his swelling vanity by inventing a scene on top of Mount Goddard, from which Arthur contemplates Lombardy stretched at his feet:

> When he was passede the heghte, than the Kyng houys
> With his hole bataylle, behaldande abowte,
> Lukand one Lumbarddye, and one lowde melys,
> "In ȝone lykand londe, lorde be I thynke."
>
> (3106–9)

Would that thinking could make it so. Recall Petrarch's famous letter describing his ascent of Mont Ventoux, where the vastness of the scene reminded him that the world is vanity and that his proper study should be the maintaining of his soul.[32] Our poet's point is similar: the prospect is an epitome of surquidry, as Arthur, lacking Petrarch's insight, imagines himself lord of that vast domain.

The Italian battles that ensue are even more reckless than the siege of Metz. When Arthur first set out for Rome after his victory of Sessoine, he vowed not to attack church properties. Now he plunders at will, church and countryside alike. The poet emphasizes Arthur's dissipation as he revels ''with riche wyne'' and

> . . . riotes hym selfen,
> This roy with his ryall men of þe Rownde Table,
> With mirthis and melodye and manykyn gamnes—
> Was neuer meriere men made on this erthe!
>
> (3172–75)

Arthur's joy is indeed presumptuous, for by this time he has cause to be the saddest man on earth. As he presses on, the ''konyngeste cardynall'' of Rome approaches him, hoping to stop the onslaught by promising Arthur the crown and all rites on Sunday eight days hence. That prospect boosts Arthur's joy to a new pinnacle as he gloats: ''Now may we reuell and riste, fore Rome es oure awen'' (3207). In his imagination he sets the coronation on Christmas day. His choice of date juxtaposes his wish with the Christmas festivity at the outset of the poem where Arthur, in his splendor at home, had assembled his counselors to consider their defense against Lucius. Somehow that court, which had seemed so magnificent, has become pale and forgotten. Rome gets its tribute from England after all, as Arthur imagines how he will dwell there and

> Ryngne in my ryalltés, and holde my Rownde Table,
> Withe the rentes of Rome, as me beste lykes.
>
> (3214–15)

The vanity of his aspiration might be compared to that of Char-
lemagne in the *Chanson de Roland*, with his hopes of being
crowned in Saragossa. Like that other worthy, Arthur is seeking
the wrong city. The poet clinches Arthur's megalomania with the
fantasy that after his coronation he will then retake Jerusalem,
"to reuenge the Renke that on the Rode dyede" (3217). Arthur
would not only rule the world; he would undertake God's task as
well.

The placing of Arthur's second dream immediately after his
plan to avenge God undercuts the heroics of Arthur's wondrous
fantasy. The review of the nine worthies is not a catalogue of
heroic achievements. Rather, it is an emblem of Fortune's
fools.[33] Fortune lures Arthur to his place atop the wheel by appealing to his desires, then whirls the wheel and destroys him. Such
is the tragedy of Fortune, as a man of high estate falls to wretchedness. But that fall, as Fortune describes it,[34] is only a surface
aspect of the real tragedy. The real loss began when Arthur
stopped defending his homeland and willfully sought possessions
that were not his own. His exile appears metaphorically in the
dream as a wilderness entangled by vines and filled with wolves,
swine, and other beasts which devour his knights. That wood is a
place of his own making: "Me thoughte I was in a wode willed
myn one" (3230). The philosophers who gloss the dream leave
no doubt about its meaning:

> Thow has schedde myche blode and schalkes distroyede,
> Sakeles, in cirquytrie, in sere kynges landis.
> Schryfte the of thy schame and schape for thyn ende;
> Thow has a schewynge, Sir Kynge—*take kepe ȝif the lyke;*
> For thow sall fersely fall . . . *þe froytez are theyn awen.*
>   (3398–3403; italics mine)

Rather than "vertous lywynge" (see lines 3–5), Arthur's conquest turns out to be "schamesdede." His fate is the fruit of his
own willful behavior, but the tragedy lies in his misunderstanding
of his proper domain. His geographical displacement is simply a
manifestation of his psychological disorder.

Immediately following the dream, Arthur learns of the rebellion in England. In the chronicles the informer is not named.[35] Our poet identifies him as Sir Craddok, "kepare of Karlyon" (3512), and makes a pilgrim of him. Caerleon, which Arthur established "be assentte of his lordys" (60) at the beginning of the poem, is an emblem of peace, the gift of a generous king to his people. Its abandonment by its keeper reflects the situation of all England, which has been abandoned by Arthur. That the keeper is an outcast is commentary on the lack of good government at home. That he is a pilgrim to Rome suggests that there might be other reasons for seeking that city besides conquest. Although Craddok was knight of Arthur's own chamber and says, "Me awghte to knowe þe Kynge: he es my kydde lorde" (3509), he fails to recognize Arthur behind all his "riche wedys" (3493). His failure to know his lord is more a commentary on Arthur than it is on Craddok. The Arthur he knew has become unrecognizable.

The conclusion to the *Morte Arthure* differs from the chronicles in several ways, but especially in the poet's treatment of Mordred and Gawain. The highly original presentation of these two vassals provides, as did the Craddok episode, a commentary on Arthur unique to this poem. The poet's sympathetic treatment of Mordred defies one of the strongest traditions in the whole of the Arthurian canon. We have seen how Mordred was presented at the outset as a dutiful though somewhat put upon kinsman. We also noted that Arthur breaks his pledge to Mordred by naming Cador his heir. None of this excuses Mordred, of course, when he betrays Arthur's trust, marries Gaynor, "corownde hym seluen" (3525), and "haldys his awen" (3541). Nevertheless, he is no simple villain. Only once does the poet call him "traytoure be tresone" (3782); the more common label is "Sir Mordrede the Malebranche" (4062, 4174), a title that reflects as much on Arthur, his progenitor, as it does upon Mordred. Mordred's loving care for Gaynor seems to be based on mutual affection. Not only do they marry, but they also have children, a detail found in neither of the chronicles. And, as Matthews notes, there is no precedent for his letter of concern to Gaynor, after Arthur attacks.[36] His most sympathetic treatment occurs, however, at that very moment when we might expect the poet to reprehend him, at the slaying of Sir Gawain. Mordred kills Gawain in self-defense and is immediately filled with remorse. When King Frederick asks the identity of the fierce opponent, Mordred laments:

> "He was makles one molde, mane, be my trowthe;
> This was Sir Gawayne the gude, þe gladdeste of othire,
> And the graciouseste gome that vndire God lyffede,
> Mane hardyeste of hande, happyeste in armes,
> And þe hendeste in hawle vndire heuen riche,
> Þe lordelieste of ledyng qwhylls he lyffe myghte,
> Fore he was lyone allossede in londes inewe;
> Had thow knawen hym, Sir Kyng, in kythe thare he lengede,
> His konynge, his knyghthode, his kyndly werkes,
> His doyng, his doughtynesse, his dedis of armes,
> Thow wolde hafe dole for his dede þe dayes of thy lyfe."
>
> (3875–85)

Perhaps one way the poet thinks to praise Gawain is by putting his eulogy in the mouth of his enemy, but the speech goes far beyond praise. Its deep-felt statement of personal loss is an insight into brotherhood as profound as any Arthur himself arrives at. As Mordred turns weeping from the fray, he curses not Arthur, but rather the time "þat euer his werdes ware wroghte siche wandrethe to wyrke" (3889). Sighing for his "sybb blode," he leaves the battle, pierced to his heart with remorseful remembrance of the joyous Round Table. He avoids Arthur as best he can, but finally is trapped, wounded by Sir Marrock, and then slain by Arthur, who cuts off his hand, an inch from the elbow, and, after Mordred faints, impales him through the vent in his armor. The literary effect of such grisly details is markedly different from those gory alliterative quatrains when Arthur slew the Giant of Gene or the Giant Golopas. There is small joy in Arthur's victory over Mordred, his son.

Perhaps the poet's positive treatment of Mordred stems from

his desire to associate him with his kinsman Sir Gawain, who is
in some ways, like Mordred and Sir Craddok, an unwitting victim of Arthur's willfulness. All three of these vassals end up
stranded in England by an absent Arthur, though Gawain, like
Mordred, is as well a victim of his own choices. The chronicles
give little attention to Gawain's death. We are merely told that he
is slain while establishing the beachhead. Our poet greatly en-
larges the scene, making it the crux in Arthur's defeat. After
winning a stunning sea victory, Gawain succeeds in landing a
small troop. Though he fights against overwhelming odds, he secures a "grene hill" (3768) which, we are told, he might have
maintained had he sat tight—"he had wirchipe, iwys, wonnen for
euer" (3769). But Gawain sees Mordred among the enemy, and
his desire for revenge overcomes him. With a "grete wyll"
(3774) he charges. As his men become entangled and slain, Gawain becomes increasingly desperate. The poet emphasizes his
madness: seeing his men destroyed, "what for wondire and woo,
all his witte faylede" (3793); "alls vnwyse, wodewyse, he
wente at þe gayneste" (3817); "his reson was passede. / He fell
in a fransye for fersenesse of herte" (3825–26); "hedlyngs he
rynys" (3829). The poet compares him to a lion:

Alls he þat wold wilfully wasten hym selfen;
And for wondsom and will all his wit failede,
That wode alls a wylde beste he wente at þe gayneste.

(3835–37)

He then draws a moral exemplum: "Iche a wy may be warre be
wreke of anoþer" (3839). The epitome functions in two ways.
First, Gawain is literally self-destroyed as he throws himself upon
the fallen Mordred. His folly anticipates Arthur's own wild encounter with Mordred where the king, blind to the warning which
the poet saw dramatically implicit in Gawain's death (3839),
rushes to his own mortal wound. Second, if we think of reason as
man's kingly part, Gawain dies in a state without a king. The
poet embellishes the idea by leaving the king literally at sea. In

the chronicles Arthur is fighting on shore at the time of Gawain's death. Our poet deliberately separates them, as if to create an emblem of headlessness.

It is the pattern of Boethian philosophical tragedy that the hero-victim becomes progressively isolated. Not only does his willfulness make him victim of Fortune, but it also removes him from the security of his rightful place. We have seen Gawain and Mordred die in isolation. The most desolate scene of all, however, is Arthur's death. The poem's conclusion is a study in barrenness. The poet has deliberately removed from the story all references to Merlin and his faery world, which were so prominent in the chronicles. There is no prophetic hope of a world beyond or a world to come which will make all things right. There is only Arthur, a "wafull wedowe" amidst a field of corpses. Much of the sadness at the end lies in the fact that Arthur, for all his destructiveness and ambition, is a great warrior with a profound love of his men. The two moments which shape his fate most decisively are the deaths of his loved ones, Sir Kay and Sir Gawain. The poet fixes our attention on this sympathetic quality in Arthur during the last battle, when Arthur, seeing Ewain in trouble, tells Idrus (Ewain's son) to go help his father. Idrus refuses, saying that his father had instructed him not to depart from Arthur's side under any circumstance. Overwhelmed with compassion Arthur cries out:

"Qwythen hade Dryghttyn destaynede at his dere will,
Þat he hade demyd me todaye to dy for ȝow all."
(4157–58)

He would rather die for his men than have for a lifetime all the lands Alexander conquered (4159–60). The problem is that Arthur's deeply felt love, though noble, is only part of what is required of a good king. It may be a heroic gesture to destroy oneself for the sake of a loved one, but it is not the mark of a good leader. Without kingly governance of the will, all the deep compassion comes to grief.

Sorrow is a forgetting, says Lady Philosophy.[37] In his grief

over Gawain's death Arthur equates Gawain with his own suf-
ficaunce (see 3956–60, where Arthur equates Gawain with "my
wirchipe," "hope of my hele," "my herte and my hardynes,"
and "my concell, my comforthe, þat kepide myn herte"). Filled
with self-hatred, he feels dispossessed: "I am vttirly vndon in myn
awen landes" (3966). But a good king must be in full possession
of himself. The incipience of Arthur's dispossession goes back
clearly to his departure from England, where his naming of his
lieutenant and heir was as much an act of will as tact. His personal security later becomes threatened when, in his exchange
with Sir Cador, he forgets his own good counsel and, in response
to Cador's declaration that he was fighting for Arthur, somewhat
sentimentally makes him his heir. Repeatedly thereafter, Arthur
ignores good counsel in the illusion of brotherhood, all the while
losing his good men. Like Gawain, who had a choice of whether
to stay on his hill or willfully attack his "sybb blode," Arthur is
given one last opportunity to choose his fate, as Sir Wichere advises him to call a council. But Arthur is determined in his revenge. It is ironic that in destroying Mordred, Arthur finds no
peace, only corpses. "A traytoure has tynte all my trewe lordys"
(4281), he laments. But the question of who has done the betraying is not easily answered.

The dying Arthur goes to Glastonbury, where a surgeon of
Salerne "enserches his wondes" (4311), but no cure can be
found. Lady Philosophy observes, "Yif thou abidest after help of
thi leche, the byhoveth discovre thy wownde."[38] The bottom of
Arthur's wound eludes "discovery." Unlike the Priamus scene,
where the enemies discovered that they were really brothers, Arthur leaves no enemies alive. After disposing of Mordred, he
calls his confessor, forgives Gaynor, and dies—but not until he
sends out men to destroy Mordred's children. The slaughter of
the children is perhaps his most empty act of all, for they are the
closest blood kin he has. Having slain his only son, he now slays
his grandchildren. R. M. Lumiansky has suggested that Arthur
regains the magnanimity, courage, and magnificence of "Christ's
knight" at the end of the poem.[39] I find it difficult to see much
fortitude in his behavior. Though he searches his wound, despite

his prayer of victory and his *In manus*, he fails to see very deeply into it. His fate is about as wretched as it can be. Instead of invoking the "once and future king" epitaph, the poet directs our attention the other way, tracing Arthur's lineage back to Troy and "Ectores blude."[40] The allusion hearkens back to the dream of Fortune's wheel with its unflattering description of Hector. Such a conclusion goes deliberately against the courtly propaganda of the time which would see the royalty of England as being descended from Arthur and claiming a glory that goes all the way back to Troy. Instead, the tone, like that of other late fourteenth-century English poems, looks upon the myth of Trojan descent as a dubious honor, the tale of a city destroyed by its own folly. One part of the conclusion's starkness lies in the fact that we as audience have, like Gawain and even Mordred, found a nobility and grandeur in Arthur, his loyalties, and his aspirations. That has all been destroyed at the end of the poem, where we find a bereft community of dignitaries and ladies "buskede in blake" (4339) putting Arthur in the ground and weeping at the tomb: "whas neuer so sorowfull a syghte seen in theire tym" (4341). Another part of the starkness lies in the Boethian reasoning whereby we see that Arthur, whom we have loved and by whom we have been thrilled, shaped his own fate. The wonder we are left with at the end is not that of a world glossed by Merlin, or embellished by some redemptive virtue. The wonder is the bleak scene itself.

NOTES

1. All quotations from the poem are taken from *The Alliterative Morte Arthur*, ed. Valerie Krishna (New York, 1976), and will be identified in the context of the argument by line number only.
2. *Confessio Amantis*, Prol. 546–49 (cf. Prol. 528 and 905), ed. G. C. Macaulay, in *English Works of John Gower* (1900; rpt. Oxford, 1975), I, 19–20.
3. The motif of right rule and good governance runs throughout the treatise, but see I, pr. 5, for discussion of sovereign rule of one's true country, and III, pr. 10, to the end of Book III on the happiness of a self-possessed and well-governed mind. All references to the *Consolation of Philosophy* are

based on Chaucer's translation, *The Works of Chaucer*, ed. F. N. Robinson, 2d ed. (Boston, 1957).

4. On the importance of self-knowledge, see I, pr. 6; and on true and false possessions, see II, pr. 5–pr. 7. On the *summum bonum*, see esp. III, pr. 10–pr. 12.

5. *Vox Clamantis,* II, iv, 203–8, *The Latin Works of John Gower,* ed. G. C. Macaulay, *Complete Works* (Oxford, 1902), IV, 90:

> Set sibi quisque suam sortem facit, et sibi casum
> Vt libet incurrit, et sibi fata creat;
> Atque voluntatis mens libera quod facit actum
> Pro variis meritis nomine sortis habet.
> Debet enim semper sors esse pedisseca mentis,
> Ex qua sortitur quod sibi nomen erit.

6. I, pr. 5, lines 4–16. I do not mean to imply that the *Morte Arthure* poet knew Chaucer's specific translation, only that he would probably have understood Boethius' ideas in somewhat the same way that Chaucer did.

7. II, pr. 2, II, 67–72. Chaucer's Monk offers a variation on the definition in his prologue, *Canterbury Tales*, Frag. VII, lines 1973–77.

8. *Mum and the Sothsegger*. Prol. 52, ed. Mabel Day and Robert Steele, EETS 199 (1936), 2. See the opening epithet to this essay.

9. William Matthews, *The Tragedy of Arthur: A Study of the Alliterative "Morte Arthure"* (Berkeley, 1960), esp. pp. 105–12 and Chap. 5, has explored some of the Boethian influences on the poem, particularly those pertaining to Fortune and world conquest. Matthews does not devote attention to questions of will, however.

10. A cursory survey of English literature of this period shows the will or willfulness to be a dominant topic in dream visions like *Piers Plowman*, Gower's *Confessio Amantis*, Usk's *Testament of Love*, and Chaucer's *Parlement of Foules*, which study the peregrinations of the will; in literature of good-counsel like *Pearl*, the *Tale of Melibee*, and the *Book of the Duchess*, which explore the debate between will and reason; in political satires like Gower's *Tripartite Chronicle, Mum and the Sothsegger*, and the *Complaint of the Plowman*, which name willfulness as chief cause of man's confusion; and in the extensive literature in the *chanson d'aventure* vein, where wonders begin as the will starts its wandering in the realm of Fortune. In fact a case might be argued that the prominence of the *chanson d'aventure* literature at the end of the fourteenth century may be attributable to that period's preoccupation with the workings and efficacy of the will. The nature and power of the will had been the principal topic of theologians at Oxford for the previous two generations.

11. References to Wace and Layamon in my subsequent discussion are based on

Le Roman de Brut de Wace, ed. Ivor Arnold, SATF, 2 vols. (Paris, 1938), and *Laȝamon's Brut, or Chronicle of Britain*, ed. Sir Frederic Madden, 3 vols. (1847; rpt. Osnabrück, 1967), and will be noted by line reference only.

12. *Morte Arthure*, ed. John Finlayson, York Medieval Texts (London, 1967), p. 12. See n. 14, which cites Lull's *Orde de Cauayleria* (ca. 1311), trans. William Caxton, *The Book of the Order of Chyualry*, ed. A. T. P. Byles, EETS 168 (1926); Honoré Bonet's *Arbre des Batailles* (ca. 1387), trans. Sir Gilbert Hay, *The Buke of the Law of Armys* (1456), ed. J. H. Stevenson, STS 44, 62 (1901, 1914), and Christine de Pisan's *Les Faits d'Armes* (1408–9), trans. Caxton, *Fayttes of Armes and of Chyualrye*, ed. A. T. P. Byles, EETS 189 (1937).

13. *Tragedy of Arthur*, pp. 105ff. See also Finlayson, *Morte Arthure*, pp. 14ff., and Robert M. Lumiansky, "The Alliterative *Morte Arthure*, the Concept of Medieval Tragedy, and the Cardinal Virtue Fortitude," *Medieval and Renaissance Studies: Proceedings of the Southeastern Institute of Medieval and Renaissance Studies*, ed. John M. Headly (Chapel Hill, N.C., 1967), pp. 97ff.

14. See Wace, 10207–36, and Layamon, 24623ff., for accounts of Caerleon's well-established prestige.

15. See *De Regno* II.2 (I.13), para. 99–101. *On Kingship: To the King of Cyprus*, trans. Gerald B. Phelan; rev. I. Th. Eschmann (Toronto, 1949), pp. 56–57.

16. In both Wace and Layamon, the feast is at Whitsuntide and at Caerleon where Arthur has come, as Layamon says, because he would "have his crune him on" (24246). Both Wace and Layamon devote several hundred lines to the splendor of the city and the grandeur of the festivity. The point is that Caerleon is "ricchere þan Rome" and the Usk more pleasant than the Tiber.

17. *The Book of Fayttes of Armes and of Chyvalrye*, trans. William Caxton, EETS 189 (1937), p. 13. Perhaps a better example of good counsel regarding war would be Dame Prudence's advice to Melibee.

18. See St. Thomas Aquinas, *De Regno* II, iv (I, 15) para. 120, on the ruler's primary obligation in carefully choosing replacements in public office.

19. E.g., in *Sir Orfeo* (another poem with strong Boethian influences), King Orfeo chooses his steward so well that the steward rules honorably in Orfeo's name until the king returns; Lycurgus, in Book VII of the *Confessio Amantis*, creates laws so true to the needs of the people and "the comun good" (VII, 2930) that Athens lives at peace long after Lycurgus disappears.

20. *Brut*, ed. Madden, III, 9. Wace is less blunt, calling Mordred a "chevalier merveillus e pruz" (11174), but noting that he is not a man of "bone fei." He then undertakes a diatribe against the evils Mordred and the queen will soon do.

21. *De Regno*, I, iii.

22. *De Monarchia* I, xii, *Tutte Le Opere di Dante*, ed. Fredi Chiappelli (Milan, 1965), pp. 738–40.

23. Ramon Lull drew parallels between the knight's arming and a priest's clothing himself with symbolic vestments, and attributed religious meaning to each piece of armor. See *The Book of the Order of Chyvalry*, trans. by William Caxton from a French version of *Le Libre del Ordre de Cauayleria*, ed. Alfred T. P. Byles, EETS 168 (1926), pp. 76–89.

24. Finlayson, *Morte Arthure*, p. 18. See Lull, p. 81.

25. There is an old woman in the chronicles who directs Sir Bedevere to the giant. She has been forced into being the giant's mistress after the giant killed the young duchess. The old woman is not presented as a widow, however, nor does she speak to Arthur of the collection of beards. The battle narrative is entirely different.

26. Larry D. Benson, ''The Alliterative *Morte Arthure* and Medieval Tragedy,'' *Tennessee Studies in Literature*, 11 (1966), 77–78, notes that such cruel actions reflect actual tactics of the Hundred Years War and would be admired as sound tactics by many in the poet's courtly audience. While I think that Benson's thesis, that the poem poses tensions between contradictory heroic attitudes within fourteenth-century Christian culture, is essentially correct, that does not mean that the poet endorses the vengeful behavior. Rather he seems sadly aware of the dire consequences induced by such behavior.

27. It is worth noting here that Malory, who draws extensively on the first half of the alliterative *Morte Arthure* in his *Noble Tale of King Arthur that was Emperor Himself through the Dignity of his own Hands* (Book V, Caxton), excludes the slaying of Sir Kay, thus removing Arthur's cause for revenge, and brings Arthur happily home at this point to rule for many years more.

28. If Christine de Pisan, *Book of Fayttes of Armes*, p. 19, can be trusted as authority on military good sense, Sir Ferrer's judgment was sound, for she says no sovereign prince should go into battle ''in his propre persone'' except in civil war, where his presence is then required.

29. See Gower's observations on the symbolic meaning of the crown in *Confessio Amantis*, VII, 1744ff.

30. Finlayson, *Morte Arthure*, p. 18.

31. See note 10.

32. Letter to Father Dionigi da Borgo San Sepolcro, from Malaucène, 26 April 1336.

33. See Matthews' discussion of the worthies, especially Alexander as a figure of vanity, *Tragedy of Arthur*, pp. 32–39.

34. See *Consolation of Philosophy*, II, pr. 2. For discussion of the limitations of Fortune's *de casibus* view of tragedy, see Lumiansky, ''The Alliterative *Morte Arthure*, the Concept of Medieval Tragedy and the Cardinal Virtue Fortitude,'' pp. 97–101, and Monica E. McAlpine, *The Genre of Troilus and Criseyde* (Ithaca, N.Y., 1978), pp. 47–115.

35. Layamon identifies the messenger as "an oht mon riden" (27993). Arthur has his troublesome dream *after* messenger arrives. Instead of a dream of Fortune's wheel, it is the message of the betrayal, which the "oht" man was afraid to tell. In Wace Arthur simply hears about the betrayal and returns to England. No mention is made of a dream.

36. *Tragedy of Arthur*, p. 30.

37. *Consolation of Philosophy*, III, pr. 12, lines 7–8.

38. *Consolation of Philosophy*, I, pr. 4, lines 3–5.

39. "The Alliterative *Morte Arthure*, the Concept of Medieval Tragedy, and the Cardinal Virtue Fortitude," p. 114.

40. Larry D. Benson, ed., *King Arthur's Death* (Indianapolis, 1974), p. 238, emends line 4343 to "Ectores kin," but the MS reading, "Ectores blude," makes better sense.

9

The Awntyrs off Arthure

A. C. SPEARING

I HAVE no new facts to offer about *The Awntyrs off Arthure*, nor even any new theories, except that it is an excellent poem, and one that deserves to be more widely read, now that it is available in two modern editions, those of Robert J. Gates and Ralph Hanna III.[1] Reviewing Hanna's most learned edition[2] provided the germ of this paper, which will be especially concerned with the poem's structure. This aspect of the *Awntyrs* has been almost universally abused by the critics and scholars who have discussed it. Albert C. Baugh writes chillingly that "an adventure of Gawain is loosely combined with a religious theme better known in the *Trental of St. Gregory*."[3] J. L. N. O'Loughlin adds that "The coupling of two such unrelated themes is certainly naïve."[4] George Kane had earlier been more vehement: "Its story is weak and meagre, and scarcely begins to move in the first half of the romance"; and he went on to refer contemptuously to "The thin little thread of narrative."[5] John Speirs praises the poetic art of *The Awntyrs off Arthure* as comparable with that of *Sir Gawain and the Green Knight*, but adds that "It remains a remarkable fragment of the same kind of poetic art, but a fragment only. It consists, as it stands, of two episodes which have not been made into an inclusive whole."[6] The fullest discussion of the *Awntyrs* is that of Ralph Hanna, in his article of 1970[7] and his edition of 1974. Hanna also is dissatisfied with the

poem's structure, so much so indeed that he returns to the theory
put forward by Hermann Lübke in 1883,[8] that the poem we know
as *The Awntyrs off Arthure* in fact consists of two poems, written
by different poets, and loosely stitched together by a not greatly
gifted third compiler. Hanna, partly following Lübke, and partly
offering the results of his own research, produces various kinds
of evidence, especially stylistic and metrical, in favor of the disintegration of the *Awntyrs*; but I think it is reasonable to suppose
that neither he nor Lübke would have set about looking for such
evidence if they had not felt dissatisfied with the poem's
structure—dissatisfied, that is, with the way that it is divided into
two quite separate adventures, the first of which concerns the apparition of Guinevere's mother to Guinevere and Gawain at the
Tarn Wadling, while the second concerns the appearance of Galeron at Arthur's court to demand the return of his lands, the combat between Galeron and Gawain, and the final amicable settle-
ment of the dispute. I do not propose to discuss the question of
authorship, as to which I find Hanna's arguments interesting but
inconclusive. My own view remains that the poem as it stands is
most likely to have had a single author, though he was of course
combining material from several different sources; on the other
hand, I think it still possible that the first adventure was written
by one poet, and that a second then added the second adventure
to it. I find it difficult to envisage the involvement of a third figure, for I would then have to attribute the structural power of
the poem, which I admire greatly, to an author different from
those who were responsible for creating its two parts; and that
third author would have had to be incredibly lucky to find two
existing poems that could be so happily combined. What I shall
have to say here will be about the poem, not about its author or
authors: about the poem as it survives, with many variant read-
ings, in four manuscripts written in four different dialect-areas,
but always as a single poem. For convenience, I shall refer to its
author in the singular, but please understand that as meaning
throughout author or authors or compiler.

  Hanna, with a footnote reference to Jordan's *Chaucer and the
Shape of Creation*, remarks that

. . . recent criticism of medieval literature has shown the distance between medieval conceptions of form and the modern belief in "organic form" or unity. Thus it would seem patronizing and unfair to attack a fifteenth-century poet by invoking a conception which he did not know.

And yet he proceeds to dismember the poem precisely by invoking this conception which the poet may not have known, separating off Part I as having "considerably more unity than is generally supposed."[9] In any case, it is not a matter of being "unfair" to the medieval poet, but of asking whether his poem implies a conception of form which we can recognize as having some validity. I think it does, and I suggest that we might think of that conception as "coherence" or "connectedness" rather than as unity.[10]

I do not in the least wish to argue that *The Awntyrs off Arthure* does not fall into two parts, the contents of which I have just outlined. But it does not appear that the two parts are juxtaposed at random. For one thing, they are of approximately equal length: the transition from one to the other occurs with the movement from the outdoor setting of the Inglewood Forest around the Tarn Wadling to the indoor setting of Randalset Hall (evidently nearby), and that transition takes place at line 340 in a poem of 715 lines, that is, very nearly halfway through. There is in fact a third setting, for the final two stanzas are set in Carlisle, where the tensions of the action are resolved: Galeron marries his lady and becomes a knight of the Round Table, while Guinevere appeases her mother's spirit with "a mylion of masses" (706). Thus the Inglewood Forest part and the Randalset Hall part are very evenly balanced indeed: 340 lines and 349 lines. (The reader will be relieved to learn that I do not propose to take my numerological analysis any further.) There are obvious contrasts between these two virtually equal parts, but there are also parallels and links which are equally obvious, though they have received less attention. In both parts of the poem, the Arthurian civilization is faced with the challenge of an apparently hostile outsider: supernatural in the first, in the form of Guinevere's

mother risen from her grave; human in the second, in the form of
Galeron, come to demand his lands. In both parts Gawain is the
leading representative of the Round Table, and in both Guinevere
also plays a leading role. We seem to be faced with a literary
structure comparable with a favorite pictorial form of the Middle
Ages, the diptych.[11] I have in mind, for example, a diptych of
which one leaf shows the Virgin and Child, the other the
Crucifixion. Each leaf is complete in itself; however, Christ and
his mother are leading figures in each, and when the two are put
together they generate a meaning and an emotion far greater than
either possesses separately. In such a case, the juxtaposition is
genuinely creative: the medieval artist is in no way limited by his
habit of composing a work in self-contained, discontinuous sections: it is precisely the discontinuity that makes possible a creative gesture in which the spectator or reader himself participates.
Sparks leap across the gap between the two parts, and the on-
looker's mind is set alight by them.

It may be that in the twentieth century we are better placed to
recognize and respond to such structures than people were in earlier postmedieval periods, because we can be familiar with them
from the arts of our own time, and especially from the art of the
cinema. The technique I have been describing is that of montage.
Eisenstein, its greatest exponent, described the origin of this
technique as lying in the discovery of the fact that "two film
pieces of any kind, placed together, inevitably combine into a
new concept, a new quality, arising out of that juxtaposition."[12]
In his later writings he was inclined to emphasize that the two
pieces must be selected so that their juxtaposition would illustrate
a chosen theme. It was not enough for them to be unrelated and
juxtaposed at random:

> *Representation* A and *representation* B must be so selected
> from all the possible features within the theme that is being
> developed, must be sought for, that their *juxtaposition*—that
> is, the juxtaposition of *those very elements* and not of alter-
> native ones—shall evoke in the perception and feelings of
> the spectator the most complete *image of the theme itself*.[13]

Now, of course, in the diptych and (as I shall argue soon) in *The Awntyrs off Arthure*, the artist or poet does indeed have in mind a theme which the parts of his work are to evoke by their juxtaposition. On the other hand, in the late writing I have just quoted, it seems to me that Eisenstein goes too far in implying that the theme is already *fully* defined in advance. At an earlier stage in his career, his emphasis had been different, and he had written of how he disagreed with his fellow director Pudovkin, whose views then were much the same as those he was to hold himself later. He wrote that Pudovkin "loudly defends an understanding of montage as a *linkage* of pieces. Into a chain. Again, 'bricks.' Bricks, arranged in series to *expound* an idea. I confronted him with my viewpoint on montage as a *collision*. A view that from the collision of two given factors arises a concept."[14] I find more help in this earlier emphasis, which implies that the theme is created or recreated by the act of juxtaposition, and that the meaning thereby produced cannot be defined by any other means. It will be a meaning relating to certain preexisting concepts, but it will not be defined by these concepts; in fact it will be a potentiality for meaning, to be drawn on by the reader or spectator, rather than a cut-and-dried proposition which the images merely illustrate. I emphasize this point, because it seems to me that there is a strong tendency in the academic interpretation of medieval poems to a kind of authoritarianism which reduces the reader's freedom of response. I do not mean, of course, that a poem with a diptych, or montage, structure can mean anything the reader chooses to imagine, or that its meaning is beyond rational discussion; but that we should not be surprised or worried to find that the poet's discontinuities leave areas of uncertainty, areas of freedom, in which it is up to us to respond to the stimulus the poem provides.

Larry D. Benson suggested some years ago that, within the alliterative tradition especially, structural variation was a common method of conveying meaning in medieval poems—or, as I would prefer to put it, of *creating* meaning. He writes of "the juxtaposition of parallel, opposing elements without an explicit statement of their relation"; he says of *Beowulf* that "The struc-

ture of the narrative is concentrated and appositional, enclosed
within the framework of the burials at the beginning and end'';
and he even mentions *The Awntyrs off Arthure*, along with the
Morte Arthure and *Golagros and Gawane*, as examples of Middle
English alliterative poems where ''one finds the same concern
with parallels, contrasts, and variations in the narrative structure.''[15] Before I proceed to examine *The Awntyrs off Arthure* in
more detail, I think it will be helpful to consider briefly some
such structural analogues. The closest is perhaps one of those
Benson mentions, *Golagros and Gawane*, another Northern poem
in rhyming alliterative stanzas, which juxtaposes two apparently
quite unconnected adventures. In the first, which is much briefer
than the second, Arthur and his knights come upon a castle, and
need provisions from it. First Kay is sent to obtain them; he
rudely seizes them from a dwarf, but is then knocked down by
the lord of the castle and returns ingloriously. Next Gawain is
sent; he makes a courteous request, admitting that the lord has
the right to do what he wishes with his own possessions, and at
this the lord offers his hospitality freely. In the second adventure,
the Arthurians come to a second castle, a place of great splendor;
and Arthur is astonished to learn that its lord, Golagros, owes
homage to no king. Gawain, Lancelot, and Ewain are sent to ask
politely for the lord's submission, and when he equally politely
declines to dishonor himself thus, Arthur makes preparations to
besiege him. There follows a series of knightly combats with no
decisive result, in one of which Kay makes a great show of being
merciful to an opponent who has unexpectedly surrendered when
Kay himself was on the verge of succumbing. At last Gawain
fights against Golagros himself and finally gets him at his mercy.
But Golagros says he prefers to die rather than submit to compulsion or even accept mercy; all that he will agree to is that Gawain
should return with him to the castle as if defeated, on the promise
that

> I sall thi kyndnes quyte
> And sauf thyn honoure.[16]

(1101–2)

Gawain takes the risk, and Golagros, after consulting his people, freely submits and does Gawain homage. Golagros then does homage to Arthur too, and Arthur stays in his castle for nine days, at the end of which he departs, freely releasing Golagros from the submission he freely made.

Even this crude summary suggests, I hope, some of the meanings that are created by the juxtaposition of the two adventures. The poem has to do with knightly courtesy, honor, and generosity: in effect, with the *franchise* of *The Franklin's Tale*, with a generosity which involves committing oneself to trust in the generosity of another man, imposing no compulsion on him, and leaving him genuinely free to act honorably or not. In the first, briefer adventure, this emerges fairly simply from the contrast between Kay's failure and Gawain's success. In the second adventure, Kay has only a minor role, in an episode which provides a comically distorted reflection of the main theme; but the chief burden is again borne by Gawain, in a situation which is far more complicated, and in which honor is shown to be almost painfully complex, for Gawain can preserve Golagros' honor only by relinquishing his own, and yet in submitting himself to apparent shame he is touching the height of honor. I do not know whether Hanna would wish to argue that *Golagros and Gawane* also must really be two poems; but its author evidently did not feel that he could leave his audience quite as free as Gawain leaves Golagros, and so he included a *raisonneur* or commentator on the story in the form of Spynagros, who for Arthur's benefit draws a moral from the first adventure—"It hynderis never for to be heyndly of speche" (368)—and repeatedly warns him that Golagros has an exceptionally high regard for his own reputation and that he will never succeed in *forcing* him to do homage. *The Awntyrs off Arthure* includes no figure equivalent to Spynagros, and it seems to me to be a purer work of art for the omission, conveying its meaning simply by the balanced relationship of its parts.

Another obvious parallel (and of course Benson's main subject) is *Sir Gawain and the Green Knight*, where, for example, we are left entirely free to respond for ourselves to the meaning and emotional effect the poet creates by his juxtaposition of the

hunting scenes with the bedroom scenes, and of the Beheading
Game with the Temptation; though, in both cases, what is presented to us is not a diptychlike composition but a sandwich
structure, in which each bedroom scene is placed between two
slices of hunt and the Temptation is placed between two slices of
Beheading Game. A less obvious parallel, perhaps, is *Patience*.
Here in one sense the principle of structure is that of a single,
causally connected narrative, taken of course as a whole from the
Book of Jonah. But cunningly superimposed on this is a diptych
structure, dividing the story of Jonah's relations with God into
two separate tests, each of which begins with his being sent to
Nineveh. In each test he finds himself in what is called a
"bower" (the whale's belly in Part I and the shelter under the
gourd in Part II); in each test he sleeps and is rudely awakened;
in each God commands the wind to blow destructively; in each
he protects and teaches Jonah while seeming to punish and destroy him; and so on.[17] The parallels between the two parts are
not geometrically exact, nor are they meant to be: they are intended to stimulate the reader's mind to work creatively for itself,
not to imprison it in a rigid doctrine.

In view of the title of this book, *The Alliterative Tradition in
the Fourteenth Century*, I would like to be able to argue that the
structural method I have been describing is one peculiar to alliterative poetry; but in fact it can be found quite commonly in
nonalliterative poems too. We are all familiar with its presence in
The Book of the Duchess, for example, where the Dreamer's encounter with the Man in Black parallels in so many ways the pre-
ceding story of Ceyx and Alcyone. There the parallels are not
merely a given structural feature, but have a causal relationship
on the level of the narrator's psychology: because he was reading
about Ceyx and Alcyone before he went to sleep, he dreamed
about the Man in Black. Still, I would guess that the method of
structural parallel with variation was far more common in alliterative poetry; and this might be connected, as Benson suggests,
with the way that, on the level of the sentence, the alliterative
style tends to "place clauses side by side and allow their meaning
to emerge from the juxtaposition."[18] Certainly, in *The Awntyrs*

off Arthure, to which I now return, one gets a strong impression of a single aesthetic governing the work at every level, from the sentence to the complete narrative.

The Awntyrs off Arthure, like a number of other poems of the Alliterative Revival, including *Sir Gawain and the Green Knight*, celebrates a noble way of life, which undergoes a serious challenge to its validity; the challenge brings out its limitations, but, despite this, the noble way of life is able to continue, at least for a time. At the opening of the poem, the noble life is expressed simultaneously on two levels. One is that of the activity described, the ritual of hunting by means of which the medieval aristocracy demonstrated its exclusive solidarity, while at once expressing and containing its violence. As in *Sir Gawain and the Green Knight,* this is a hunt in the close season, the *fermyson,*[19] and aristocratic violence is therefore very strictly limited; though, as the combat between Gawain and Galeron in the second part will demonstrate, it is none the less real. The second level of expression is that of the language—the traditionally conventional and pleonastic style which Marie Borroff has shown to correspond to social elevation.[20] Superlative expressions are common: the courtiers are "wlonkest in wedes" (9), and Gawain is "grayþest on grene" (12). The style is full of semantically empty asseverations: a single stanza contains "by boke and by belle" (30), "þe trouthe for to telle" (34), and "ho þe trouth trowes" (35). Epithets frequently add nothing to our information, but are merely what is expected: "bonkes so bare" (41), "holtes so hare" (43), "cliffes so colde" (44), "greues so grene" (61, 69). In such a style, with its conspicuous consumption of words and of time, formalized in the highly repetitive stanza-linking, a leisure class confirms its identity; and at the same time an atmosphere of normality is established, in which the abnormal is to intrude with shattering force.

The sudden storm of snow and rain, which makes the day "als dirke / As hit were mydniȝt myrke" (75–76), breaks up the hunt, and then the howling apparition terrifies even the greyhounds (126), so that the hunters become the hunted. On the level of language, the very repetitions now become more sharply

and individually expressive. Thus one stanza ends with the apparition's first speech: "I gloppen, and I grete" (91); the next stanza
repeats the words, but with a new subject, transferring the activities mentioned from the ghost to Guinevere, in whom they are
less expected: "Then gloppenet and grete Gaynour þe gay" (91).
There is a similar transference later, when the ghost ends, "Be
war be my wo" (195), and Guinevere begins, "Wo is *me* for þi
wirde" (196). The traditional phrases are now set in a new context: it profits little to be "hendest in halle" (131) when one is
not in hall, but in a wintry forest confronted with a shrieking
thing from the grave; and it profits the apparition little now, that
once

> I was radder of rode þen rose in þe ron,
> My ler as þe lelé lonched so light.

(161–62)

The poem's style is spikily Gothic, and seems at first to offer
only a restlessly decorative ingenuity of surface, with little regard
for specific meaning either locally or overall, and we may have
to learn to recognize the significant variations within it. As in *Sir
Gawain and the Green Knight*, the impact of the apparition encourages sharp and critical observation of the limitations of the
courtly characters. The comforting masculine superiority of Gawain's scientific explanation of the terrifying experience—"Hit ar
þe clippes of þe son, I herd a clerk say" (94)—is all too clearly
threadbare, though the poet's explanation in the following line
should prevent us from feeling too superior ourselves toward a
knight who is doing his duty as best he can: "And þus he con-
fortes þe quene for his kniȝthede" (95). Guinevere is observed
with a more wholeheartedly critical eye: she blames the other
knights for abandoning her on what she calls, with hysterical ex-
aggeration, "my deþday" (98), yet it appears that she had voluntarily stayed in the forest after Arthur had blown the assembly-
call, perhaps in order to enjoy a little innocent dalliance with
Gawain.
    The first of the poem's many instances of parallel with varia-

tion occurs with the juxtaposition of Guinevere with the apparition of her mother. John Speirs has summed this up well: "Each is confronted with herself in the other—the daughter as she will be, and the mother as she once was."[21] But even before the ghost identified itself, it seemed to come as a kind of serious parody of Guinevere's shallowness in lamenting the absence of her usual circle of knights: "Hit waried, hit waymented, as a woman" (107). We have already seen how the repetitions that link the stanzas are used to transfer activities from one of the pair to the other. Another example occurs when the ghost ends one stanza by telling Gawain,

> I am comen in þis cace
> To carpe with your quene
>
> (142–43)

and then begins the next with "Quene was *I* somwile" (144), and adds, "Gretter þen Dame Gaynour" (147). Later the ghost explains that her punishment is for "luf paramour" (213), and thereby suggests another parallel with Guinevere, though it is left to us to decide whether the poet is referring to her notorious affair with Lancelot, to her seduction by Mordred as indicated in the *Morte Arthure* (that would link this part of the *Awntyrs* with the ghost's message to Gawain), or simply to her predilection for being surrounded with glamorous knights.

The apparition is both like and unlike Guinevere. Guinevere's elaborate dress is described in the poem's second stanza, but of the apparition we are told, "nauthyr on hide ne on huwe no heling hit hadde" (108); and whereas Guinevere wears a blue hood on her head, the ghost has only a revolting toad. The ghost warns Guinevere that she will come to the same state, "For al þi fressh foroure" (166). The emphasis on Guinevere's dress might seem to suggest that she is concerned only with externals, mere trimmings; and indeed the widespread tendency in medieval literature and art to convey courtly grandeur and luxury through exhaustive representations of costume must always have this as a potential meaning. The same suggestion emerges more strongly from the

conversation between Guinevere and her mother. The first action
that the ghost urges upon Guinevere is, "Haue pité on þe poer
while þou art of power" (173), for when Guinevere comes to be
as the ghost is now, "Þe praier of þe poer may purchas þe pes"
(178). Guinevere asks whether "matens or mas" (198) can do
anything to alleviate her mother's state, and the answer is that
"To menne me with masses grete menske hit were" (230), but
her mother goes on to reiterate her plea for practical charity:

> For him þat rest on þe rode,
> Gyf fast of þi goode
> To folke þat failen þe fode
> While þou art here.
>
> (231–34)

Guinevere, however, disregards this, and promises the ghost that
she will have her commemorated with "a myllion of masses"
(236). When she asks again how she can aid her mother in the
next world, the ghost speaks for a third time of her concern for
the poor:

> Mekenesse and mercy, þes arn þe moost,
> And haue pité on þe poer, þat pleses Heuenking.
>
> (250–51)

In medieval courtly poetry courtly values are rarely tested in this
way by the larger social concern that is associated rather with
noncourtly works such as *Piers Plowman* and *Peres the
Ploughman's Crede*; and one possibility of development would
seem to be toward Lear's recognition that in this world "Robes
and furred gowns hide all," his "Off, off, you lendings," and
his acknowledgment that he has taken too little care of the suffer-
ings of the poor. But Guinevere is no Lear: she does not respond
to the ghost's attempts to turn her attention beyond outward observances to practical charity. On the other hand, she is no
Goneril or Regan either: her observances include religious observances, and the poem is certainly not arguing or implying that the

masses in themselves will do no good. They will be better than nothing; indeed, they will be a kind of food for the dead soul in its spiritual poverty, and before the apparition departs she couples a last reference to feeding the poor with a striking development of the courtly theme of the rich feast:

> Fede folke for my sake þat fauten þe fode
> And menne me with matens and masse in melle.
> Masses arn medecynes to vs þat bale bides;
> > Vs þenke a masse as swete
> > As eny spice þat euer ye yete.
>
> (319–23)

Before these parting words, the ghost has turned her attention from Guinevere to Gawain. Gawain seems to be more perceptive than the queen about the limitations of the Arthurian way of life, and his very questions to the ghost already imply her answers. He knows that in their warfare the knights "defoulen þe folke on fele kinges londes" (262) and that they invade kingdoms "withouten eny right" (263), and no more than the audience does he really need to be told what the end will be. They perhaps knew, as the poet certainly did, the *Morte Arthure*, or at least they would have been familiar with the Arthurian legend in general; and so the poet is able to make the ghost prophesy the future in a most effectively condensed and allusive way. Arthur is "to couetous" (265); for this moment, while Fortune's wheel stands still, he seems unconquerable, but soon "That wonderfull whelewright" (271) will bring him low. In this section of the poem, the sense of standing at one particular moment in a predestined legendary history is unusual and moving. France has already been conquered, Italy remains to conquer, but bad news will be brought to Tuscany, and in the end "In Dorsetshire shal dy þe doughtest of alle" (295), Gawain himself. Mordred's rebellion is foretold, though Mordred is never identified by name, only by his armorial bearings; and, at this very moment, the seeds of the future are growing:

> In riche Arthures halle,
> The barne playes at þe balle
> Þat outray shall you alle,
> Derfely þat day.
>
> (309–12)

I find this the most poignant moment in the poem: at this point of
equilibrium, Mordred is only a child, playing harmlessly and in-
nocently in Arthur's court, yet he is Mordred all the same, and
must play the terrible part we know in the coming destruction.

Her errand complete, the apparition disappears; as if by
magic, the clouds part, the sun shines, and normal life resumes
with a blast from Arthur's bugle. The Arthurians all ride off to
supper at Randalset Hall, courtly luxury apparently unchanged by
the messages from beyond the grave. But the purpose of the diptych structure is to show change as well as repetition. Hanna sees
in the poem a simple rather than a complex meaning; simple failure on the part of both Guinevere and Gawain to understand that
the way of life they share and represent is superficial and inadequate.[22] But in my view that simple meaning can be read in
The Awntyrs off Arthure only by separating the first part from the
second. The two parts together compose a meaning more complex and less rigidly compelling.

Hardly has the feast at Randalset Hall begun when there is a
second intrusion, which at once parallels and contrasts with the
first. A scene of aristocratic recreation, but this time feasting instead of hunting, is disrupted by a challenge from outside, but
this time there are two intruders instead of one, and they are human, not supernatural. Indeed, they are themselves courtly, and
whereas before luxurious and elaborate clothing were attributes of
the court, now they belong to the intruders as well. The descriptions of the clothing and equipment of Galeron and his lady are
developed into full-blown Gothic fantasies, with every inch of
surface crowded with outlandish detail, culminating in the horse
transformed into a unicorn by the thorn-sharp spike on its
forehead armor (387–90). Such descriptions are intended to be
pleasing in themselves, quite apart from any contribution they

may make to the poem as a whole, and it would be foolish to demand that every detail should have a larger significance. The hypothesis of the reader is connectedness—not unity, but connectedness—and we shall sense as we read a readjustment of the balance that was struck in the first part. Elegant dress does not necessarily imply shallowness, and the courtly world has a magnificence that is not totally negated by its transience and its imperfection.

The stranger-knight introduces himself as Galeron of Galloway, and his purpose is at once related to the theme of the first part of the poem. Arthur, he claims, has displayed precisely the covetousness and the habit of unjustly seizing others' lands of which the ghost accused him earlier. He has taken Galeron's lands—"**Þou has wonen hem in werre with a wrange wile**" (421)—and bestowed them on Gawain; and Galeron is determined to fight to get them back, either against Gawain himself or against any other knight assigned by Arthur. Arthur explains why this cannot be done immediately, and his explanation provides yet another link between the two parts of the poem—a causal, not a thematic link. The Arthurian party is out on a hunting expedition, and is therefore unprepared for a duel:

> We ar in þe wode went to walke on oure waith,
> To hunte at þe herdes with hounde and with horne.
> We ar in oure gamen; we haue no gome graiþe. . . .
>
> (434–36)

But if Galeron will wait till the next day, an opponent will be found. The hospitality shown to Galeron during his overnight stay is described in detail, as an exemplary display; and once more we are made to feel the impressive magnificence of Arthurian courtliness.

Gawain himself volunteers to fight Galeron, and the duel between them is described at length. It is another case of a subject appealing to the audience in its own right, but we should note the special effect created by the poet's double emphasis on luxury and on violence, the warlike and the peaceful aspects of aristocra-

tic life. Frequently the luxurious and the violent are brought together, with a piquant aesthetic quality: the carefully burnished
sword smeared with blood; or

> Shene sheldes wer shred,
> Bright brenés bybled;
>
> (569–70)

or Gawain's splendid and beloved warhorse with its head severed;
or the warriors who

> beten downe beriles and bourdures bright.
> Shildes on shildres þat shene were to shewe,
> Fretted were in fyne golde, þei failen in fight.
> Stones of iral þey strenkel and strewe.
>
> (587–90)

The effect is not only aesthetically disturbing and pleasing; it perfectly expresses the nature of the aristocratic life, which consists
in a generous willingness to waste those material possessions that
seem to be its essence. And, as I suggested earlier, the ample and
often redundant style of this description is itself an enactment of
such aristocratic waste, a form of conspicuous consumption of the
poet's verbal substance and of his listeners' leisure. The poet's attitude to the combat, at the one point where he directly expresses
it, is of interest. Galeron raises his sword to aim devastatingly
at Gawain, "But him lymped þe worse, and þat me wel likes!"
(615). This momentary participation, by its very openness,
paradoxically conveys detachment, as though the poet is revealing
that his enthusiasm is only for a game. It contrasts strikingly with
the earnest commitment of the *Morte Arthure*, a commitment
which displays itself at its least likable early in that poem, in the
relations between Arthur and the Roman ambassadors. (For
example, there is a kind of bad faith in the scene where the ambassadors return to their master and praise Arthur to the skies, for
the poet is *pretending* to give a Roman view of the British king,
without really stepping outside his own partisanship.)[23] The later

poem, in my view, conveys a surer poise in the poet's attitude toward Arthurian civilization. The bloody and extravagant combat is no more than a game, just as the poem itself in its verbal extravagance is a game, too.

Gawain seizes Galeron by the collar, and at this point Galeron's lady intervenes with an appeal to Guinevere to have mercy on Galeron. This creates a further unexpected parallel with the first adventure, for the lady now shrieks and groans in a way which reminds us of the earlier apparition's appeal, also directed to Guinevere:

> Þen his lemman on loft skrilles and skrikes;
> Ho gretes on Gaynour with gronyng grylle.
>
> (619–20)

The apparition had urged "Mekenesse and mercy" (250) as the means to salvation, and it seemed as though Guinevere had failed to understand her appeal; but now, within the familiar courtly context, she responds promptly and generously, by kneeling meekly before Arthur and begging him mercifully to "Make þes knightes accorde" (635). Her appeal at once touches off generosity in others. Galeron abandons his claim to the return of his lands, and offers the king his sword. The king in turn makes Gawain a further huge grant of land, on condition that he will be reconciled with Galeron, and will release his lands to him. And Gawain finally releases them all, on condition that Galeron remains with the Round Table for a while. It is not only Guinevere who seems to have learned something from the first adventure, which she puts into practice in the second. Arthur had been accused by the apparition of being "to couetous" (265), but he now voluntarily gives up great tracts of land in Wales, Ireland, and Brittany in order to bring peace with honor to the two warring knights. The pattern is formally completed by the admission of Galeron to the Round Table, and Guinevere's arrangement of the "mylion of masses" (706) that she had promised to her mother's ghost. As at the end of *Sir Gawain and the Green Knight*, however, we are left to decide for ourselves whether the formal completion of the pattern, marked by the ending of the poem with the words with which it began, does or does not correspond to a psychological and spiritual fulfillment. Has Guinevere failed to learn the most important lesson of all, to be charitable to the poor, who lie outside the courtly circle? Does the poem close so neatly in on itself only at the expense of excluding a tract of experience so important as to render its completion trivial? Enigmatically, life continues in the poetic court, as no doubt it did in the court for which the poem was written.

In the poetic court, the continuation is under a shadow, that of the ghost's prophecy of a doom whose seeds lie within the court itself. I think it of great importance—and it is this that makes me most reluctant to believe that *The Awntyrs off Arthure* was not planned as a diptych—that the admiring descriptions of knightly dress and courage and Arthurian hospitality, and the generosity of Guinevere, Arthur, and Gawain, come *after* the prophecy. The poet reverses the flow of time, and in the poem's second part we are made to feel intensely the poignancy of this moment of Arthurian civilization—courage, compassion, generosity—knowing as we do of the destiny that awaits it when the boy Mordred is a man. It was a stroke of genius to make the glorification of what was doomed come after the prophecy of doom. All human achievement is only imperfect and provisional: individuals die and civilizations collapse. But, for this and other medieval poets, that did not make human achievement worthless. They saw in courtly civilization, for all its limitations, an admirable resilience, which enabled it to continue the game even while knowing that it was only a game, and must come to an end. What I most admire in *The Awntyrs off Arthure*—and I think this is a quality to which its diptych structure makes a major contribution—is its civilized poise, a respect in which it is surely much superior to the *Morte Arthure*, though it could scarcely have been written if the *Morte* had not already existed. The poet of *The Awntyrs off Arthure* sets before us a pair of moving images, intriguingly similar and yet dissimilar to each other. The conclusions are for us to draw.

NOTES

1. Respectively (Philadelphia, 1969) and (Manchester, 1974). I quote from the latter.
2. *The Times Higher Education Supplement*, 2 May 1975, p. 18. I must express my gratitude to Ralph Hanna, both for what I have learned from his edition and for his generosity in supplying me with a copy of his article and in subsequent discussion.
3. A. C. Baugh, "Middle English," in *A Literary History of England*, 2nd ed. (London, 1967), I, 190, n. 22.
4. J. L. N. O'Loughlin, "The English Alliterative Romances," in *Arthurian Literature in the Middle Ages*, ed. R. S. Loomis (Oxford, 1959), p. 527.
5. George Kane, *Middle English Literature* (London, 1951), pp. 52–53.
6. John Speirs, *Medieval English Poetry: the Non-Chaucerian Tradition* (London, 1957), p. 252.
7. Ralph Hanna, *"The Awntyrs off Arthure*: An Interpretation," *Modern Language Quarterly,* 31 (1970), 275–97. Other discussion of the poem's structure is to be found in S. O. Andrew, "Huchown's Works," *Review of English Studies,* 5 (1929), 17, and David N. Klausner, "Exempla and *The Awntyrs of Arthure,"* *Mediaeval Studies,* 34 (1972), 307–25.
8. Hermann Lübke, *"The Aunters of Arthur at the Tern-Wathelan, Teil* I: Handschriften, Metrik, Verfasser" (Diss. Berlin, 1883).
9. Hanna, "Interpretation," p. 277.
10. D. S. Brewer, discussing the form of Malory's work, proposes a contrast between "cohesion" (a term suggested to him, he remarks, by Eugène Vinaver) and "organic unity": "the hoole book," in *Essays on Malory,* ed. J. A. W. Bennett (Oxford, 1963), p. 42 and n. 1.
11. For discussion of the general idea of diptych structures in medieval narratives, see William W. Ryding, *Structure in Medieval Narrative* (The Hague, 1971), pp. 25–27, 40, and passim.
12. Serge Eisenstein, *The Film Sense* (London, 1943), p. 14.
13. Ibid., p. 19.
14. Written in 1929 about the situation of 1926; published in Serge Eisenstein, *Film Form* (London, 1951), pp. 37–38. I am much indebted to Dr. Stephen Heath for directing me to this passage, and for disentangling the chronology of Eisenstein's thought.
15. Larry D. Benson, *Art and Tradition in Sir Gawain and the Green Knight* (New Brunswick, N.J., 1965), p. 163.
16. *Scottish Alliterative Poems in Rhyming Stanzas*, ed. F. J. Amours, STS 1S, 27 and 38 (1892–97).
17. The bipartite structure of *Patience* was first noted by E. D. Cuffe, "An Interpretation of *Patience, Cleanness,* and *The Pearl*, from the Viewpoint of Imagery" (Diss. North Carolina, 1951).

18. Benson, p. 155.
19. *Awntyrs*, 8; *Gawain*, 1156.
20. Marie Borroff, *Sir Gawain and the Green Knight: A Stylistic and Metrical Study* (New Haven, 1962), Part I, passim.
21. Speirs, p. 257.
22. E.g., "The failure of Guinevere to recognize the danger of her regal posturing is matched by Gawain's parallel failure to see that neither warfare nor courage provides a viable mode of existence" (loc. cit., p. 291).
23. See *Morte Arthure*, 530–79, in *King Arthur's Death*, ed. Larry D. Benson (Indianapolis, 1974).

Index

The Contributors

RUTH M. AMES, who received her doctorate from Columbia University, is Professor of English at Queensborough Community College in the City University of New York. Her publications on Chaucer and Langland, especially *The Fulfillment of the Scriptures: Abraham, Moses, and Piers,* reflect her interest in the diverse ways in which writers have transformed Scripture into poetry.

JOHN V. FLEMING, Professor of English and Comparative Literature at Princeton University, has worked in several fields of medieval English and Continental literature. His principal publications include *The Roman de la Rose: A Study in Allegory and Iconography; An Introduction to the Franciscan Literature of the Middle Ages;* and most recently *Two Poems Attributed to Joachim of Fiore* (with Marjorie Reeves).

JOHN B. FRIEDMAN has been Professor of English at the University of Illinois at Urbana-Champaign since 1971. His special interests are iconography and manuscript studies. His publications include *Orpheus in the Middle Ages* and an edition of parts of Thomas of Cantimpré's encyclopedia, *De Naturis Rerum.*

MAUREEN FRIES is Professor of English at the State University of New York College at Fredonia, where she has taught since

1969. Besides writing the book *A Bibliography of Writings by and About British Women Authors, 1957–69,* she has written numerous articles on Chaucer, Malory, and the images of women in literature. She is currently completing another book, *Mirrors, Ribs and Vessels: Women in Late Medieval British Literature.* She holds a State University of New York Chancellor's Award for Excellence in Teaching.

DAVID LAMPE is Professor of English at the State University of New York College at Buffalo. He has written numerous articles on the poetry of fourteenth-century England, both the Chaucerian and the non-Chaucerian traditions. Currently working with Chaucer's lyrics, he is President of the Western New York Medievalists' Association.

DEREK PEARSALL is Professor of English at York University in England. His published work includes editions of *The Floure and the Leafe* and *Piers Plowman,* as well as these critical studies: *John Lydgate, Landscapes and Seasons of the Medieval World* (with Elizabeth Salter), and *Old English and Middle English Poetry,* which is Volume I of the *Routledge History of English Poetry.*

RUSSELL A. PECK is Professor of English at the University of Rochester. His publications include essays on Chaucer, Shakespeare, medieval aesthetics, numerology, dream poetry, and intellectual history. Editor of Gower's *Confessio Amantis,* he recently wrote a critical study of that poem entitled *Kingship and Common Profit in Gower's "Confessio Amantis."*

EARL G. SCHREIBER, a Fellow of the American Academy of Rome, has taught at the State University of New York at Stony Brook and at the University of Illinois. He has written about medieval mythography and about drama. With Thomas E. Maresca, he translated Bernardus Silvestris's *Commentary on the Aeneid* for the University of Nebraska Press.

A. C. SPEARING is a Fellow of Queen's College and University Lecturer in English at Cambridge University, where he has taught for twenty years. His publications include *Criticism and Medieval Poetry; the Gawain-Poet: A Critical Study; Medieval Dream-Poetry;* and *Chaucer: Troilus and Criseyde.*

The Editors:

BERNARD S. LEVY, who received his doctorate from the University of California at Berkeley, teaches at the State University of New York at Binghamton. His special interests are Middle English literature and Chaucer. He has written essays on Chaucer, *Sir Gawain and the Green Knight*, and Dante's *La Vita Nuova.* He is the editor of *Mediaevalia*, the interdisciplinary journal published by the Center for Medieval and Early Renaissance Studies at the State University of New York at Binghamton.

PAUL E. SZARMACH is Associate Professor of English and Director of the Center for Medieval and Early Renaissance Studies at the State University of New York at Binghamton. His special interest is Old English prose and its backgrounds. With Bernard S. Levy, he is an editor of *The Fourteenth Century*, and he is also editor of the *Old English Newsletter.*